SIXTH EDITION

Technical Communication

商务沟通与写作（下）

（第6版）

Rebecca E. Burnett

IOWA STATE UNIVERSITY

北京大学出版社
PEKING UNIVERSITY PRESS

北京市版权局著作权合同登记号 图字 [01-2010-4301] 号

图书在版编目 (CIP) 数据

商务沟通与写作·下 = Technical Communication (Sixth Edition) /（美）伯奈特 (Burnett R. E.) 著. —北京：北京大学出版社，2011.1

（商务英语写作系列丛书）

ISBN 978-7-301-18346-5

Ⅰ.商… Ⅱ.伯… Ⅲ.①商业管理—公共关系学—教材—英文 ②商务—英语—应用文—写作—教材 Ⅳ.①F715 ②H315

中国版本图书馆 CIP 数据核字（2010）第 260413 号

Technical Communication (Sixth Edition)
Rebecca E. Burnett
Copyright © 2005, 2001, 1997, 1994, 1990, 1986 by Thomson Wadsworth. Thomson Wadsworth and the Thomson logo are trademarks used herein under license.

本书原版由圣智学习出版公司出版。版权所有，盗印必究。

Peking University Press is authorized by Cengage Learning to publish and distribute exclusively this edition. This edition is authorized for sale in the People's Republic of China only (excluding Hong Kong SAR, Macao SAR and Taiwan). Unauthorized export of this edition is a violation of the Copyright Act. No part of this publication may be reproduced or distributed by any means, or stored in a database or retrieval system, without the prior written permission of the publisher.

本书由圣智学习出版公司授权北京大学出版社独家出版发行。此版本仅限在中华人民共和国境内（不包括中国香港、澳门特别行政区及中国台湾）销售。未经授权的本书出口将被视为违反版权法的行为。未经出版者预先书面许可，不得以任何方式复制或发行本书的任何部分。

Cengage Learning Asia Pte. Ltd.
5 Shenton Way, # 01-01 UIC Building, Singapore 068808

本书封面贴有 Cengage Learning 防伪标签，无标签者不得销售。

书　　　　名：	Technical Communication (Sixth Edition) 商务沟通与写作（第 6 版）（下）
著作责任者：	[美] Rebecca E. Burnett 著
责 任 编 辑：	黄瑞明
标 准 书 号：	ISBN 978-7-301-18346-5/H·2728
出 版 发 行：	北京大学出版社
地　　　　址：	北京市海淀区成府路 205 号　100871
网　　　　址：	http://www.pup.cn
电　　　　话：	邮购部 62752015　发行部 62750672　编辑部 62754382　出版部 62754962
电 子 邮 箱：	zbing@pup.pku.edu.cn
印 　刷 　者：	山东省高唐印刷有限责任公司
发 　行 　者：	新华书店
	787 毫米 ×960 毫米　16 开本　18.25 印张　280 千字
	2011 年 1 月第 1 版　2011 年 1 月第 1 次印刷
定　　　　价：	38.00 元

未经许可，不得以任何方式复制或抄袭本书之部分或全部内容。

版权所有，侵权必究　举报电话：010-62752024
　　　　　　　　　　电子邮箱：fd@pup.pku.edu.cn

专家委员会

顾问 文秋芳

主任 王立非

委员 （按姓氏笔画排序）

丁言仁	于兰祖	卫乃兴	马广惠	王东风	王俊菊
文旭	文军	方琰	邓鹂鸣	朱源	刘世生
许德金	严明秦	苏刚	杨永林	杨达复	杨鲁新
李小华	李文中	李正栓	李生禄	李炳林	李霄翔
肖德法	吴红云	汪红	张世耘	张佐成	陈法春
陈新仁	周平	郑超	封一函	赵永青	胡一宁
胡健	战菊	俞洪亮	洪刚	袁洪庚	晓晴
徐珺	郭海云	黄国文	常玉田	梁茂成	程幼强
程晓堂	程朝翔	傅似逸	蔡金亭		

总 序

北京大学出版社继《英语写作原版引印系列丛书》之后，2010年，又专题引进商务英语写作原版系列教材。这套教材体系完整，应用性强，商务内容丰富，十分贴近英语教学改革的需要和广大学生提升未来就业能力的需求，填补了我国商务英语写作领域内没有高质量商务英语写作教材的空白，并得到15所商务英语专业院校教学协作组和中国英语写作教学专业委员会相关专家的联合推荐。

随着我国对外开放的不断深入，高水平的商务英语写作人才一将难求，能用地道规范的英文起草法律合同、撰写咨询报告的专业写作人才更是凤毛麟角，部分国际咨询机构提供的一份英文公司咨询报告价格高达百万美元，如此激烈的竞争值得我们认真反思现有的写作教学。即将出台的高等学校商务英语专业本科教学要求（试行）明确指出，商务英语写作是学生的核心能力，商务英语专业应加大毕业设计的比重，鼓励学生采用商务报告（如市场调研报告、商业计划书、营销方案等）多种形式。而全面提升商务英语写作能力，按照过去传统的写作教学模式，已无法适应，必须要有新的改革思路，要改变"费时低效"的困境，就必须做到以下几个转变：(1) 从重写作技能转向技能与内容并重；(2) 从传统写作教学转向机辅写作教学模式；(3) 从开设单一写作课转向开设写作课程群；(4) 从大班课堂写作教学转向个性化写作教学中心。通过对美国普林斯顿大学、英国华威大学等世界名校的考察，我们建议，可分阶段分层次为不同水平的学生开设商务英语写作课程群（Writing Portfolio），具体可包括：基础英语写作、国际贸易写作、国际营销写作、金融英语写作、法律英语写作、学术英语写作、财经新闻写作、商务函电写作、商务报告写作、职业应用文写作等，全面提升学生的写作能力。

本套系列教材在国外畅销经久不衰，多次再版或重印，此次由北京大学出版社首批引进出版10本：《商务沟通：以读者为中心的方法》（上、下册）、《商务沟通与写作》（上、下册）、《最新商务报告写作》（上、下册）、《职场英语写作》（上、下册）、《成功商务英语写作》（上、下册），由对外经济贸易大学商务英语写作教学团队的教师魏明博士、冯海颖博士、杨颖莉博士、李玉霞博士、尹珏林博士分别撰写导读。

本套丛书既是职场英语写作的优质教材，又是商务写作的经典教材，教材深入浅出，语言简明，可帮助学生理解、记忆和应对多种国际商务场合下的写作需求。通过本丛书的学习和训练，学生可提高写作水平，为踏入职场做好准备。本套丛书可用作全国大专院校的商务英语学生和教师的写作课教材和参考书，还可供经管类学生学习商务英语写作之用，同时也可供爱好商务英语写作的广大社会读者和各类公司企业人员提高英语写作使用。

中国英语写作教学专业委员会主任
对外经济贸易大学英语学院院长
教授、博士生导师
王立非
2010年国庆节于北京

导　读

一、本书的特色

1. 作者简介

Rebecca Burnett 现为佐治亚理工学院教授。2007 年自依阿华州立大学退休，曾任该大学修辞与专业交流高级教授，获"杰出教师"之美誉。Burnett 为《商务与专业交流》杂志前主编。她同时在多家美国大型公司担任专家鉴定人与交流顾问等职。她的研究领域包括专业交流、团队合作、交流评估、跨文化交流和风险沟通等。

2. 本书特色

《商务沟通与写作》自 1986 年以来已再版五次。本书内容覆盖面广，涉及从商务领域到学术领域各行各业的专业交流；交流的形式也不仅限于文本，而把口头报告、视图设计、网络交流也考虑在内；不仅详细介绍了交流的过程与步骤，还具体分析了职场常见的各种体裁。

作者提出评估专业交流的标准是可读性、可理解性与可用性，并以此标准贯穿全书。此书自身其实就是可读性、可理解性与可用性的典范。全书设计精致，插图丰富，结构清晰；有来自不同领域的新鲜实例，示例文本有边际注解以鼓励读者批判性的评估；每章有边栏讨论相关的一个职业道德问题；本书还有配套网站，每章附有众多网络链接，学习者因而可以了解更多相关内容；每章后的个体与协作任务也极具实用价值。

3. 使用对象与方法

鉴于其可读性和实用性，无论是在校学生还是职场人士，阅读此书都将获益匪浅。对于开设商务交流或高级写作的大学教师来说，此书也是难得的好教材；配套的教师专用网站可为教师提供丰富的教学资料。

二、本书内容

本书共有十六章，分为四部分。

第一部分　职场中的交流

第一章　职场交流特点

定义了职场交流为各行各业之话语活动，如撰写与制作专业文件、口头报告，以及视图等。讨论了职场交流的重要性，引导读者思考体裁、科技与职业道德在职场交流中的角色；以具体的例证说明如何使职场交流更具可读性、更易懂、更可用，以及影响交流的各种限制性因素。

第二章　理解文化与职场的关系

定义并解析了国家文化、机构文化以及身处文化中的个体。文化影响着工作场所的交流，因此无论机构/公司采取全球化或本地化策略，都应增强文化意识，了解并尊重不同文化。

第三章　阅读技术信息

专业人士需阅读文件、聆听口头报告和观看视图文件来了解背景信息，评估并做出决定，学习并最终完成某项任务。该章讨论了读与写之间的相互影响，以及有效的阅读策略。

  第四章 满足交流对象需求

    职场交流服务于两大目的：传递信息并说服读者/听众关注此项信息。因此了解读者/听众，分析他们的教育背景、工作经历、阅读能力、工作环境与职务都至关重要。该章讨论了如何针对读者/听众不同水平的专业技能调整材料的复杂度，针对他们不同的职务调整内容的选择。

  第五章 职场中的合作

    讨论了合作在职场中的重要性，合作中可能出现的问题，以及合作者应有的行为与技巧。良好的合作须避免情感（人际）冲突，协调潜在的程序冲突，鼓励关于实质问题的冲突。

  第二部分 掌握信息筛选过程

  第六章 搜集与使用信息

    讨论了在交流前如何搜索与使用各类电子资源；如何采用其他手段如访谈、调查等收集资料；在采用信息资源的同时如何避免踏入剽窃的误区。

  第七章 设计与起草

    介绍了在交流前勘察、设计以及起草的技巧。勘察阶段可采用头脑风暴法、因果或综合分析法等技巧。设计阶段采用项目管理工具，思考所需交流的内容、目的、对象、结构和设计等因素，评估交流的内在逻辑。起草阶段则需考虑如何选择恰当的人称和动词语气，使用平实的语言，采用"已知—新信息"的组句结构等。

  第八章 修改与编辑

    修改侧重于整体，而编辑侧重于具体与局部。该章介绍了修改与编辑的过程、技巧以及需要注意的问题，并以一可行性报告为例分析了修改与编辑的重要性。

  第九章 确保可用性

    专业交流需确保可用性，即把使用者放在首位，满足不同目的与技巧的人们在各种复杂情境下的需求。该章介绍了三类可用性测试（基于文本的、基于专家的和基于使用者的），以及可用性测试的全过程（从建立可用性测试计划，到分析使用者与任务，到实施测试，到最后报告测试结果）。

  第三部分 信息梳理

  第十章 组织信息

    介绍了如何利用大纲、故事板和表格来组织信息，如何利用主题句和过渡词/句来标志结构，如何利用六种传统结构形式——整体/部分、时间顺序、空间顺序、升/降序、比较/对比、因果——来展示信息。

  第十一章 设计信息

    为了有效地结合视图和文字来组织和展示信息以增加可读性、可理解性和可用性，该章介绍了一些利用页面空白、对齐方式、行间距和行长、标题、字体等来设计信息的技巧。

  第十二章 使用视觉形式

    介绍了各种视觉形式——图表、绘画、地图、照片等——在现代职场交流中的重要性及功能，并建议了如何正确、妥当地使用颜色。

  第十三章 设计电子交流

    基于网络的电子信息交流，是互动而非线性的，虚拟而开放的，复杂而动态的。为满足可读性和可用性，该章介绍了设计网站所需注意的几个因素：信息架构、网页设计和内容；具体讲解了如何组织、标识以及导航信息，如何设计界面，包括留白、滚屏、导航、颜色和图片，如何使内容更适应屏幕阅读的特点等。

第四部分 理解交流者采用的策略

第十四章 创建定义

在职场沟通中，情境化的定义是必不可少的。针对多变的词义及读者不同的理解能力，该章介绍了正式定义、非正式定义、归纳步骤的操作性定义以及扩充性定义。非正式定义包括同义、反义、否定、限定、类比、例释六类；而扩充性定义包括介绍词源、历史及举例。

第十五章 创建技术描述

技术描述概括物质特性，解答读者关于某一物体、物质、机制、有机组织、系统或位置的外观及组成的疑问。写一篇好的技术描述，我们需要了解读者的需求和目的，确定物质的结构和功能组成，选择精确而生动的措辞，设计直观而有效的视图，以空间顺序来安排说明文的结构。

第十六章 创建过程解释

过程解释不同于操作指南（后者见第二十一章）；过程解释提供足够的信息让读者了解某一行为或过程，而非引导读者完成这一行为或过程。写过程解释，我们同样需要了解读者需求，确定具体步骤，使用各种视图（如流程图），选择恰当措辞（如根据具体情况选择主动或被动语态），以时间顺序来组织文章结构。

三、推荐相关参考书

1. 常玉田，2010，《商务报告写作》，高等教育出版社。
2. 段平等编，2010，《专业信息交流英语教程》，中国人民大学出版社。
3. Jean Wyrick, 2008，《成功写作入门》(英文版)(第 10 版)，北京大学出版社。
4. Bonnie L. Tensen, 2008，《数字时代写作研究策略》(英文版)(第 2 版)，北京大学出版社。
5. Steven H. Gale, 2008，《公司管理写作策略》(英文版)，北京大学出版社。
6. David Rosrnwasser, 2008，《分析性写作》(英文版)(第 5 版)，北京大学出版社。
7. Edward P. Bailey, 2010，《实用写作》(英文版)(第 9 版)，北京大学出版社。
8. Cheng, W. & Kong, K. (2009). *Professional communication: Collaboration between academics and practitioners.* Hong Kong: Hong Kong University Press.
9. Guffey, M. E. & Du–Babcock, B. (2008). *Essentials of business communication.* Singapore: Thomsom.
10. Lannon, J. M. (2008). Technical communication. Longman.
11. Pfeiffer, W. S. (2006). Technical communication: A practical approach. Beijing: Publishing House of Electronics Industry.

对外经济贸易大学

冯海颖

译者序

《商务沟通与写作（第6版）》的主要目的是帮助学生和在职人员面对各种读者（客户）需求时进行有效的书面、口头和视觉上的信息交流。本书依据最新理论、研究和实践成果，用简明直白的语言解释了进行有效信息交流的方式和方法。设计精巧实用，提供了很多文本、数据和表格实例。本书设计的讨论和课堂练习可以帮助使用者成为更好的交流者。本书易读易教，强调创作有效书面和电子文档的过程是反复综合的过程，鼓励学生把创作和修改看成是不断发展的过程，把视觉方式看成是展现信息的手段，并重视语言在影响读者对信息内容评判中的重要作用。

本书使用者在进行信息交流的过程中将学会对修辞相关因素如语境、内容、目的、对象、组织、视觉手段及设计等的使用做出决断，并且了解做出各种交流方式决定的原因。本书不仅涉及信息交流中与修辞技巧相关的传统内容，即技巧（如定义、描述及过程）和形式（如信件、指南、提案和报告），而且详细描述了关于合作、职业道德、视觉手段及设计方面的内容以及扩展了国际交流、可用度测试和技术方面的讨论。与以前的版本相比，本书有以下变化：

- 增加了评估标准。第一章介绍了本书采用的可访性、理解性及可用性等标准来分析和评估书面、口头和视觉交流的效果。
- 增加了新例子。这些例子多与国际热点相关，如科技革新、药学发展、疾病控制、食品生产、生态平衡。
- 国际流行重点。许多国家的国际性企业的业务交流强调使用文本和视觉例子。
- 增加了关于文化的章节。第二章"理解文化与职场的关系"阐释了国际和企业文化及其对本企业员工的影响。
- 增加了关于可用性的章节。第九章"确保可用性"描述了可用性和可用性测试的特点，介绍了进行各种测试的指导原则，区分了可访性和可用性。
- 增加了关于技术的章节。技术内容贯穿全书。第十三章"设计电子交流"突出了各种新媒体的特点。
- 更多注释。本书样例配有更多的注释。
- 增加了职业道德注释栏。每个章节都有一个职业规范注释栏，讨论专业人士可能遇到的职业道德方面的冲突。
- 增加了网址链接。本书每个章节列举的网址可以通过本书的网址链接。这些网址提供了很多相关例子和文章，供进一步讨论。
- 增加了图片。本书新增图片阐释了工作中如何创作和使用技术文件、口头展示和视觉手段。

本书共分四部分十六章。第一部分包括五章，介绍了职场交流的主要内容。第二部分包括四章，讨论了信息筛选的主要过程。第三部分包括四章，讨论了如何整理收集到的信息。第四部分包括三章，讨论了交流者在信息交流准备中采用的策略。

北京外国语大学英语学院
杨鲁新

CONTENTS IN BRIEF
简要目录

PART I Communicating in the Workplace 职场中的交流 1

1. Characterizing Workplace Communication 职场交流特点 3
2. Understanding Culture and the Workplace 理解文化与职场的关系 37
3. Reading Technical Information 阅读技术信息 77
4. Addressing Audiences 满足交流对象需求 111
5. Collaborating in Workplace Communication 职场中的合作 143

PART II Managing Critical Processes 掌握信息筛选过程 183

6. Locating and Using Information 搜集与使用信息 185
7. Planning and Drafting 设计与起草 227
8. Revising and Editing 修改与编辑 261
9. Ensuring Usability 确保可用性 305

PART III Shaping Information 信息梳理 343

10. Organizing Information 组织信息 345
11. Designing Information 设计信息 377
12. Using Visual Forms 使用视觉形式 409
13. Designing Electronic Communication 设计电子交流 467

PART IV Understanding the Communicator's Strategies
理解交流者采用的策略 515

14. Creating Definitions 创建定义 517
15. Creating Technical Descriptions 创建技术描述 547
16. Creating Process Explanations 创建过程解释 579

CONTENTS 目 录

Preface 前言 xvii
Acknowledgments 致谢 xxii

PART I Communicating in the Workplace 职场中的交流 1

1. Characterizing Workplace Communication 职场交流特点 3

- Objectives and Outcomes 学习目标 3
- Importance of Effective Communication 有效交流的重要性 4
- Defining Technical Communication 定义技术交流 5
- Contexts for Constructing Meaning 构建意义的环境 9
  - Genre in Technical Communication 技术交流文体 9
  - Communities 社团 10
  - Technology in Technical Communication 技术交流中的技术运用 11
  - Ethics in Technical Communication 技术交流中的职业道德规范 12
    - **Ethics Sidebar:** Public vs. Private: Ethics and the Technical Professional 职业道德规范知识吧：公共与隐私：职业规范和专业技术人员 12
- Accessibility, Comprehensibility, and Usability 可访性，理解性及可用性 13
- Communication in the Workplace 职场中的交流 15
  - *Providing Information* 提供信息 16
  - *Identifying Problems* 发现问题 18
  - *Reporting Progress* 报告进展 20
  - *Managing Web Resources* 掌控网上资源 22
  - *Directing Action* 指导行动 24
- Constraints that Communicators Encounter 交流中可能遇到的局限 26
  - Time Constraints 时间局限 26
  - Subject and Format Constraints 主题与格式局限 26
  - Audience Constraints 读者（或客户）局限 26
  - Collaboration as a Constraint 合作带来的局限 26
  - Constraints in Data Collection 数据收集的局限 27
  - Constraints in Technology 技术中的局限 27
  - Constraints Caused by Noise 噪音引起的局限 27
- Individual and Collaborative Assignments 个人作业和小组作业 28

2. Understanding Culture and the Workplace 理解文化与职场的关系 37

- Objectives and Outcomes 学习目标 37
- Noticing Culture in the Workplace 关注职场中的文化 38
  - What's Normal? 什么是常规？ 40
  - Cultural Blindness 文化盲点 40
  - Defining Culture 文化定义 40

Understanding the Importance of Culture 理解文化的重要性 41
    Globalization and Localization 全球化与本地化 42
    Ethics Sidebar: Minimizing Cultural Bias in International Web Sites
    职业道德规范知识吧：减少国际网站的文化偏见 44
    Cultural Values 文化价值 51
Analyzing Culture 分析文化 52
    National Culture 民族文化 52
    Organizational Cultures 机构文化 58
    Gansu Province Project in the People's Republic of China 中国甘肃省项目 60
    Individuals and Their Culture 个体与其文化 62
Increase Cultural Awareness 增强文化意识 65
Individual and Collaborative Assignments 个人作业和小组作业 68

3. Reading Technical Information 阅读技术信息 77

Objectives and Outcomes 学习目标 77
Identifying Purposes 确定目的 78
Reading-Writing Relationships 阅读与写作的关系 79
Strategies for Effective Reading 有效阅读技巧 81
    Skim, Scan, and Predict 略读、速读、预测 81
    Identify Structure and Hierarchy 识别结构特点 84
    Determine the Main Points 确定主要内容 89
    Draw Inferences 运用推理 91
    Generate Questions and Examples 发现问题和例子 92
    Ethics Sidebar: "It's only a report": Ethics and Context
    职业道德规范知识吧："只是一个报告"：职业规范与工作环境 94
    Monitor and Adapt Reading Strategies 调整学习策略 95
Individual and Collaborative Assignments 个人作业和小组作业 104

4. Addressing Audiences 满足交流对象需求 111

Objectives and Outcomes 学习目标 111
Identifying Purposes 确定目的 112
Identifying Audiences 确定交流对象 113
Analyzing Audiences 分析交流对象 116
    Context 环境 117
    Purpose and Motivation 目的与动机 119
    Prior Knowledge 背景知识 120
    Reading Level 阅读水平 121
    Organizational Role 机构管理机制 126
Adjusting to Audiences 根据交流对象调整交流内容与形式 127
    Differences in Expertise 专业知识差异 127
    Differences in Role and Stances 交流对象职位差异 129
    Ethics Sidebar: "Their approaches are culturally insensitive":
    Ethics and Public Policies
    职业道德规范知识吧："他们的方式没有考虑文化因素"：职业规范与公共政策 132
Individual and Collaborative Assignments 个人作业和小组作业 133

5. Collaborating in the Workplace 职场中的合作 143

Objectives and Outcomes 学习目标 143
Reasons to Collaborate . . . or Not 合作与不合作的原因 145
    Subject 课题内容 146
    Process 过程 146
    Product 产品 147
    Benefits 利益 149
    Reasons Collaboration is a Problem 合作产生问题的原因 150
Types of Collaboration 合作的种类 151
    Coauthoring 合著 151
    Consulting with Colleagues 咨询同事 152
    Contributing to Team Projects 为团队项目献计献策 153
Being a Good Collaborator 成为一个好的合作者 153
    Self-Assess 自我评估 154
    Be Engaged and Cooperative 工作投入及善于合作 154
    Listen 倾听 155
    Conform to Conversation Conventions 遵守对话规范 158
    Ask Questions 问问题 159
    Share 分享 159
    Use Technology Effectively 有效运用技术 161
    Reflect 反思 164
Negotiating Conflicts 化解冲突 164
    Affective Conflicts 情感冲突 166
    Procedural Conflicts 过程冲突 167
    Ethics Sidebar: "They were there to grasp all the credit for themselves":
    Ethics and the Culture of Credit
    职业道德规范知识吧:"他们来这儿索取功劳":职业道德与文化 169
    Substantive Conflicts 实质性冲突 170
    Cultural Differences and Expectations 文化差异与期望 173
Individual and Collaborative Assignments 个人作业和小组作业 174

PART II   Managing Critical Processes 掌握信息筛选过程 183

6. Locating and Using Information 搜集与使用信息 185

Objectives and Outcomes 学习目标 185
Locating Primary and Secondary Sources 找到第一手和第二手信息资源 187
    Ethics Sidebar: On-the-Job Pressures: Ethics and Technology
    in the Workplace 职业道德规范知识吧:工作压力:职业道德与技术 189
Finding Information Using Electronic Resources 运用电子资源发现信息 190
    Finding Electronic Resources 发现电子资源 191
    Searching Electronic Resources 搜索电子资源 198
Finding Information Using Other Resources 运用其他资源发现信息 202
    Internal Records 内部记录 202
    Corporate Libraries 企业图书馆 202
    Personal Observations 个人观察 203

　　　　Interviews and Letters of Inquiry　访谈和信件咨询　206
　　　　Surveys and Polls　问卷调查　210
　　Using Sources Ethically　使用资源应符合道德规范　212
　　　　Assessing Credibility　评估可信度　212
　　　　Avoiding Plagiarism　避免剽窃　213
　　　　Avoiding Unintentional Plagiarism　避免无意剽窃　216
　　Individual and Collaborative Assignments　个人作业和小组作业　218

7. Planning and Drafting　设计与起草　227

　　Objectives and Outcomes　学习目标　227
　　Differences Between Writing Processes　写作过程差异　228
　　Inventing and Exploring　创作与探索　230
　　　　Problem-Solving Processes　解决问题过程　231
　　　　Problem-Solving Strategies　解决问题策略　231
　　Planning and Organizing　谋篇与组织　234
　　　　Types of Expert Planning　写作高手的谋篇方式　234
　　　　Project Planning　项目设计　235
　　　　Considering Rhetorical Elements　考虑修辞方式　237
　　　　Ethics Sidebar: "Is the communication honest?": Ethics and the Writing Process　职业道德规范知识吧："交流是诚实的吗?"：职业道德与写作过程　239
　　　　Assessing the Logic　逻辑检测　240
　　　　Drafting　起草　245
　　　　Selecting Person　人称选择　245
　　　　Verb Mood　动词语气　246
　　　　Selecting Active or Passive Voice　主动或被动语态　247
　　　　Using Plain Language　使用通俗语言　248
　　　　Avoiding Density　避免晦涩　251
　　　　Using Given-New Analysis　采用已有—新增信息构建写作模式　253
　　Individual and Collaborative Assignments　个人作业和小组作业　254

8. Revising and Editing　修改与编辑　261

　　Objectives and Outcomes　学习目标　261
　　Revising　修改　264
　　　　The Revision Process　修改过程　264
　　　　Redesigning Documents　重新设计文件　266
　　　　Revision Strategies　修改策略　266
　　Editing　编辑　271
　　　　Levels of Edit　编辑层次　271
　　　　Readability Formulas Don't Do What Their Name Claims　可读性方程　272
　　　　Common Copyediting Problems　常见编辑问题　276
　　　　Ethics Sidebar: Author, Audience, and Company: Ethics and Technical Editing　职业道德规范知识吧：作者，读者和公司：职业规范与技术编辑　282
　　　　Proofreading　校对　284
　　Examining Revision and Editing Decisions　检查修改和编辑内容　284
　　Individual and Collaborative Assignments　个人作业和小组作业　301

9. Ensuring Usability 确保可用性 305
Objectives and Outcomes 学习目标 305
Characterizing Usability 可用性特点 306
    Definition of Usability 可用性定义 308
    Critical Principles 重要原则 308
Characterizing Usability Testing 可用性测试特点 310
    Definition of Usability Testing 可用性测试定义 310
    Limitations 局限 311
    Benefits 益处 312
Types of Usability Testing 可用性测试种类 313
    Text-Based Testing 文本测试 314
    Expert-Based Testing 专家测试 316
    User-Based Testing 使用者测试 317
Conducting Usability Testing 进行可用性测试 320
    Creating a Usability Testing Plan 创建可用性测试计划 320
    Analyzing Users and Tasks 分析使用者和任务 322
    Implementing the Test Plan 执行测试计划 324
    Reporting Test Results 报告测试结果 328
Ensuring Accessibility 确保可访性 331
    Principles of Accessibility 可访性原则 332
    Accessibility and Electronic Communication 可访性与电子交流 333
    Ethics Sidebar: "What You Say!" 职业道德规范知识吧："你说什么！" 335
    Accessibility and Government Regulations 可访性与政府规章 337
    Accessibility and Attitude 可访性与态度 338
Individual and Collaborative Assignments 个人作业和小组作业 340

PART III Shaping Information 信息梳理 343

10. Organizing Information 组织信息 345
Objectives and Outcomes 学习目标 345
Transforming Information into Knowledge 把信息转化为知识 346
Developing the Organization for Information 确定信息组织方式 348
    Outlines 大纲 348
    Storyboards 故事板 351
    Tables and Spreadsheets for Organizing Information 表格 354
Implementing the Organization of Information 组织信息 356
    Alphabetical Order, Numeric Order, and Continuums
    字母排序，数字排序，物体或实践发展过程排序 356
    Topic Sentences and Transitions to Signal Organizations 主题句和过渡语 357
    Whole/Parts Organization 整体与局部 360
    Chronological Order 时间顺序 361
    Spatial Order 空间关系 363
    Ascending/Descending Order 升序或降序 364
    Comparison/Contrast 对照比较 366
    Cause and Effect 因果关系 367

Using Organization　信息的组织　371
　　　Ethics Sidebar: "Is This Ethical?": Ethics and Document Design
　　　职业道德规范知识吧："这符合职业道德吗?"：职业道德与文件设计　372
　　Individual and Collaborative Assignments　个人作业和小组作业　372

11. Designing Information　设计信息　377

Outcomes and Objectives　学习目标　377
Chunking and Labeling Information　集中与标注信息　379
　　Principles of Design in Action　设计原则　380
　　White Space to Chunk Information　用空白集中信息　384
　　Headings to Label Chunked Information　用标题标注集中的信息　389
Arranging Related Chunks of Verbal and Visual Information　整理文字和视觉信息　390
　　Using Design Conventions　使用设计原则　390
　　Avoiding Problems in Arranging Information　避免信息整理中的问题　391
　　Ethics Sidebar: "A Wound to the Hand": Ethics and Document Design
　　职业道德规范知识吧："手上的伤口"：职业道德与文件设计　394
Emphasizing Information　强调信息　395
　　Typefaces　字体与字号　395
　　Typographic Devices　文档符号　400
Individual and Collaborative Assignments　个人作业和小组作业　403

12. Using Visual Forms　使用视觉形式　409

Objectives and Outcomes　学习目标　409
　　Ethics Sidebar: "With no sacrifice to truth": Ethics and Visuals
　　职业道德规范知识吧："没有牺牲事实"：职业道德与视觉手段　411
Incorporating Visuals　应用视觉手段　412
　　Visual/Verbal Combinations　视图与文字结合　412
　　Adapting Visuals to Audiences　根据交流对象调整视觉手段　415
　　Conventions in Referencing and Placing Visuals　视觉手段参考和放置原则　415
Visual Functions　视觉手段的作用　417
　　Function 1: Provide Immediate Visual Recognition　作用1：即刻视觉辨认　418
　　Function 2: Organize Numeric or Textual Data　作用2：组织数字或文字数据　419
　　Function 3: Show Relationships　作用3：展示关系　421
　　Function 4: Define Concepts, Objects, and Processes　作用4：定义概念、物体及过程　430
　　Function 5: Present Action or Process　作用5：展示行动与过程　433
　　Function 6: Illustrate Appearance, Structure, or Function
　　作用6：示例说明外表、结构或作用　436
　　Function 7: Identify Facilities or Locations　作用7：确定设施或地点　441
Conventions in Use of Color　颜色使用原则　447
　　Cautions against Misuse of Color　谨慎使用颜色　447
　　Suggestions for Appropriate Use of Color　恰当使用颜色的建议　447
　　Color in Designing Electronic Documents　设计电子文档时的颜色使用　456
Individual and Collaborative Assignments　个人作业和小组作业　457

13. Designing Electronic Communication　设计电子交流　467

Objectives and Outcomes　学习目标　467
Characterizing Electronic Communication　电子交流特点　468
　　Types of Electronic Communication　电子交流种类　469

Ethics Sidebar: We Know Who You Are and Where You've Been
职业道德规范知识吧：我们知道你是谁和去过哪里 471
  Web Sites and Web-Enabled Environments 网站和网络支持环境 472
  Audiences and Electronic Communication 交流对象与电子交流 475
Principles and Practices of Effective Design 有效设计的原则与实践 478
  Information Architecture 信息建构 479
  Page/Screen Design 页面或屏幕设计 487
  Developing Effective Content 建立有效内容 496
Standards and Tools 标准与工具 498
  Markup Languages, Scripts, and Programming 置标语言、文字及程序 498
  Style Sheets and Templates 格式模板 500
  Style Guides 格式指南 500
Understanding the Iterative Design Process 理解设计过程 502
  Planning the Iterative Process 计划设计过程 502
  Analyzing Existing Sites 分析已有网站 502
  Creating Prototypes of Your Web Site 创建你的网站原型 503
  Coordinating the Process 协调过程 503
Ensuring Usability and Accessibility 确保可用性和可访问性 507
  Features of Accessible Electronic Communication 可访问性电子交流特点 507
  Meeting the Challenges of a Web Accessibility Policy 面对网站可访问性原则的挑战 508
  Checking Web Sites for Accessibility 检查网站的可访问性 510
Individual and Collaborative Assignments 个人作业和小组作业 510

PART IV Understanding the Communicator's Strategies
理解交流者采用的策略 515

14. Creating Definitions 创建定义 517

Objectives and Outcomes 学习目标 517
The Need for Definitions 定义的需要 519
    Multiple Meanings 词的多义 519
    Complexity of Meaning 意义的复杂性 520
    Technical Jargon 技术术语 521
    Symbols 符号 523
Construction of Definitions 构建定义 524
    Formal Definitions 正式定义 525
    Informal Definitions 非正式定义 526
    Operational Definitions 操作定义 529
    Expanded Definitions 扩展定义 530
        Ethics Sidebar: Professional Codes of Conduct 职业道德规范知识吧：职业行为规范 530
Placement of Definitions 定义的位置 533
    Glossary 词汇表 533
    Information Notes and Sidebars 注释 535
    Appendixes 附录 535
    Online Help 网上帮助 535
Individual and Collaborative Assignments 个人作业和小组作业 537

15. Creating Technical Descriptions 创建技术描述 547
    Objectives and Outcomes 学习目标 547
    Defining Technical Description 定义技术描述 550
        Ethics Sidebar: "The decision was flawed": Ethical Responsibility and the Challenger Explosion 职业道德规范知识吧："决定不是完美的"：职业责任与"挑战者号"爆炸 551
    Using Technical Description 使用技术描述 552
        Observation Notes 观察记录 553
        Training Materials 培训手册 553
        Technical Manuals 技术手册 554
        Proposals and Reports 研究提案与研究报告 556
        Marketing and Promotional Pieces 市场营销材料 558
        Public Information and Education 公众宣传和教育 558
    Preparing a Technical Description 准备技术描述 562
        Audience's Task 交流对象的需求 562
        Components 组成部分 562
        Diction 语言使用 563
        Visuals 视觉手段 564
        Organization 信息组织 568
    Individual and Collaborative Assignments 个人作业和小组作业 571

16. Creating Process Explanations 创建过程解释 579
    Objectives and Outcomes 学习目标 579
    Defining Processes 定义过程 580
        Ethics Sidebar: Whistleblowers: Ethical Choices and Consequences 职业道德规范知识吧：告发者：职业道德的选择与后果 582
    Using Process Explanations 使用过程解释 583
        Reports 报告 583
        Task Manuals 使用手册 583
        Orientation and Training Materials 培训材料 586
        Marketing and Promotional Materials 市场营销材料 586
        Public Information and Education 公众宣传与教育 590
    Preparing Processes 准备过程 591
        Audience and Purpose 交流对象与目的 591
        Identification of Steps 确定步骤 591
        Visuals 视觉手段 592
        Diction 文字使用 593
        Organization and Format 组织与格式 594
    Examining a Sample Process Explanation: Developing Low-Cost Roofing Materials 过程解释案例分析：开发低耗屋顶材料 595
        Processes Involving Sockeye Salmon 捕获、保存、烹调三文鱼的过程 598
    Individual and Collaborative Assignments 个人作业和小组作业 600

15. Creating Technical Descriptions 574

Objectives and Outcomes 574
Defining Technical Description 576
Ethics Sidebar: The Decision was Delayed, Ethical Responsibility, and the Challenger Explosion 578
Using Technical Description 581
Observation Notes 581
Training Materials 581
Technical Manuals 581
Proposals and Reports 581
Marketing and Promotional Pieces 581
Public Information and Education 581
Preparing a Technical Description 582
Audience's Task 582
Components 582
Diction 583
Visuals 584
Organization 584
Individual and Collaborative Assignments 571

16. Creating Process Explanations 579

Objectives and Outcomes 579
Defining Processes 580
Ethics Sidebar: Whistleblowers, Ethical Choices and Consequences 582
Using Process Explanations 585
Reports 585
User Manuals 585
Orientation and Training Materials 586
Marketing and Promotional Materials 586
Public Information and Education Materials 586
Preparing Process Explanations 587
Audience and Purpose 587
Identification of Steps 587
Visuals 587
Diction 588
Organization and Format 589
Combining a Sample Process Explanation, Developing Low-Cost Promotional Materials 595
Processes Involving Decision Making, A Flow Chart 596
Individual and Collaborative Assignments, A Flow Chart 600

PREFACE
前 言

Technical Communication, Sixth Edition, has a clear goal: to help students and workplace professionals communicate technical information — written, oral, and visual — to audiences in a variety of complex workplace contexts.

Technical Communication, Sixth Edition, presents straightforward explanations and guidelines based on current theory, research, and practice. The elegant, usable design of this edition enables students to use many of the text's pages, figures, and tables as models. The discussions and the classroom-tested exercises and assignments, both individual and collaborative, help users become better communicators. This highly readable and teachable edition stresses the integrated, recursive nature of producing effective print and electronic documents, encouraging students to think of invention and revision as ongoing processes, to think of visuals as ways to present information, and to think of language as having the power to shape and influence users' perceptions.

What's the approach? This edition emphasizes a rhetorical, problem-solving approach. Users of this text will learn to make decisions about rhetorical elements such as context, content, purpose, audience, organization, visuals, and design as they engage in the process of communicating technical information. In addition, they will learn the *reasons* behind their communication decisions.

Users of this text — both traditional and nontraditional students as well as workplace professionals — will learn that effective technical communication contains both creativity and craft, a point I make by the continued use of Leonardo da Vinci's technical drawings on all the chapters openers throughout the book. Like Leonardo da Vinci's technical drawings, technical communication should be precise, detailed, functional, and focused. That's not all it should be; it's the least it should be.

Creativity and craft play out in another way with this edition's new cover featuring a photograph of wind turbines. The image is not only aesthetically pleasing, but it also represents the leading edge of a centuries' old technology that captures many of the challenges that technical professionals and technical communicators face. Traditions exist, but to endure they must adapt to a dramatically changing world.

Throughout the text, the traditional concerns of technical communication — techniques such as definitions, descriptions, and processes; and forms such as correspondence, instructions, proposals, and reports — are always related to rhetorical elements. Beyond these concerns, the text continues to include detailed information about collaboration, ethics, visuals, and design and has significantly expanded its discussion of international communication, usability testing, and technology.

What's new in this edition? This sixth edition of *Technical Communication* maintains the strengths of the previous editions while incorporating important new information. The changes in this edition are drawn from current theory and research, leading-edge practices from the workplace, and helpful tools and strategies from practitioners. Twelve of the changes are particularly important:

- *Evaluation criteria.* Chapter 1 introduces easy-to-use evaluation criteria — *accessibility, comprehensibility,* and *usability* — which are used as a heuristic throughout the book to analyze and assess written, oral, and visual communication.
- *New examples.* New examples come from a variety of disciplines and professions. Many relate to global themes — scientific/technological innovation, medical advances/disease control, food production, and ecological/environmental balance — which demonstrate that scientific and technological concerns are global.
- *International emphasis.* The international workplace is emphasized with textual and visual examples from many countries and in many languages.
- *Special features.* Two-page spreads highlight interesting situations where technical documents, oral presentations, and visuals are created and used.
- *New chapter about culture.* Chapter 2, "Understanding Culture and the Workplace," addresses international and organizational cultures as well as characteristics that influence individuals in those cultures.
- *New chapter about usability.* Chapter 9, "Ensuring Usability," characterizes usability and usability testing, introduces guidelines for conducting various types of tests, and differentiates usability from accessibility.
- *New chapter about technology.* Throughout the new edition, you will find increased information about technology, including Chapter 13, "Designing Electronic Communication," which highlights critical features of new media, ranging from e-mail and PowerPoint® to animated Web sites.
- *More annotations.* More extensive marginal annotations for the sample documents include questions and comments to encourage critical evaluation.
- *New Ethics Sidebars.* Each chapter includes an Ethics Sidebar that focuses on a complex ethical issue considered by workplace professionals. Several of these sidebars are new to this edition.
- *WEBLINKS.* Numerous WEBLINKS in each chapter are accessible through the book's Companion Web site, which also has a wide array of relevant examples and articles for discussion.

- *Photographs throughout.* New photographs throughout the text illustrate workplaces where technical documents, oral presentations, and visuals are created and used.
- *Improved design.* The sophisticated, usable design features full-color pages that demonstrate ways in which color can be functional and contribute to interpreting and using technical information.

What critical concerns are addressed? While accuracy is arguably the most critical aspect of any technical document, oral presentation, or visual, technical accuracy is not enough. This text balances theory and research, pedagogy and practice, and classroom and workplace needs. The balance is demonstrated in ten critical concerns:

- *Rhetorical base.* Most problems communicating technical information occur in complex workplace environments. In addressing this challenge, *Technical Communication,* Sixth Edition, uses rhetorical elements — for example, the context of the communication; the constraints of the situation; needs of the audience(s); purposes of the writers, speakers, and designers; conventions of the genres; strategies for organizing and designing information — which influence the process of creating documents, oral presentations, and visuals.
- *Communicating with audiences, including international audiences.* The text provides early and ongoing in-depth coverage of audience analysis, focusing on practical suggestions for evaluating audiences and developing strategies for adjusting material to different audiences, including those in a variety of international and organizational cultures.
- *Visuals and document design.* The text emphasizes the rhetorical nature of visuals and establishes parallels between visual and verbal information. The text also explores the role of color and emphasizes the impact of information design, both in print and electronic documents. The design of this text models ways to make information accessible, comprehensible, and usable.
- *Collaboration.* The text not only presents a chapter about collaboration, but the end of each chapter includes collaborative assignments. Throughout the text, students are reminded that the workplace is a collaborative environment and that written, oral, and visual information is seldom produced or used in isolation. Students not only learn the importance of collaboration and teamwork, but they also learn how to be productive collaborators.
- *Testing.* Creating effective documents, oral presentations, and visuals should include text-based, expert-based, and user-based testing. The results of testing can be used as the basis for revising and editing.
- *Process and product.* This edition shows how technical professionals are involved in a complex process to create as well as interpret technical

documents, presentations, and visuals. The text discusses ways to approach communication problems; explains options available to writers, speakers, and designers; offers suggestions about logical organization; and illustrates appropriate language use.

- *Technology.* Because technical communication takes place in a rapidly changing electronic environment, this text discusses the impact of technology on creating and interpreting documents, oral presentations, and visuals. Users learn ways to make informed decisions about technology as well as ways that enable them to take advantage of the power of new media.

- *Examples.* Throughout the text, annotated examples from students and workplace professionals around the world illustrate the key points and serve as models.

- *Style. Technical Communication* is a reader-based text; it directly addresses students and workplace professionals in a straightforward manner that is both appealing and accessible.

- *Apparatus and computer support.* The extensive marginal annotations prompt critical thinking and offer opportunities to discuss ideas and apply the practices presented in *Technical Communication.* The Individual and Collaborative Assignments at the end of each chapter encourage planning and developing a wide array of documents, oral presentations, and visuals.

What support materials are available? This new edition of *Technical Communication* has a greatly expanded *Instructor's Manual* and a Book Companion Web Site.

- The *Instructor's Manual (IM)* is a valuable resource both for highly experienced and for new instructors. It offers strategies for teaching each chapter successfully, including the use of a new convenient heuristic: RADAR (Read, Act, Discuss, Assess, and Reflect). The *IM* also includes suggestions for planning and preparing course material, additional activities and assignments, strategies for managing different classroom formats (traditional, computer lab, and online), PowerPoint® presentations for introducing or reviewing concepts, and tools and strategies for assessing student work (written, oral, and visual; individual and collaborative; print and electronic). In addition, the *IM* includes essays by nationally recognized researchers and educators; written specifically to accompany *Technical Communication,* Sixth Edition, these essays discuss innovative approaches and practices being used in technical communication classrooms. Many of the articles are new to this edition's manual. The *IM* is available free to all adopters of this new edition of *Technical Communication.* (You may request a copy of the *IM* from your Thomson representative or download the PDF version from the instructor side of the Book Companion Web Site, available at www.english.wadsworth.com/burnett6e.)

- *Student side of the Book Companion Web Site.* The student side of the Web site includes for each chapter an overview, tools and tips, "Workplace Realities" (videotapes with workplace professionals), annotated interactive examples, a variety of classroom and Internet activities, key terms, Web links to chapter-related content, and a tutorial quiz. Additionally, the student side of the Web site includes many cases, new assignments, a complete handbook, and career resources. To access the Book Companion Web Site, go to **www.english.wadsworth.com/burnett6e**.

- *Instructor side of the Book Companion Web Site.* The instructor side of the Web site includes for each chapter an instructor overview, chapter teaching tips, PowerPoint® lecture slides, and answers to chapter quizzes as well as suggestions for integrating the additional examples and assignments into the course. The instructor side of the Web site also includes course management tools, sample syllabi, rubrics for assessing student work, and suggestions for using the Web site's cases and career resources. To access the Book Companion Web Site, go to **www.english.wadsworth.com/burnett6e**.

I have made changes in each edition based on the recommendations of colleagues from colleges, universities, agencies, businesses, and companies around the world. If you have suggestions about changes I should consider, please contact me. If you have examples that would work well for the next edition, please contact me as well. I value your feedback.

Rebecca E. Burnett

Rebecca E. Burnett, PhD
University Professor of Rhetoric & Professional Communication
Iowa State University
c/o Thomson Higher Education
25 Thomson Place
Boston, MA 02210

Acknowledgments 致 谢

Technical Communication would not exist without the personal and professional support of family, friends, and colleagues.

Researchers. In preparing this edition, I have been thankful for the skillful and thorough researchers from Iowa State University who assisted me in preparing this revision: Brian Hentz, Katherine Miles, and Rebecca Pope-Ruark. They posed alternative approaches, updated information, located examples, suggested two-page spreads, provided valuable editing, and drafted new activities, glossary lists, PowerPoint presentations, and quizzes. Their assistance has been essential.

Co-author. Donna Kain, at East Carolina University, has been my trusted and expert co-author for Chapters 9 and 13, my co-author for the expanded and updated *Instructor's Manual,* and the creative and insightful developer of the content on the Book Companion Web Site. She has been invaluable in this revision.

Personal thanks. As always, Dorothea Burnett, Margaret Burnett, Christopher Burnett, and Paula Thompson provide me with the confidence and support to make the revision possible. William Jeffries continues in his unwavering support and serves as a voice of reason.

Friends and colleagues. I appreciate the support and contributions provided by friends and colleagues around the world: Philippa Benson, Mort Boyd, Shelly Boyd, Linda Driskill, Marcia Greenman Lebeau, Muriel McGrann, Susie Poague, Bev Sauer, Don Stanford, Judith Stanford, Anette van der Mescht, and Ben Xu. They have helped to shape my thinking as I went about this revision.

I want to thank my friends and colleagues at Iowa State University who see wisdom in balancing theory, research, workplace practice, and pedagogy. Their curiosity, dedication, and insight are an inspiration to me. My undergraduate and graduate students at Iowa State University and technical professionals in university seminars have also been important to this edition. I want to acknowledge the valuable discussions and contributions of various kinds provided by ISU friends and colleagues, most especially Gloria Betcher, Daniel Coffey, Dan Douglas, Laura Hannasch, Carl Herndl, Lee Honeycutt, Denny Howe, Robert Martin, Linta Meetz, Michael Mendelson, Neil Nakadate, Elizabeth Orcutt-Kroeger, Lorrie Pellack, Lee Poague, Diane Prince-Herndl, David Roberts, Caskey Russell, Geoff Sauer, Sarah Stambaugh, Lana Voga, and Loren Zachary. And in this revision, I also want to thank my friends and colleagues at Rice University who provided many opportunities that have enabled me to select useful new examples.

Contributors. I especially appreciate the colleagues and workplace professionals who contributed examples for this edition: Paul Boyd from the US Army Corps of Engineers; Maria Cochran, Marisa Corzanego, Mark Gleason, Oskana Hlyva, Ken Jolls, and Arvid Osterberg — all from Iowa State University; Sarah Helland from Pioneer; Zachary Lavicky from Emporia State University; Melissa Poague from University of Washington; Lee Tesdell from Minnesota State University–Mankato; and Tara Barrett Tarnowski from University of Georgia.

Previous editions. The contributions by the following people to the fifth edition have been substantially retained: Jill Bigley, Arricka Brouwer, Christopher Burnett, Larry Chan, David Clark, Irene Faass, Patty Harms, Elizabeth Herman, William Jeffries, Ken Jolls, Kari Krumpel, Muriel McGrann, Walden Miller, Kate Molitor, Matt Turner, Peggy Pollock, Janet Renze, Daryl Seay, Doug Schaapveld, Clay Spinuzzi, Don Stanford, Judith Stanford, Melissa Waltman, and Julie Zeleznik as well as friends, colleagues, and students at Iowa State University.

The contributions by the following people to the fourth edition have been substantially retained: Susan Booker, Kaelin Chappelle, David Clark, Andrea Breemer Frantz, Woody Hart, William Jeffries, Lee-Ann Kastman, Elenor Long, Muriel McGrann, Ron Myers, Tom Myers, Mike Peery, Clay Spinuzzi, Don Stanford, Judith Stanford, Gary Tarcy, Lee Tesdell, Christianna White, Dorothy Winchester, Mark Zachry, and Stephanie Zeluck as well as friends, colleagues, and students at Iowa State University.

The contributions by the following people to the third edition have been substantially retained: Reva Daniel, Michael Hassett, William Jeffries, Muriel McGrann, Cindy Myers, and Christianna White as well as colleagues and students at Iowa State University.

The contributions by the following people to the second edition have been substantially retained: Philippa Benson, William Jeffries, and Barbara Sitko as well as my friends, colleagues, and students at Carnegie Mellon University.

The contributions by the following people to the first edition have been substantially retained: Geraldine Branca, Christopher Burnett, Robert Carosso, Bernard DiNatale, Arline Dupras, Elizabeth Foster, Nancy Irish, Elizabeth Carros Keroack, Marcia Greenman Lebeau, Muriel McGrann, Stephen Meidell, Leon Sommers, and Judith Dupras Stanford as well as students at Northern Essex Community College, Merrimack College, and the University of Massachusetts at Lowell.

Reviewers. I appreciate the helpful feedback from colleagues around the country who suggested revisions, sometimes in a quick e-mail message, sometimes in a short conversation at a conference. The official reviewers' practical and often insightful suggestions were, of course, instrumental in revisions for this edition. Detailed reviews were provided by

Scott Chadwick	*Creighton University*
Dave Clark	*University of Wisconsin–Milwaukee*
Lee Ann Kastman Breuch	*University of Minnesota*
Cezar Ornatowski	*San Diego State University*
Penny Sansbury	*Florence-Darlington Technical College*
Geoffrey Sauer	*Iowa State University*
Karen Schnackenberg	*Carnegie Mellon University*
Stuart Selber	*Pennsylvania State University*
Clay Spinuzzi	*University of Texas–Austin*
Cindy Raisor	*Texas A&M University*

The Thomson Wadsworth team for *Technical Communication* has been extraordinary. Dickson Musslewhite, my trusted and supportive Acquisitions Editor, provided excellent editorial direction. Michell Phifer, Senior Development Editor, kept me on track in this complex revision with intelligence, patience, expertise, and humor — for which I am immensely grateful. Linda Beaupre redesigned the book, creating a design that is elegant and usable (a remarkable and wonderful combination); her design reflects the spirit of the text. Joe Gallagher and Cara Douglas-Graff supported the development of the Web site for the book. Janet McCartney copyedited the manuscript and the endnotes, saving me from embarrassing errors. Sally Cogliano, Senior Production Editor, began the production process with efficiency and good humor. Lianne Ames, Senior Production Editor, saw the book through the production process with remarkable energy, insight, flexibility, patience, and grace. Christina Micek was invaluable as the photo researcher for this edition. Karyn Morrison handled the complex task of permissions with thoroughness. Joy Westberg wrote wonderful marketing materials. Beth Callaway from Graphic World supervised and coordinated the composition process with care and deliberation. For all, I am immensely thankful.

PART III

Shaping Information
信息梳理

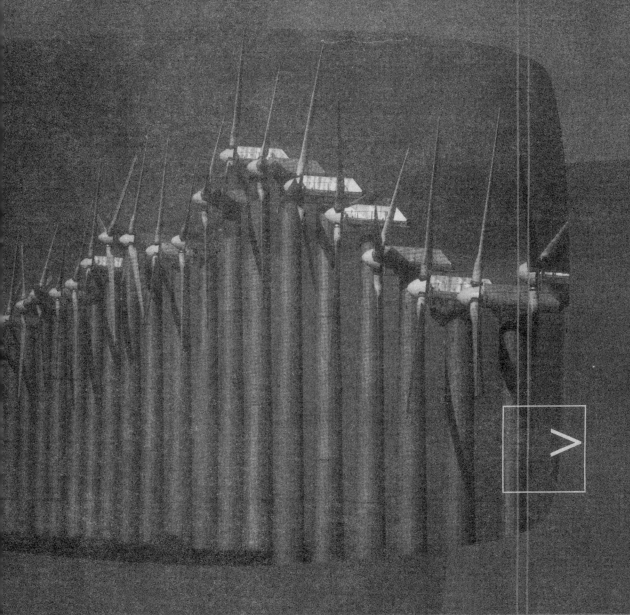

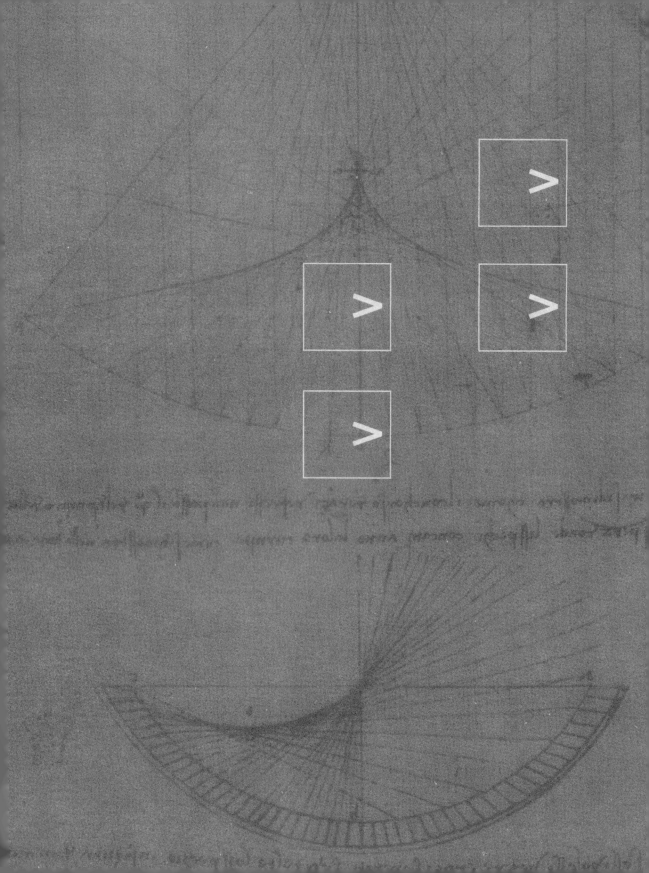

CHAPTER 10

Organizing Information
组织信息

　　组织信息是知识管理的一个重要步骤。本章介绍了如何整理和转化搜集的信息。具体地讲，可以采用大纲、故事板及表格等方式来整理信息，以确定最佳的信息组织方式。一旦确定信息组织的方式，下一个任务就是如何让读者或观众理解许多信息之间的关系。本章最后阐释了如何运用常规的写作方式（如整体与局部、时间顺序、空间关系、信息排序、对照比较、因果关系）来呈现搜集的信息。

Objectives and Outcomes 学习目标

This chapter will help you accomplish these outcomes:

- Organize information as part of knowledge management

- Use outlines, storyboards, and tables as tools to test various ways to organize information

- Use topic sentences and transitions to signal organization

- Use conventional organizational patterns — whole/parts, chronology, spatial order, ascending/descending order, comparison/contrast, cause and effect — to present information verbally and visually

The way you choose to organize information affects the way you interpret it and, necessarily, the meaning you make from it. While Chapter 6 discussed the beginning steps of knowledge management (finding and selecting information), this chapter is about organizing and transforming that information. If you skimp on this part of the communication process — organizing information — you will have difficulty producing high-quality documents, oral presentations, and visuals. Outlines, storyboards, and tables are valuable tools for organizing information in various ways. Additionally, six conventional patterns enable you to organize verbal information (for both documents and oral presentations) and visual information.

Transforming Information into Knowledge
把信息转化为知识

Decontextualized information doesn't carry meaning, but once information is transformed into knowledge, that information does carry meaning. This transformation requires you to make sense of the information, organizing it so that you can compare it to your prior knowledge, consider the implications and consequences, and talk about it with informed colleagues.

The process of transforming information into knowledge — and, thus, making meaning — is messy, sometimes unpredictable, often difficult, and always contextualized. When you change the context, you change the meaning. The organization of your information affects the rest of the project, so if you're involved in an important or complex project, you should allow time during your planning to organize your information in more than one way because you'll see different things every time you rearrange it. Why? The meaning you construct from information is contingent on a range of things, including national and organizational

Informal Settlements in Durban, South Africa.[1] This is housing in an "informal settlement." These overcrowded residential areas present complex social, economic, and engineering challenges since these areas typically do not have sanitation systems, fresh water, or electricity.

culture, the local context and specific situation, and the perspectives of you and the audience(s). If you do nothing to organize and interpret the information you present, other people will organize it to suit themselves, perhaps seeing meanings different from what you might have presented.[2]

The strategies for organizing information are widely recognized, but you should apply them purposefully rather than mechanically — that is, have reasons for what you do rather than just following convenional practices. The purpose of a document, oral presentation, or visual is to communicate information to an audience; thus, making your information understandable is critical. As you initially explore a topic, you may initially create a *writer-based* document (or presentation or visual), one that helps you examine and organize the information. However, it doesn't consider whether the information will be effective for your audience. Your goal should be to create an *audience-based* document, presentation or visual, one that considers the needs and reactions of your audience and organizes information so that these readers, listeners, and viewers can understand the issues.

Can you have too much relevant information? Probably not. But you can have too much information that's irrelevant, badly organized, and inaccessible. To read a short version of how one company handled this problem, go to **http://english.wadsworth.com/burnett6e**.
  CLICK ON WEBLINK
    CLICK on Chapter 10/information silos

WEBLINK

Informal Settlements in Context. Audience reactions to the same housing may be different when the informal settlement is put in context — adjacent to more elaborate housing. Even though the problems with sanitation systems, fresh water, and electricity don't change, the context influences interpretation.

Developing the Organization for Information
确定信息组织方式

The overall persuasiveness of your documents, oral presentations, and visuals depends on their organization. You can use strategies such as outlines, storyboards, and tables to experiment with and test various ways to arrange and rearrange your information to determine the most effective organization.

Outlines 大 纲

You may decide to outline your information simply because (as you read in Chapter 6) changing an outline is usually easier than changing the draft of a text. Any outline you develop should be flexible and easy to change as you arrange and rearrange ideas, add new information, and delete unnecessary material. Outlines are not intended to restrict you; rather, they are tools to help you manage the material for a document. Think of them as blueprints that show the overall structure and primary features. As with buildings that exist only as blueprints, changes in documents or oral presentations are easier to make in their preliminary stages.

Outlines can help you arrange and examine and then rearrange collected information. They do not have to be formal, complete-sentence outlines. Initially, you can just jot down information and then rethink, rearrange, and reorganize it

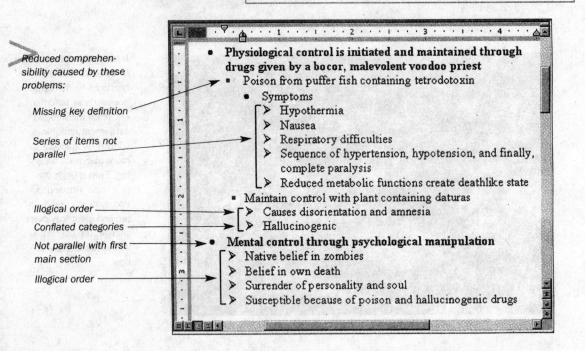

FIGURE 10.1 Online Outline Showing Problems in Completeness, Organization, and Parallelism

Part III Shaping Information

in an outline. For example, a simple list of unorganized points about native beliefs and practices reports the work of Wade Davis, a Harvard ethnobotanist, who used pharmacology to discuss the zombies of traditional Haitian voodoo.[3]

Figure 10.1 shows a computer screen of an outline that was developed from this preliminary list. Outlining is an option with most word-processing software. An electronic outline offers you a different view of your document rather than creating a separate document. The electronic changes you make in the outline automatically become part of the document, and vice versa. You can easily switch back and forth between an outline view of your document and a full text view.

The writer could examine the electronic outline in Figure 10.1 to determine whether the information is complete and parallel — equivalent in importance, sequence, and wording. In this case, the outline has incomplete information, needs reordering, and isn't parallel. But without the outline (whether paper or electronic), the writer might not see these inadequacies.

Figure 10.2 shows a revised electronic outline in which the writer has corrected the problems. The changes are more than cosmetic. First, expressing ideas in parallel structure demonstrates that the writer intends to treat them equally, as shown in the revision. Next, the sequence must be logical, as shown in

FIGURE 10.2   **Online Outline Showing Revisions**

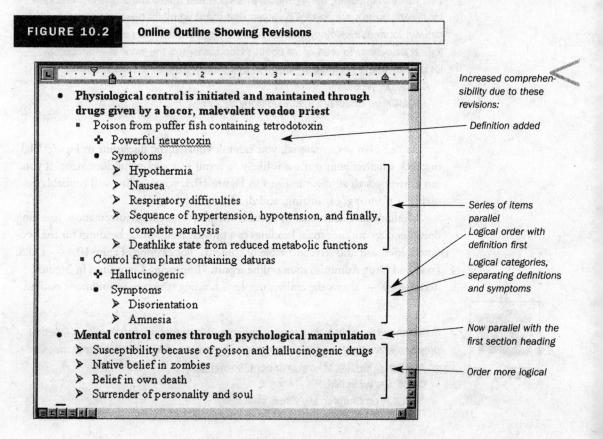

the revision in the order of entries. Here, indicating susceptibility logically comes first; instances of beliefs resulting from this susceptibility follow. Finally, essential information must not be inadvertently omitted, as shown by the omission of the type of poison in the first section. In each case, changing the outline is easier than changing the draft of the paper.

The original and revised outlines about zombies (Figures 10.1 and 10.2) show how helpful outlines can be to organize and reorganize information before starting to draft a document. These outlines identify gaps in data, inconsistencies in the relative importance of various segments, and problems in sequencing information. If you use outlines as tools for planning and revision, you may save yourself a great deal of frustration and time.

WEBLINK

Ethnobotonists study the connections between plants and people. Harvard ethnobotonist Wade Davis has "traveled to Haiti to investigate legends of a 'zombi poison.' The so-called poison was supposedly made from human bones and parts of lizards, poisonous toads, sea worms, puffer fish, and other items; it was said to lower the metabolism of anyone who swallowed it and paralyze his or her vital functions, leaving the individual in a condition that could easily be mistaken for death. Davis's supporters believed that the drug might have important applications for anesthesiology and artificial hibernation,"[4] which might control neurological diseases. To read more about Wade Davis and the work of ethnobotonists, go to http://english.wadsworth.com/burnett6e for a series of links.
CLICK ON WEBLINK
CLICK on Chapter 10/ethnobotony

As you plan your material, you can ask yourself the questions in Figure 10.3 to check whether your outline is likely to result in a successful document. If you can answer yes to all the questions in Figure 10.3, your outline will probably be useful in planning, organizing, and drafting your document.

Outlines have additional uses besides helping to organize information. In a long document, an outline's main headings can provide ready-made headings for the document itself and also serve as a table of contents. For example, Figure 10.4 — a U.S. Food and Drug Administration online report, "Improving Innovation in Medical Technology" — shows the entire three-level heading structure as a numeric outline.

WEBLINK

Sometimes the most useful way to organize information is visually. For a link that provides examples of ways to organize using tables, diagrams, lists, and maps, go to http://english.wadsworth.com/burnett6e.
CLICK ON WEBLINK
CLICK on Chapter 10/visual strategies

FIGURE 10.3 — Questions to Ask about Your Outline

Content and context	■ Is all important information included and all unnecessary information omitted? ■ Are contextual factors that will influence the document's interpretation acknowledged?
Audience	■ Do the headings give readers an accurate overview of the document? ■ Is the level of detail appropriate for the purpose and audience?
Purpose and key points	■ Are the main headings and subheadings logically arranged? ■ Is the organization in the outline appropriate to the content, purpose, audience, and genre?
Organization	■ Is all information in the outline in the appropriate places — both in the main sections and the subsections?
Professional standards	■ Do the details in each subsection reflect the emphasis for that heading? ■ Are main headings in the outline written in parallel grammatical form (so that you can use them as headings in the document)?

Storyboards 故事板

Storyboards are a second way of experimenting with and testing your organization of information. They have two broad purposes and audiences: (1) a powerful organizing tool for the writers and designers who create them; and (2) a short, dramatic visual summary showing the gist of the final project for clients or customers. Storyboards are a related sequence of hand-drawn or electronic sketches of pages or screens that organize their critical points. Basically, storyboards create shorthand stories that have a setting, characters, and actions for a particular audience. They also convey the purpose, hierarchy, and sequence of the information as well as the navigation. Using them enables you to plan highly visual projects such as tutorials, training videos, ads, and Web sites.

Storyboards have been around for a long time; even Leonardo da Vinci put ideas up on a wall and examined the layout. Modern storyboards can trace their origins to the beginnings of cinema with Sergei Eisenstein. Then, in 1928, Walt Disney and his staff developed a storyboard system allowing writers and designers to trace the overall story and see connections between the various parts.[5]

Some storyboards are passive — simply a sequence of thumbnail sketches or drafts of screenshots of a Web site. With a *passive* storyboard, the writer or designer usually walks a client through the sequence, explaining what happens.

Other storyboards are *active* (animated on a timed program) or *interactive* (requiring the user to be engaged in the process, for example, using PowerPoint so a client can independently walk through the sequence of a presentation).[6] And,

FIGURE 10.4 Outline Headings in FDA Report[7]

Improving Innovation in Medical Technology

1.0 Background
    1.1 FDA Product Approvals and Challenges
    1.2 Factors contributing to decline in new product applications.

2.0 Reducing Delays and Costs in Product Approvals by Avoiding Multiple Review Cycles
    2.1 Factors that cause unnecessary delays in new product approvals
    2.2 Reducing avoidable delays in time to approval
        2.2.1 Addressing the root causes of longer review times for human drugs and biologics
        2.2.2 Reducing Delays in Medical Device Reviews
        2.2.3 Reducing Delays in Animal Drug Reviews

3.0 Improving the review process through a quality systems approach to medical product review
    3.1 Instituting quality systems in review of new drugs and biologics
    3.2 Implementing medical device quality initiatives

4.0 Improving Product Development and FDA Review Process through Developing Clear Guidance
    4.1 Better Guidance for Targeted Clinical Areas
    4.2 Better Guidance for Emerging Technology Areas
        4.2.1 Cell & Gene Therapy
        4.2.2 Pharmacogenomics
        4.2.3 Novel Drug Delivery Systems

4.2.2 Pharmacogenomics
Certain new therapies will b[e]
identify the responding sub[...]
find people who are prone [...]
combinations must be faci[...]
benefits while minimizing [...]
uncertainty. Over the next [...]

- Issue guidance on [...] FDA during drug d[...] pharmacogenomic [...] information would [...] next 6 months)
- Hold a workshop [...] test and a drug.(this year)
- Issue joint guidance (CDRH-CDER) on the regulatory pa[...] combinations. (In 18 months)

4.2.3 Novel Drug Delivery Systems
Novel drug delivery systems present a wide diversity of technologies and applications, e.g., infusion pumps, drug-eluting stents, lasers for photodynamic therapy, hyperthermia devices, etc. Most of these products require application submissions to, and reviews by multiple centers, and multiple offices and divisions within those FDA centers. The complexity of the review issues vary dramatically from product to product, ranging from simple device/complex drug combinations to simple drug/complex device products. The novel technologies and regulatory uncertainties can present challenges for product innovators.

finally, some storyboards have evolved to *animatics,* which are drafts of animated presentations that are "produced by photographing storyboard sketches on a film strip or video with the audio portion synchronized on tape."[8]

WEBLINK

> Animatics are similar in function to storyboards. They are animated presentations — for example, short Quicktime videos — that give clients a sense of the focus, tone, and content of the final product. For some examples of animatics, go to
> http://english.wadsworth.com/burnett6e.
>   CLICK ON WEBLINK
>   CLICK on Chapter 10/animatics

Typically, storyboards identify the context or setting and display the relationships between the players and their activities. The individual frames in storyboards often have annotations or captions, especially if they are active or interactive. If you include a separate text, you should cross-reference each chunk of text with the number of the appropriate storyboard frame. In general, storyboards have one of two layouts:[9]

- A storyboard might be in a linear layout when you want users to visit each page sequentially without skipping around. What kinds of projects might use linear storyboards? Introductory computer-based tutorials or training modules. Procedural task instructions. Slide shows. PowerPoint presentations.
- A storyboard might be in a hierarchical layout to structure Web documents. This layout can begin with a homepage and show links that lead to other pages, each with additional links to other pages. For the usability of your site, create no more than three or four levels of linked pages. What kinds of projects might use hierarchical storyboards? Complex Web sites. Interactive tutorials. Training modules.

What are the benefits of storyboarding? A large portion of the project planning and revising takes place up front, which saves time and money. Why? The revisions are done to a plan, not to a product. This reduces changes later in the process. People involved in the project can review and revise storyboards as a way to explore alternative ideas.

Some companies have templates for storyboards, which often include a box for information such as the name and purpose of the project, people who are involved (including client, subject matter experts, writers, and designers), the projected start and completion dates, and the media that will be used. Other kinds of information on (or accompanying) most storyboards include the text that goes with each frame; typographic specifications; and the nature of the visuals, animation, audio, and video. Storyboards let you try out various designs without the effort of a fully developed project. Many professionals see storyboards as a way to increase efficiency while encouraging creativity in content, structure, and design.

WEBLINK

Storyboarding is an easy way to accomplish a lot of planning. For links to some useful sites about storyboarding, go to **http://english.wadsworth.com/burnett6e**.
CLICK ON WEBLINK
CLICK on Chapter 10/storyboarding

Storyboards are tools, so don't make too big a production out of them. You can use them frequently to plan/organize and to get user feedback. These guidelines will save your time and money:

- Don't invest too much time and effort in storyboards. Keep storyboards sketchy.
- Make storyboards easy to modify. If you don't change anything, you don't learn anything.
- Whenever possible, make storyboards interactive. The user's experience will generate more feedback and will elicit more new requirements than passive storyboards.
- Create storyboards early and often. Always use storyboards on projects that have new or innovative content.[10]

Tables and Spreadsheets for Organizing Information 表 格

Tables and spreadsheets are a third way to experiment with and test ways to organize information. They enable you to classify information into comparable groups and then identify categories of details (features, functions, applications, and so on) about each group. As you collect information, you can organize it in the table or spreadsheet.

If you create the tables and spreadsheets on a computer, you can rearrange the rows and columns to consider additional comparisons. Electronic spreadsheets have a further benefit for numeric data: You can easily organize and interpret the data using various formulas, both standard equations and ones that you create for special purposes.

An example illustrates how useful tables can be for organizing information. The use of color is critical for a number of professionals, including scientists, designers, and printers. Differentiating these color systems is sometimes confusing, especially if you learned in elementary school that red, yellow, and blue are the only primary colors, and now you realize that scientists and artists talk about the CMYK Subtractive Color System and the RGB Additive Color System. So you sketch the information you mini-

Color Systems	CMYK~ Subtractive	RGB~ Additive
Identifying Primary Colors		
Mixing Primary Colors		
Using Color Systems		
Creating Other Colors		

mally need to organize in a table, as shown on the previous page: What are the primary colors in both the CMYK and RGB systems? What happens when you mix the colors in each system? What are the applications for each color system? What are the specific ways of colors can be combined in each system? This rough sketch can then be refined into a table for organizing the information you collect about the CMYK and RGB systems. Figure 10.5 shows this simple table for organizing information.

FIGURE 10.5   Table for Organizing Information

Color Systems	CMYK ~ Subtractive Color	RGB ~ Additive Color
Identifying primary colors	CMYK = cyan, magenta, yellow, black cyan magenta yellow	RGB = red, green, blue red green blue
Mixing primary colors	In their purest form, cyan, magenta, and yellow cannot be made by mixing other pigments. When any two subtractive primary colors come together, they form one of the additive primary colors. cyan yellow magenta	When additive primary colors — beams of light of dots of colored light — are combined, they form different colors than mixing subtractive colors. red green blue
Using color systems	Subtractive color applies to print documents, photography, lithographs, and paintings by combining physical pigments such as paint, dyes, or inks.	Additive color applies to stage lighting, computer monitors, and television by combining colored light such as spotlights or the dots of color on computer monitors and TV screens.
Creating other colors	• Mix paint together. • Combine clear color liquids. • Place one color glass in front of another. • Print several color inks on top of each other on the same paper during several press runs. • Use several transparent color layers to make a photo, a slide, or movie film.	• Shine colored lights or spotlights on the same area. • Visually combine the separate dots of colored light on a television screen or computer monitor.

WEBLINK

Color can be a critical part of documents, oral presentations, and visuals. Understanding subtractive and additive color is important. You might also be wondering why school children are usually introduced to red–yellow–blue as primary colors. To learn more about these issues and to see how the colors work together, go to http://english.wadsworth.com/burnett6e for useful links.
CLICK ON WEBLINK
CLICK on Chapter 10/color

Implementing the Organization of Information
组织信息

The way information in a print or electronic document, oral presentation, or visual is organized affects the meaning that the audience constructs.

- *Print documents* chunk information into paragraphs that readers can see; the paragraphs can be signaled by indentation or extra line spacing as well as by topic sentences and transitions.
- *Electronic documents* chunk information into paragraphs as well; they have the additional benefit of hyperlinks (usually signaled visually by color and underlining), so users can organize personal sequences of information.
- *Oral presentations* also chunk information, often in similar ways to the chunks in documents; the audience has to listen for cues about shifts to another topic, so changes in vocal pacing, pitch, and inflection take the place of indentation and line spacing, and the topic sentences and transitions need to be much more explicit than in documents.
- *Technical visuals* also chunk information; labels and cues direct movement through the visual.

Sometimes information can be organized in lists and continuums, sometimes in paragraphs, and sometimes in visuals. These various options are explained and illustrated in the rest of the chapter.

Alphabetical Order, Numeric Order, and Continuums 字母排序，数字排序，物体或实践发展过程排序

Information can be organized in alphabetical order, numeric order, or continuums.[11] One of the most basic organizational patterns is alphabetical order, which is useful for quite a range of documents, such as dictionaries, encyclopedias, glossaries, indexes, and phone books. Another common organizational pattern is *numeric order,* which arbitrarily associates a particular number (or range of numbers) with some category, as in the Dewey Decimal System categories:

000	general reference	500	science
100	philosophy and psychology	600	technology
200	religion	700	arts and recreation
300	social science	800	literature
400	language	900	history and geography

A numeric system is effective because each item — whether a book or an automotive part — is identified by a single number. However, the assigned number doesn't indicate a rank ordering.

WEBLINK

If you want to learn more about the complexities of an enormous numeric classification system, go to **http://english.wadsworth.com/burnett6e** for a link. On the home page for the Dewey Decimal System, select the link *Introduction to the DDC*, which takes you to a 37-page introductory list related to managing such complex systems.
CLICK ON WEBLINK
CLICK on Chapter 10/dewey decimal

A third way of organizing information is to use a *continuum,* which ranks or rates the objects or practices being organized, such as runs batted in (RBIs), an airline's on-time record, a company's safety record, a division's manufacturing performance. Figure 10.6 displays an edited excerpt from an online list of changes in several updates of a computer program ("Common Gateway Interface [CGI], a set of rules that describe how a Web server communicates with other software on the same machine and how the other piece of software, the CGI program, talks to the Web server").[12] Referring to this list of earlier changes helps CGI users trace the product's history and also identify current capabilities. Because the releases are on a continuum, the numbers — 1.01 through 2.01 — show that version 2.0 was a major revision.

Topic Sentences and Transitions to Signal Organizations 主题句和过渡语

Sometimes alphabetical or numeric lists and continuums are not sufficient because you need to explain the relationship between the ideas or objects you're organizing. Once you've decided how to organize the information, you can help the audience by using signals that identify the organization. Two tools help signal the organization of information, whether written or oral:

- A *topic sentence* identifies both the content and organization of a paragraph so that the audience anticipates what forthcoming information is about and how the information will be sequenced.

FIGURE 10.6 Continuum: Changes in CGI Program Releases[13]

The continuum makes the chronology clear.

The newest release is version 2.01.

A big change in features and capabilities came in release 2.0. The release prior to that had been 1.07.

What's new in version 2.01?
- Makefile supports "make install"
- Compiles without warnings under both C and C++ with strict warnings and strict ANSI compliance enabled . . .

What's new in version 2.0?
1. CGIC 2.0 provides support for file upload fields. User-uploaded files are kept in temporary files, to avoid the use of excessive swap space. . . .

What's new in version 1.07?
A problem with the cgiFormString and related functions has been corrected. These functions were previously incorrectly returning cgiFormTruncated in cases where the returned string fit the buffer exactly.

What's new in version 1.06?
1. A potentially significant buffer overflow problem has been corrected. . . .

What's new in version 1.05?
Non-exclusive commercial license fee reduced to $200.

What's new in version 1.04?
For consistency with other packages, the standard Makefile now produces a true library for cgic (libcgic.a).

What's new in version 1.03?
Version 1.03 sends line feeds only (ascii 10) to end Content-type:, Status:, and other HTTP protocol output lines, instead of CR/LF sequences. . . .

What's new in version 1.02?
Version 1.02 corrects bugs in previous versions. . . .

The first revision after the initial release was 1.01.

What's new in version 1.01?
Version 1.01 adds no major functionality but corrects significant bugs and incompatibilities . . .

For a reader who is an expert in the subject, why are transitions necessary? Won't an expert understand the relationships among the ideas?

- *Transitions* are words, phrases, and sentences that act as the glue connecting ideas and sentences within a single paragraph, linking one paragraph to another, and relating one section of a document or presentation to the next section.

Technical communicators organize information to make it clear and accessible to an audience. Some common ways to organize information are whole/parts organization, chronological order, spatial order, ascending/descending order, comparison/contrast, and cause and effect. With few adaptations, these ways of organization apply to written documents, oral presentations, and visuals.

No communicator settles down to write and says, "I'm about to plan a document or presentation using chronological order." Instead, the communicator asks questions like these: "What's the situation or problem I'm responding to?" "What's my purpose?" "Who's the audience, and what are their expectations?" "How can I help my audience understand this information?" "What's the appropriate genre?" And then the communicator may ask, "What's the most appropriate way to organize the information given the situation, purpose, audience, and genre?" In organizing written and oral information, technical communicators use topic sentences and transitions to help make the information more accessible and appealing to the audience.

Does every paragraph need a topic sentence? Not necessarily. Some paragraphs are transitional, connecting one main paragraph or section to the next. Occasionally, an excessively long paragraph in a document is separated into two or more to make the information easier to read and give readers a chance to breathe. Usually, however, most of the paragraphs in a well-constructed document have clear topic sentences that can be listed together as a summary. If the message from this topic sentence summary is clear and logical, then the information is probably well organized.

In what ways do topic sentences make technical information easier to read?

These points about organizing information for documents naturally extend to Web sites. However, Web sites not only have available the strategies that work for written documents, they also have additional organizational strategies because hyperlinks can be incorporated. Jakob Nielsen, an expert of Web usability, reports on some of the problems that result from poorly organized Web sites:[14]

- In one recent study of 15 large commercial sites, users went to the correct home page before they started the study's test tasks; even with that help, they found information they needed only 42 percent of the time.
- In a study of electronic shoppers, 62 percent gave up looking for the item they wanted to buy because they couldn't find it.
- A third study analyzed 20 major sites to determine whether these sites followed simple Web usability principles: Is the site organized by user goals? Does a search list retrievals in *order* of relevance? Only slightly more than half of the sites — 51 percent — complied with basic principles of organization.

What's the impact of such poorly organized Web sites?

- Sites lose approximately 50 percent of potential sales because people can't find what they want.
- Sites lose repeat visits from up to 40 percent of users who do not return to a site after an initial negative experience.

What's the most effective solution? Jakob Nielsen recommends usability testing of all Web sites. If a site is well organized, users should be able to find what they want. The strategies in this chapter can be part of your repertoire for organizing print and Web documents. These strategies are useful tools for making both print and electronic documents comprehensible and usable, but in some remarkably different ways. For example, print documents can be organized chronologically; however, you can be quite sure that users of a Web site will follow links in different ways and thus necessarily create different sequences of information. Therefore, a Web author needs to ensure that information makes sense in the various ways that users might access it. If a specific sequence is critical for comprehension, a Web author needs to tell users to follow the prescribed sequence.

WEBLINK

Organizing information for your Web site gives you more options than organizing an effective print document. You should create logical chunks, determine a hierarchy, establish relationships, implement your plan, and analyze its effectiveness. For a link to a more detailed discussion, go to
http://english.wadsworth.com/burnett6e.
   CLICK ON WEBLINK
      CLICK on Chapter 10/organizing information for the Web

Whole/Parts Organization 整体与局部

A document that uses *whole/parts organization* presents readers with a relationship between the whole (whether an idea, object, or entire system) and parts of that whole (whether on a micro level or a macro level). Sometimes whole/parts organization involves separating a single item into individual components. At other times, it involves identifying related types of an item. It may also involve identifying the broad category to which something belongs.

A whole/parts organization to present the categories of integrated circuits is shown in Figure 10.7. The paragraph shows the relationship between the whole

FIGURE 10.7   Whole/Parts Organization

A clear topic sentence identifying the whole increases comprehensibility.

Bullets signaling the three types of circuits make the information more accessible.

Transitions signaling the parts of the whole make the information more comprehensible.

A simple visual (referred to in the text) reinforces the whole/parts relationship.

> Integrated circuits are divided into three categories, depending on their function and capability in the final product. (See the diagram below.)
> - The first type is a programmable integrated circuit, a multifunctional component designed to be programmed by the supplier or by in-house technicians.
> - The second type of integrated circuit is the memory device, used to store memory in an end product.
> - The third type is a linear device designed to do many specific predetermined functions and used in conjunction with other components to operate computers.
>
> integrated circuits
> ├── programmable devices
> ├── memory devices
> └── linear devices

(the category of devices called integrated circuits) and the parts of that whole (three types of circuits: programmable devices, memory devices, and linear devices). This example (and the following related ones) was written by the testing line supervisor in an inspection group of a plant that manufactures and assembles integrated circuits. This supervisor was required to train the unskilled entry-level workers assigned to her area. She decided to provide these workers with short, easy-to-read explanations about the inspection process, believing that helping workers understand how their specific job fit into the larger process would increase the quality of their work. Although she hoped they would learn this information during their initial job orientation, she knew she would need to review it periodically in ongoing training sessions.

> What additional examples of using a whole/parts organization for information are likely in the workplace?

> A new researcher is organizing a report about a six-month project he just completed. He wants his readers to follow his experiments step by step, not being able to know the results until they read his conclusion and recommendations at the end. He says he worked hard; he wants readers (especially his manager) to appreciate his efforts. What do you think of his decision? What would you say to persuade him to reconsider his plan?

Chronological Order 时间顺序

Chronological order presents readers with material arranged by sequence or order of occurrence. When the purpose is to give instructions, describe processes, or trace the development of objects or ideas, chronological order is appropriate. For example, chronologically organized information about CDs might include a description identifying each step of the manufacturing process or an explanation of the historical development of electronic storage media. Information can be presented chronologically in visual forms, as shown in Figure 10.8, which also lists an example of each form.

FIGURE 10.8 Visual Forms for Chronological Order

Form	Example
Schedules	Plane, train, or bus schedule
Flow chart	Sequence of manufacturing process
Time line	Development of synthetics for medical use
Genealogy chart	History of family with Huntington's disease
Sequential photos	Embryo development
Sequential drawings	Steps in resuscitation of drowning victim
Storyboard	Public service ad urging water conservation
Time-lapse photos	Emergence of butterfly from cocoon
Line graph	Increase in eye movement during REM sleep
Calendar	Production schedule for new product
Chart	Stratification of rock layers according to geologic periods

A topic sentence conveying chronology includes words or phrases that indicate a process or a sequence of actions, as illustrated in the following examples:

- Seven operations are necessary to fabricate sheet metal.
- Most poultry farms are vertically integrated, from breeding to egg to packaged product.

Readers can justifiably expect the paragraph that follows the first topic sentence to identify the seven steps of sheet-metal fabrication. The paragraph that follows the second topic sentence should identify each stage in the process of poultry production.

Transitions in chronological paragraphs can indicate the sequence of events or the passage of time. Figure 10.9 presents an example that explains the chronology of incoming inspection that integrated circuits go through. Readers can easily follow the process because the chronological transitions highlight each step of the five-step process.

FIGURE 10.9 Information Organized Using Chronological Order

Chronological transitions:
- the first stage
- then
- Next
- After this
- The final step

Integrated circuits received at incoming inspection go through a five-step process. As the flowchart shows, the first stage of inspection ensures that the parts have been purchased from a predetermined qualified vendor list. The parts are then prioritized according to daily back-order quantities and/or line shortages assigned by the production floor. Next the parts are moved into the test area, where a determination is made as to which lots will be tested at 100 percent and which will be sample tested. After this, the parts are electrically tested for specific continuity and direct current parameters using MCT handlers. The final step of incoming inspection is distributing the parts according to need on the production floor.

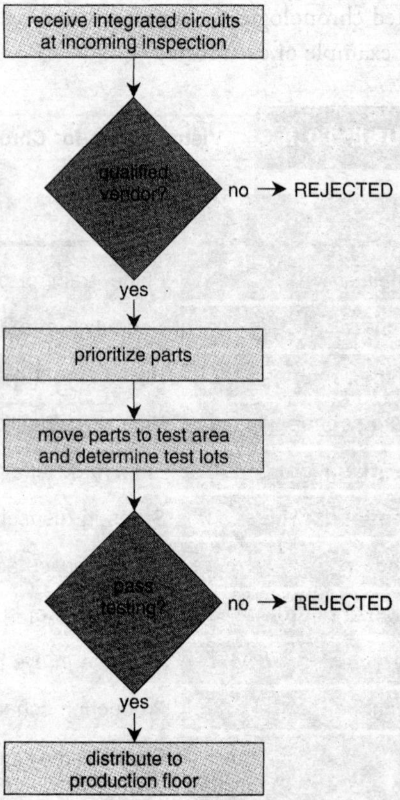

What additional examples of using chronological order for organizing information are likely in the workplace?

Spatial Order 空间关系

Spatial order — arrangement by relative physical location — describes the physical parts of nearly anything, from cellular structures to the orbital path of a satellite. Spatial organization could explain parts of a CD or the location of the hard drives in relation to the other parts of the computer. Figure 10.10 presents examples of several visual forms. You may find that visuals are particularly effective for spatially arranged material because they help your readers see the actual physical relationships.

Because spatial arrangement deals with the relative physical location of objects, the topic sentence suggests their placement, as seen in these examples.

- Unnecessary or damaged inventory that is scheduled to be scrapped is placed on skids in one of six bin locations in the Defective Stockroom.
- Sound is a ripple of molecules and atoms in the air that travels from its source to our ears.

Readers of the first sentence anticipate the identification of each bin's location according to type of scrap material. The second topic sentence indicates to readers that the paragraph will track the sound as it moves through the air from source to listener.

Transitions in spatial paragraphs suggest the relative physical location of components or objects. Figure 10.11 presents an example that uses spatial order to describe the incoming inspection of an integrated circuit.

FIGURE 10.10 Visual Forms for Spatial Order

Form	Example
Map	Identification of migration stopovers
Blueprint	Specification of dimensions for machined part
Navigational chart	Location of sand bars and buoys
Celestial chart	Sequence of moons around Jupiter
Exploded view	Assembly of disk brake
Cutaway view	Interior components of pool filter
Wiring diagram	Wiring of alarm system
Floor plan	Workflow in busy area
Set design	Arrangement of furniture/props for *Hamlet*
Architectural drawing	Appearance of building with solar modifications

FIGURE 10.11 | Information Organized Using Spatial Order

Spatial transitions:
- through the test area from the supplier
- into a removable channel within a clear tube
- in the same direction
- into the MCT handler
- in the upper left
- through a slot
- to the manufacturing area
- to another engineering station

The movement of the IC (integrated circuit) chip through the test area is very efficient. The chips arrive from the supplier, already set—24 at a time—into a removable channel within a clear tube. The chips are aligned in the same direction within the tube. This tube is inserted by the operator into the MCT handler so that pin 1 of the first chip, marked by a small dot, is in the upper left. The tube slides through a slot, into the testing compartment, where each chip is tested individually. Automatically, the good chips are placed in one channel, the rejects in another. The channels are moved so the operator can slip on the protective tubes. The good chips are sent to the manufacturing area; the rejects are sent to another engineering station for further testing.

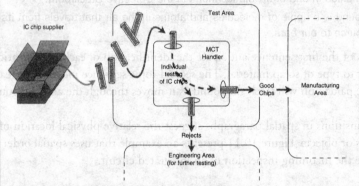

What additional examples of using spatial order for organizing information are likely in the workplace?

Ascending/Descending Order 升序或降序

Ascending and *descending orders* present readers with information according to quantifiable criteria.

appeal	durability
authority	ease of manufacture, operation, repair
benefit	frequency
cost	importance
delivery	size

Descending order uses a most-to-least-important order; ascending order, a least-to-most. Descending order is found in workplace writing more frequently than ascending order because most readers want to know the most important points first. Readers generally form opinions and make decisions based on what they read initially; they expect descending order in nearly all technical documents. Either descending or ascending order would be appropriate for organizing the relative convenience of various forms of electronic data storage or for identifying the CD specifications in various price ranges. If you wanted to arrange information visually, one of the forms illustrated in Figure 10.12 would work.

FIGURE 10.12	Visual Forms for Ascending/Descending Order
Form	Example
Numbered list	Priority of options for treating breast cancer
Bull's-eye chart	Population affected by nuclear explosion
Percent graph	Percent of different economic groups receiving balanced nutrition
Pareto diagram (bar graph of ranges of data arranged in descending order)	Productivity using different methods
Line graph	Increasing success for breeding endangered species in captivity over 20-year period

Unlike topic sentences for paragraphs organized in other ways, those beginning descending or ascending paragraphs do not give an immediate clue about the subsequent organization. The reader understands that the paragraph presents a series of related ideas, but the specific relationship is not clear until the second sentence. The topic sentence in the next example begins a paragraph about the master satellite station in Beijing by presenting the characteristics of the Beijing antenna in descending order of importance.

> The largest earth station in China is a 15-to-18-meter-diameter dish antenna in Beijing for domestic satellite communications.

A paragraph using a descending organization to identify the various sized antennas in China begins with a general statement before going on to identify each type of station.

> Three types of earth stations are planned for domestic satellite communication in China. The largest is a 15-to-18-meter-diameter dish antenna of the master station in Beijing. . . . Regional stations are equipped with a 10-to-13-meter-diameter antenna. . . .[15]

Readers would expect the remainder of the paragraph to identify a series of satellite dish antennas, arranged by size, from largest to smallest.

Transitions in ascending/descending paragraphs indicate the relative priority of points in the paragraph or document. Figure 10.13 uses *descending order* to identify the priorities for testing circuits.

FIGURE 10.13 Information Organized Using Descending Order

Cues to the organizational pattern:
- ... the most important integrated circuits ...
- ... first priority ...
- ... priority parts are further separated ...
- ... All other integrated circuits are then prioritized ...

What additional examples of using ascending and descending order for organizing information are likely in the workplace?

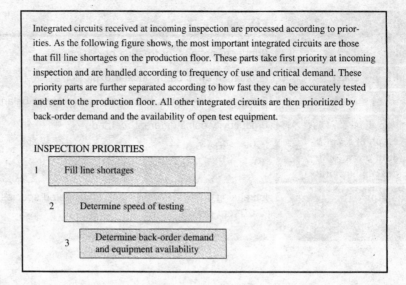

Comparison/Contrast 对照比较

Comparison and contrast tell readers about similarities and differences. *Comparison* identifies the similarities of various ideas, objects, or situations; *contrast*, the differences. A comparison or contrast organization could present the advantages and disadvantages of certified versus uncertified computer disks or the ease or difficulty of various methods of storing electronic data. Any of the techniques in Figure 10.14 could visually present information that you want to compare and contrast.

Readers expect comparison and contrast topic sentences to present ideas dealing with similarities and differences, or both, as illustrated by the following two sentences:

- The Honey Bee Lens, with three telescopic lenses for each eye, is patterned after the compound eye of a bee.
- Computers can now analyze measurable differences between the cries of healthy newborns and high-risk infants.

The first sentence introduces a paragraph that compares new lenses to the compound eyes of bees. The second sentence leads readers to expect the paragraph to deal with characteristics that differentiate cries of healthy and high-risk infants.

Transitions in comparison and contrast paragraphs identify various similarities and differences. Figures 10.15 and 10.16 use comparison and contrast to differentiate the responsibilities of incoming inspection and in-process inspection of integrated circuits. Figure 10.15 shifts between incoming inspection and in-

FIGURE 10.14 Visual Forms for Comparison and Contrast

Form	Example
Paired photos or drawings	Before/after of patient treated for scoliosis
Multiple or paired bar graphs	Expenditures for utilities for each quarter of the fiscal year
Multiple or paired percent graphs	Utilization of nutrients with and without coconut oil to increase absorption
Line graph	Changes in toxicity of emissions since installation of scrubbers
Multiple or paired gauges	Illustration of danger/no-danger in training manual for pilots
Table	Data collected on size of bats according to age, sex, and location
Dichotomous key	Distinction of edible wild plants
Pareto diagram	Distinction between major and minor causes of shipping delays
Histogram	Women, grouped by age, affected by lung cancer
Columned chart	Physical symptoms of substance abuse

process inspection, explaining how each deals with specific responsibilities. Figure 10.16 takes the same paragraph and rearranges it to present all the information about incoming inspection first and discuss the in-process inspection second.

Cause and Effect 因果关系

The *cause-and-effect* organization of information focuses on precipitating factors and results. You can move from cause to effect or from effect to cause. For example, you could carry a CD through an electronic surveillance scanner and then trace the effects — the various disk errors that appear. Or beginning with the effect, a damaged disk, you could investigate the causes of the damage. Figure 10.17 identifies and illustrates various visuals that are effective for presenting cause-and-effect relationships.

Understanding inductive and deductive reasoning is critical in constructing effective cause-and-effect arguments. Making strong arguments involves considering the ways to organize the information and avoiding errors in logic.

One type of cause and effect — *inductive reasoning* — moves from specific instances to broad generalizations, forming the basis for the *scientific method* used in much research and experimentation. You begin by collecting data in support of

FIGURE 10.15 | **Information Organized Using Comparison and Contrast**

Organization of information:
- *incoming inspection*
- *in-process inspection*
- *incoming inspection*
- *in-process inspection*
- *mutual goal*

Integrated circuits are inspected and/or tested by two separate quality control departments: incoming quality control and in-process quality control. Incoming quality control is responsible for ensuring that all integrated circuits sent to the production floor meet all electrical standards set by the Component Engineering Department. In-process quality control is only responsible for ensuring that the parts are properly mounted on the printed circuit board. Incoming quality control also has to verify the markings on the integrated circuits in order to do proper testing and make certain that the company has purchased a qualified product. In contrast, in-process quality control only has to do random inspections of the circuit markings to ensure that qualified parts are being used in the manufacturing process. Although incoming and in-process inspection are two different areas, they do share the same goal of building a quality product. The following lists summarize each department's responsibilities.

Component Engineering Department responsible for *incoming inspection*
- verify parts meet standards
- verify IC markings
- confirm qualified vendors

Quality Control Department responsible for *in-process inspection*
- ensure proper mounting
- do random inspections

FIGURE 10.16 | **Information Organized Using Comparison and Contrast**

Organization of information:
- *incoming inspection*
- *in-process inspection*
- *in-coming inspection*
- *in-process inspection*
- *mutual goal*

Integrated circuits are inspected and/or tested by two separate quality control departments: incoming quality control and in-process quality control, as shown in the lists below. Incoming quality control is responsible for ensuring that all integrated circuits sent to the production floor meet all electrical standards set by the Component Engineering Department. Incoming quality control also has to verify the markings on the integrated circuits in order to do proper testing and make certain that the company has purchased a qualified product. In-process quality control is only responsible for ensuring that the parts are properly mounted on the printed circuit board. In-process quality control only has to do random inspections of the circuit markings to ensure that qualified parts are being used in the manufacturing process. Although incoming and in-process inspection are two different areas, they do share the same goal of building a quality product.

What additional examples of using comparison and contrast for organizing information are likely in the workplace?

Component Engineering Department responsible for *incoming inspection*
- verify parts meet standards
- verify IC markings
- confirm qualified vendors

Quality Control Department responsible for *in-process inspection*
- ensure proper mounting
- do random inspections

FIGURE 10.17   **Visual Forms for Cause and Effect**

Form	Example
Paired photos or drawings	Effects of two different treatments for removing facial birthmarks
Weather map	Impact of cold front on majority of Midwest
Bar graph	Efficiency of various methods for harvesting cranberries
Line graph	Destruction of American chestnut by blight during the 1900s
Cause-and-effect diagram	Identification of multiple contributing factors to contamination of drinking water
Pareto diagram	Identification of major causes of low birth weight

an unproved hypothesis. After you have organized and examined a sufficient body of data, you draw a conclusion. When your conclusion proves consistently to be valid, it is considered a generalization. Most scientific principles and theories are based on this method of inquiry.

Because no way exists to test every instance, inductive reasoning has a certain risk, and professionals must be careful to avoid basing their conclusions on invalid assumptions. Two kinds of errors will put your cause-and-effect thinking at risk: You cannot assume chronology is the same as causality, and you need to examine a large sample before drawing a conclusion.

The first problem equates chronology with causality. Just because B follows A does not mean that A causes B. Because inductive reasoning moves from specifics to a generalization, an investigator should not assume that sequence of events alone causes the effect. (Such an error in reasoning is called *post hoc, ergo propter hoc,* Latin for "after this, therefore because of this.") For example, a donor may become ill the day after donating blood to the Red Cross, but she cannot logically conclude that donating blood caused her to become ill. Guard against fallacious reasoning by examining all possible causes. A closely related problem is using *non sequiturs,* or arguments that begin with an unwarranted assumption, so its inference isn't correct.

The second problem deals with sample size. You need to examine a large enough number of instances before drawing a conclusion. For example, before a new drug is allowed on the market, the Food and Drug Administration requires extensive tests with a broad segment of the target population. As a result of testing, a powerful painkiller such as propoxyphene, when taken according to directions and under a physician's care, is certified as safe even though all propoxyphene tablets and capsules have not been individually tested. Unfortunately, errors occur, although rarely, causing some people to suspect all inductive reasoning. So make sure your methodology is sound, your sample large, and your analysis free from bias or distortion.

When a generalization is widely accepted, you can use it as a base from which to predict the likelihood of specific instances occurring. This process is called *deductive reasoning* — moving from general premises to specific causes. A patient taking propoxyphene trusts that the pills are safe even though those particular ones have not been tested.

In paragraphs that use cause and effect as a way to organize information, both the cause and the effect should be identified in the topic sentence, as seen in the next examples:

- One hypothesis about the formation of mineral-rich marine nodules suggests that marine bacteria break down organic material into free-floating minerals that eventually collect to form nodules.
- The Zephinie Escape Chute (ZEC) can rapidly evacuate people from 10-story burning buildings because of its unique construction.

Readers of the first sentence expect the information in the paragraph to explain how minerals form marine nodules. The second sentence develops a paragraph that explains how the ZEC's unique construction aids rapid evacuation.

Transitions in cause-and-effect paragraphs signal the relationship between an action and its result. The example in Figure 10.18 uses cause and effect to organize information about integrated circuit (IC) testing. In this example, the cause-and-effect transitions indicate the descending order of the reasons an IC chip can be rejected.

FIGURE 10.18 Information Organized Using Cause and Effect

Causal transitions:
- because
- therefore
- so

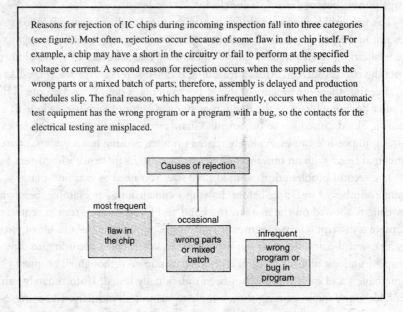

What additional examples of using cause and effect for organizing information are likely in the workplace?

Using Organization

信息的组织

These ways of organizing information are frequently used in technical documents, both as short, self-contained segments (like the examples about integrated circuits) and also combined in longer pieces of writing.

By organizing information so that it meets the needs of the content, purpose, and audience, you can make a paragraph or document more understandable, as well as overcome some of the noise that interferes with readers' acceptance or comprehension of information. For example, processes, procedures, and directions are best organized chronologically for all audiences. Descriptions of physical objects, mechanisms, organisms, and locations frequently make the most sense if the information is organized spatially. Reasons and explanations are usually presented in descending order so that the audience reads the most important information first. Explanations of problems and their solutions often make the most sense if the information is organized using comparison/contrast and cause and effect.

You can also use organization of information to adapt your material to readers' attitudes by taking advantage of what you know about induction (specific to general) and deduction (general to specific). If you think readers might be reluctant to accept your conclusions or recommendations, you can organize the material inductively, moving from various specifics to your conclusion. Thus they can follow your line of reasoning and, perhaps, be persuaded by your analysis. If you think readers will agree with your conclusions, you can organize the information deductively, presenting the conclusion initially and then following it with the specifics that led to it. Deductive organization is more common in technical documents.

Sometimes decisions about organizing information aren't obvious or easy. The ethics sidebar on this page focuses attention on unethical design choices, ones that distort information and thus mislead readers because of the way information is organized. Decision making might be easier if workplace professionals could agree about what is unethical, but, as you'll read in the sidebar, opinions are divided.

ETHICS SIDEBAR 职业道德规范知识吧

"Is This Ethical?": Ethics and Document Design
"这符合职业道德吗？"：职业道德与文件设计

Consider the following scenarios:

> Scenario 1: "You have been asked to evaluate a subordinate for possible promotion. In order to emphasize the employee's qualifications, you display these in a bulleted list. In order to de-emphasize the employee's deficiencies, you display these in a paragraph. Is this ethical?"

Scenario 2: "You are designing materials for your company's newest product. Included is a detailed explanation of the product's limited warranty. In order to emphasize that the product carries a warranty, you display the word 'Warranty' in a large size of type, in upper and lower case letters, making the word as visible and readable as possible. In order to de-emphasize the details of the warranty, you display this information in smaller type and in all capital letters, making it more difficult to read and thus more likely to be skipped. Is this ethical?"[16]

Are these ethical or unethical document design choices? If you are uncertain, then you are not alone. Technical professionals and teachers, responding to these same scenarios (and others) in a survey, revealed differing opinions about the ethics involved. A majority of respondents (54.6%) considered the design choices of the evaluation ethical, although a significant number were uncertain (26.7%) or found the evaluation unethical (18.7%). The warranty divided opinions even more: ethical (33.3%), unethical (44.1%), uncertain (22.6%).

Researcher Sam Dragga, who coordinated the survey, believes it indicates the thin line separating rhetorically savvy design from deceptive design. He did find, however, that the survey revealed a general guideline most technical professionals follow for producing ethical document design: "The greater the likelihood of deception and the greater the injury to the reader as a consequence of that deception, the more unethical is the design of the document."[17] Determining the degree of deception and injury requires a technical communicator to weigh different items, "including typical communication practices, professional responsibilities, explicit specifications and regulations, as well as rhetorical intentions and ideals."[18] Dragga recognizes that workplace pressures can sometimes lead us to choose convenience over ethics. To avoid making unethical document design choices, Dragga advises "periodic self-examination" for technical professionals to help them create ethical communications.

Follow Dragga's advice for self-examination by reviewing the scenarios. Is the reader deceived by the different formats in the evaluation? Does the difference in font size in the text of the warranty increase the likelihood of deception for the reader?

What can help you decide whether a document's design is misleading?

Individual and Collaborative Assignments
个人作业和小组作业

1. **Identify expectations based on topic sentences.** Read the following topic sentences and identify expectations that readers might have if they read them. What content would readers expect in each paragraph? One example is provided.

    Example The use of a sulfur-asphalt mixture for repaving the highway will result in several specific benefits.

    Analysis The sentence presents a cause-and-effect relationship between using a sulfur-asphalt mixture and specific benefits. The paragraph will identify these benefits.

    a. The CAT scan creates an image resembling a "slice" that clearly visualizes anatomical structures within the body.

b. The human fetus is in the birth position by the ninth month of a normal pregnancy.

c. The routine use of drugs in labor and delivery sometimes has adverse effects on otherwise healthy, normal infants.

d. The stages of normal labor and delivery begin at term when the fetus reaches maturity and end with the expulsion of the placenta.

e. Two major forms of leukemia — chronic myelocytic and acute myelocytic — have distinct differences.

f. Improper downstroke and follow-through can cause the golf ball to either hook and fade to the left or slice and fade to the right.

g. Three main types of parachutes are used for skydiving. The most widely used parachute has a round, domelike canopy.

h. A square parachute provides more maneuverability and a better overall ride than does a conventional round parachute.

i. Two methods of disinfecting treated wastewater are chlorination and ozonation.

j. The chlorinator room contains the evaporators, chlorinators, and injectors, three of each. The evaporators are used only when liquid chlorine is being drawn from the containers.

2. **Revise a memo by improving organization.** Read the memo below. Revise it so that the subject line in the heading, the topic sentences, and the paragraphs are well organized, unified, and coherent. The intended readers are interested in information that will help decrease rejects during manufacturing. They are not particularly concerned with personnel or cost.

Stanford Engineering, Inc.

February 14, 20—

To Quality Control Supervision
From T. R. Hood, Engineer *TRH*
Subject Increased scrap and customer rejects

The Engineering Department is recommending the purchase of an International glue line inspection system to strengthen standard visual inspection. Machine operators will not be slowed down by the addition of this new glue line inspection system. The system will detect breaks in the glue line and eject a carton from the run before it reaches shipping. If the system detects more than five consecutive rejects, it will automatically stop the machine.

Purchasing this International system is a better solution than purchasing a new glue pot for $6,500. The savings in purchasing the $4,000 International system will allow us to rebuild the existing glue pot.

3. **Revise paragraphs by adding topic sentences.** Read the two paragraphs below and write topic sentences that help readers anticipate the content and organization.

   Paragraph 1 Buss bars, the smallest of the parts the Sheet Metal Fabrication Shop produces, are made of grade-A copper and are tin-plated before being used for internal grounding. Paper deflectors, used in printers, are made of stainless steel and do not require any plating or painting. Deflectors guide the paper through the printer and usually measure 4" in width and 15" in length, depending on the size of the printer. A larger box-like structure, made of aluminum and requiring plating in the enclosure chassis, is designed to hold a variety of electronic devices within an even larger computer main frame. A steel door panel requiring cosmetic plating and painting is the largest of the parts produced by the Sheet Metal Fabrication Shop.

   Paragraph 2 The fetal causes for spontaneous abortion are infectious agents: protozoa bacteria, viruses, particularly rubella virus. Drugs such as thalidomide cause fetal abnormalities. When radiation is given in therapeutic doses to the mother in the first few months of pregnancy, malformation or death of the fetus may result.

4. **Characterize and evaluate the organization of a Web site.** Work with a small group of people in your major or a closely related field of study.

   (a) Visit several Web sites that are related to your field of study. How would you characterize the organizational strategies used: whole/parts, chronological, spatial, ascending/descending, comparison/contrast, or cause and effect?

   (b) Establish criteria for evaluating the effectiveness of Web site organization based on your responses to Assignment 4(a).

   (c) Create a rubric for these criteria, and evaluate one Web site from your list.

   (d) Share your rubric and evaluation with your classmates.

5. Tour and evaluate the organization of a Web site. Visit one of the following Web sites:

   www.ashastd.org/   www.centerforfoodsafety.org/
   www.hhs.gov/   www.avert.org/condoms.htm
   www.ostrich.ca/index-2.htm   www.ercim.org/
   www.hc-sc.gc.ca/pphb-dgspsp/sars-sras/index.html   www.epa.gov/

   Follow the links to learn as much as you can about the Web site's audience and purpose. Pay special attention to the overall organization of the site — that is, the site architecture. Write a one-page review for your instructor about the comprehensibility and usability of the site's organization, given the audience and purpose.

Chapter 10 Endnotes

1. Jeffries, W. L. (2003). *Informal settlements* and *Informal settlements in context.* © William L. Jeffries. Durban, South Africa.
2. Allee, V. (n.d.). A delightful dozen principles of knowledge management. In *The knowledge evolution: Expanding organizational intelligence.* Retrieved November 8, 2003, from www.vernaalee.com/library%20articles/A%20Delightful%20Dozen%20Principles%20of%20Knowledge%20Management.pdf
3. Modified from Jordon, N. (1984). What's in a zombie. [Review of the book *The serpent and the rainbow*]. *Psychology Today,* (May), 6.
4. H. W. Wilson Co. (2003, January). Wade David. In *Current biography.* Retrieved November 8, 2003, from http://www.hwwilson.com/currentbio/cover_bios/cover_bio_1_03.htm
5. *Storyboarding.* (n.d.). Retrieved November 8, 2003, from http://members.ozemail.com.au/~caveman/Creative/Techniques/storyboard.htm
6. HM Customs and Excise. (2002, January 25). *Business change lifecycle — storyboarding.* Retrieved October 18, 2003, from http://www.ogc.gov.uk/sdtkdev/examples/HMCE/Guidance/RequirementsManagement/Storyboarding.htm
7. U.S. Food and Drug Administration. (n.d.). *Improving innovation in medical technology: Beyond 2002.* Retrieved November 7, 2003, from http://www.fda.gov/bbs/topics/news/2003/beyond2002/report.html
8. Arens, W. F. (n.d.). Glossary. In *Contemporary advertising* (8th ed.). Retrieved November 7, 2003, from http://highered.mcgraw-hill.com/sites/0072415444/student_view0/glossary.html
9. *Storyboarding.* Retrieved November 8, 2003, from CalPolyWeb Authoring Resource Center Web site: http://www.calpoly.edu/warc/plannning/layout/storyboarding.html
10. HM Customs and Excise. (2002, January 25). *Business change lifecycle — storyboarding.* Retrieved October 18, 2003, from http://www.ogc.gov.uk/sdtkdev/examples/HMCE/Guidance/RequirementsManagement/Storyboarding.htm
11. The discussion expands the examples provided by Shedroff, N. (1994). Information interaction design: A unified field theory of design. Retrieved November 8, 2003, from http://www.nathan.com/thoughts/unified/index.html
12. 1001homepages.com (n.d.). CGI. In *Glossary of terms.* Retrieved November 9, 2003, from http://1001resources.com/hosting/glossary.htm1#C
13. Boutell, T. (2003). *CGIC 2.02: An ANSI C library for CGI programming.* Retrieved November 9, 2003, from http://www.boutell.com/cgic/
14. Nielsen, J. (1998). Failure of corporate websites. *Jakob Nielsen's Alertbox for October 18, 1998.* Retrieved November 9, 2003, from http://wwwuseit.com/alertbox/981018.html
15. Modified from Lenorovitz, J. M. (1983, November 21). China plans upgraded satellite network. *Aviation Week & Space Technology, 65,* 71–75.
16. Dragga, S. (1996). 'Is this ethical?': A survey of opinion on principles and practices of document design. *Technical Communication, 43*(1), 29–38, p. 30.
17. Dragga, S. (1996), p. 35.
18. Dragga, S. (1996), p. 35.

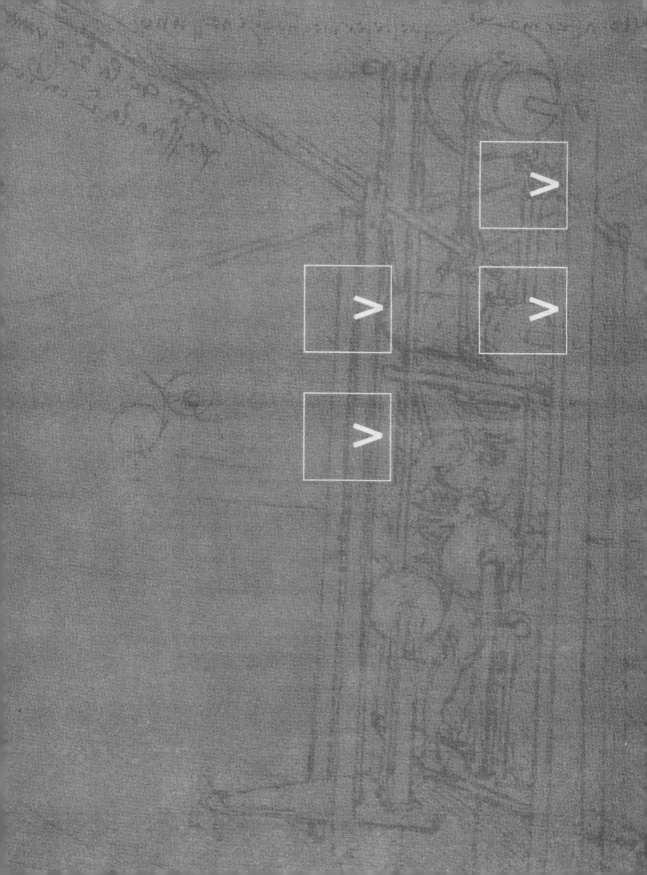

CHAPTER 11

Designing Information
设计信息

如何有效地呈现信息是很多工作中必不可少的一个环节。信息呈现的方式直接影响读者或客户对信息的理解。本章介绍了设计信息的基本原则,并讨论了信息呈现的技巧。然后,本章主要阐释了处理文件中的文字、空间、图片、颜色、动漫等的三项原则:(1) 有效利用空白和标题等归类和标注信息;(2) 通过合理搭配文字和图片来组织信息;(3) 通过合理使用文档符号(如下划线、数字编码、方框、颜色)、字体、字号等方法来强调信息。

Outcomes and Objectives 学习目标

This chapter will help you accomplish these outcomes:

- Understand the relationship between the design of information and the critical goals of accessibility/legibility, comprehensibility/readability, and usability

- Use chunking and labeling to group topically related information

- Arrange visual and verbal information using a page grid

- Emphasize information by appropriate use of typographic and design elements such as lists, boxes, and color

Regardless of your technical specialty, from aviation to biology to computers, from mechanical engineering to nursing to oceanography, from writing to xerography to zymurgy, part of your job will involve the design of information in both print and electronic documents, for both presentations and Web sites. Your knowledge of ways to effectively combine visual and verbal elements to communicate to audiences may distinguish you from other professionals. And if you are lucky enough to have designers and graphic artists to work with, you need to be able to communicate your vision of a document to them.

Whether information is in print form or electronic form, a number of general principles about design apply. This chapter presents principles that affect accessibility/legibility, comprehensibility/readability, and usability for paper documents and also notes variations and adjustments that are often necessary when technical information is presented in other ways, such as PowerPoint presentations, technical and scientific posters, and Web sites.

Information design is concerned with the ways in which you organize and present information to increase audience comprehension. *Document design*, a term you're probably more familiar with, is part of information design. As you design the information in your documents, you manage five categories of elements:[1]

> Take a quick look at this page and the facing page. Identify the textual, spatial, graphic, color/textural, and dynamic design elements. Then open some other book, journal, or Web site that's close at hand and identify the design elements.

- ■ ***Textual elements*** — letters, numbers, and symbols (for example, the characters that form the words in a document, as well as headings, labels, and page numbers)

- ■ ***Spatial elements*** — the spaces between elements (for example, the spacing between letters, sentences, paragraphs, and margins, sometimes called *white space* or *negative space*), as well as the size and placement of textual and graphic elements

- ■ ***Graphic elements*** — punctuation marks, typographic devices (for example, bullets and icons), geometric forms (for example, lines and arrows; boxes on flowcharts), and visual images (for example, tables, graphs, diagrams, drawings, photographs, maps)

- ■ ***Color and textural elements*** — the hue (what the color is), saturation (how pure the color is; the amount of color), and value/brightness/luminescence (how bright the color is; the color's lightness or darkness), which are called HSV, HSB, or HSL color model; texture is the tactile or virtual features of a surface (for example, smoothness, glossiness, hardness, and so on)

- ■ ***Dynamic elements*** — the motion that is implied in a print document (by, for example, layout, typography, placement of images); often actual motion in an electronic document that uses various kinds of animation

For a better understanding of hue, saturation, and value in color, go to
www.english.wadsworth.com/burnett6e for a link to useful examples.
  CLICK ON WEBLINK
    CLICK on Chapter 11/HSV

WEBLINK

These five categories of design elements are important whether you're designing print documents or Web pages. Regardless of how carefully you design information, though, reading electronic documents is about 25 percent slower than reading from paper. Furthermore, many people simply do not like to read extended chunks of text on a computer screen. And, finally, many people don't like to scroll, so brief electronic pages are likely to get more attention. To compensate for these reading preferences, when you're designing an electronic document, you should consider writing "50 percent less text and not just 25 percent less since it's not only a matter of reading speed but also a matter of feeling good."[2]

This chapter begins by illustrating basic principles of information design in an excerpt from an online report and then discussing strategies of information design that use the following principles for managing text, space, graphic elements, color, and movement in both print and electronic documents:

- Chunking and labeling information by effective use of white space and headings
- Arranging information by appropriate integration of visual and verbal chunks
- Emphasizing information by effective use of typographic devices and typefaces

Chunking and Labeling Information
集中与标注信息

You can apply the design principles in your print document or Web site by grouping, or chunking, topically related information and then labeling that information for the audiences. In simple terms, chunking makes the information in undifferentiated text accessible to audiences. Decisions about chunking information involve two factors:

- Logical topical relationships
- Audience needs for the information

PRINCIPLES OF DESIGN IN ACTION
设计原则

You can use a number of widely accepted principles that enable designers to effectively integrate text, space, graphics, color, and implied or actual movement in print and electronic documents. The example here applies the most critical of these principles in a typical document — in this case, the beginning of an online technical report about tropical deforestation[3] — to show that design principles apply even in everyday print and online documents.

Direction. Where should people begin reading? In what direction should they move? People begin a document where the design directs them; the upper left part of the page or screen contains the most important information — the title and the primary text. The entry is prompted by column width and placement, typography, and visual emphasis.

Proportion/Scale. How big are elements of the design in relation to the audience? In relation to each other? Scale helps the audience understand how big various elements are in relation to human size. Proportion helps the audience understand the relationship between the various elements of the design.[4] The photo lets readers know the scale of the forest.

Contrast. What creates contrast — size, color, shape, or placement? Is the contrast obvious — even dramatic? The primary contrast here is provided by differences in size: the wider column of the primary text contrasts with the narrower column of the supplemental text, not only letting the audience know which is more important but also creating visual variety.

Rhythm. How dynamic is the design? Do the elements have a pace or rhythm? The elements of a design — text, space, graphics, color, and implied or actual movement — are repeated to help the audience move through the design and better understand and interpret information. Selected elements are usually repeated. When people access the information online, the right-hand information is repeated on every screen, so the links are always accessible.

Balance. How are the various elements in the design balanced?
- Symmetrical — each half of the design (horizontal or vertical) is a mirror image
- Asymmetrical — design has uneven number of elements and/or elements that are not placed evenly
- Radial — design moves out from the center (or near the center) of the page or screen

Most designers envision horizontal and vertical grids for a design. The example uses a three-column grid, but the site looks like it has two asymmetrical columns. Why? The primary text takes up two columns in the grid (making it appear as a single, wider column). The third column serves as a site menu, so it has a large amount of white space that balances the text.

Alignment. How do various chunks of the text line up with each other? How does the text line up with the visuals? Text can align in columns on a page or screen:
- Left aligned text (also called flush left, left justified, or ragged right) lines up evenly on the left.
- Right aligned text (also called flush right, right justified, or ragged left) lines up evenly on the right.
- Centered text has equal white space on both sides.
- Justified text lines up evenly on both sides.

The primary text in this example has left justified/ragged right margins, which is easy for readers.

You can read the full report about tropical deforestation by going to www.english.wadsworth.com/burnett6e for a link.
  CLICK ON WEBLINK
   CLICK on Chapter 11/tropical deforestation

WEBLINK

earth observatory
home • data & images • features • news • reference • missions • experiments • search
glossary   on ○ off ●

REFERENCE

TROPICAL DEFORESTATION
By Gerald Urquhart, Walter Chomentowski, David Skole, and Chris Barber

The clearing of tropical forests across the Earth has been occurring on a large scale basis for many centuries. This process, known as deforestation, involves the cutting down, burning, and damaging of forests. The loss of tropical rain forest is more profound than merely destruction of beautiful areas. If the current rate of deforestation continues, the world's rain forests will vanish within 100 years-causing unknown effects on global climate and eliminating the majority of plant and animal species on the planet.

Why Deforestation Happens
Deforestation occurs in many ways. Most of the clearing is done for agricultural purposes-grazing cattle, planting crops. Poor farmers chop down a small area (typically a few acres) and burn the tree trunks-a process called Slash and Burn agriculture. Intensive, or modern, agriculture occurs on a much larger scale, sometimes deforesting several square miles at a time. Large cattle pastures often replace rain forest to grow beef for the world market.

Commercial logging is another common form of deforestation, cutting trees for sale as timber or pulp. Logging can occur selectively-where only the economically valuable species are cut-or by clearcutting, where all the trees are cut. Commercial logging uses heavy machinery, such as bulldozers, road graders, and log skidders, to remove cut trees and build roads, which is just as damaging to a forest overall as the chainsaws are to the individual trees.

The causes of deforestation are very complex. A competitive global economy drives the need for money in economically challenged tropical countries. At the national level, governments sell logging concessions to raise money for projects, to pay international debt, or to develop industry. For example, Brazil had an international debt of $159 billion in 1995, on which it must make payments each year. The logging companies seek to harvest the forest and make profit from the sales of pulp and valuable hardwoods such as mahogany.

"THE CAUSES OF DEFORESTATION ARE VERY COMPLEX."

Tropical Deforestation
Why Deforestation Happens
The Rate of Deforestation
Deforestation and Global Processes
After Deforestation

Related Data Sets:
Biosphere
1km^2 AVHRR Fires
4km^2 TRMM Fires
Vegetation

Related Case Studies:
Fire!

Recommend this Article to a Friend

Emphasis. What's the focus? What draws audience attention? What's important? The hierarchy visually differentiates the title and headings from the primary text by placement (set off from text) and by typestyle (small caps and boldfacing).

Gestalt. How do all the elements work together? This report has a coherent gestalt (also called unity, consistency, variety, harmony, wholeness, oneness). All the elements look as if they belong together in their current location and sequence.

Proximity. Where are the elements — text, space, graphics, color, and implied or actual movement — placed? How are elements grouped? The primary text is placed close to the heading and photograph. The supplementary information is grouped in a narrower column.

Hornbills are an exotic bird found in Africa and Asia. The female nests in a tree cavity or rock crevice and then seals the nest entrance, leaving only a narrow slit for receiving food from the male.

Figure 11.1a–c shows the sequence of chunking and labeling information. The first chunk, Figure 11.1a, includes information about several topics related to hornbills. Unfortunately, the information is in no particular order and is without any design elements to aid audiences.

The second chunk, Figure 11.1b, groups all the information about the various subtopics and then visually separates these topical chunks into paragraphs. The third chunk, Figure 11.1c, labels the subtopics and uses a bulleted list to make reading easier.

Decisions about the most appropriate way to chunk and label information are not necessarily as simple as grouping topically related information, as in Figures 11.1a–c. For example, if you are preparing a fact sheet about the rivets your company sells, you could chunk the information by such characteristics as types of materials, strength of materials, applications, dimensions, resistance to corrosion, distinctions from competitors, price, and so on. Information from all these categories could appear on the fact sheet, but you could make a decision about how to chunk the information based on the needs of your audience. For example, the top list on the right chunks information about rivet material according to type; the second list chunks information about material according to strength.

> What other information could you chunk in two (or more) different ways, similar to these lists categorizing rivets?

Types of Rivet Materials
Steel
Aluminum
Brass
Plastic

This topical chunking would be useful for audiences interested in marine applications, where anticorrosion is a critical factor.

Strength of Rivet Materials
Tensile strength
Compressive
Flexure
Torsion
Shear

This topical chunking would be useful for audiences interested in bridge construction, where strength is a critical factor.

FIGURE 11.1 Sequence from (a) Undifferentiated Text to (b) Chunked Text to (c) Labeled Text[5]

(a) Twenty-three species of hornbills inhabit the savannas and forests of Africa, and twenty-seven more species are found in Asia, mostly in tropical rain forests. The Tangkoko red knobs are a species bothered by few dangerous predators; their unusual nesting behavior seems a holdover from earlier times. The nesting behavior of the Tangkoko red knobs is thought to have evolved from one or more of these reasons: protection from predators; defense against intruding hornbills; ensurance of mate fidelity (female can't escape to the nest of another; or, variously, male is too exhausted feeding one female and chick to seek an additional mate). Tangkoko red knobs weigh more than five pounds and produce a variety of honks, croaks, squawks, and barks, some of which can be heard more than 300 yards away. The female Tangkoko red knob nests in a tree cavity or rock crevice and then seals the nest entrance — with mud delivered by the male and her own fecal matter — leaving only a narrow slit for receiving food from the male. One of the Borneo species of hornbills, the Tangkoko red knobs, is large and loud. Only four species are found to the east of the biogeographical boundary between Borneo and Sulawesi.

The information about hornbills is raw, run-together text. It is undifferentiated, except for capital letters and periods to mark the beginning and end of sentences. The information is unordered and is in a sans serif font, without any spatial or graphic elements to aid audiences.

(b) Twenty-three species of hornbills inhabit the savannas and forests of Africa, and twenty-seven more species are found in Asia; mostly in tropical rain forests. Only four species are found to the east of the biogeographical boundary between Borneo and Sulawesi.

One of the Borneo species of hornbills, the Tangkoko red knobs, is large and loud. They weigh more than five pounds and produce a variety of honks, croaks, squawks, and barks, some of which can be heard more than 300 yards away.

The female nests in a tree cavity or rock crevice and then seals the nest entrance — with mud delivered by the male and her own fecal matter — leaving only a narrow slit for receiving food from the male. This behavior is thought to have evolved from one or more of these reasons: protection from predators; defense against intruding hornbills; ensurance of mate fidelity (female can't escape to the nest of another; or, variously, male is too exhausted feeding one female and chick to seek an additional mate). However, the Tangkoko red knobs are bothered by few dangerous predators, so their unusual nesting behavior seems a holdover from earlier times.

All the information about the three subtopics, now in a serif font, is topically chunked and then visually separated into paragraphs with a ragged-right margin.

(c) **Hornbill Territory.** Twenty-three species of hornbills inhabit the savannas and forests of Africa, and twenty-seven more species are found in Asia, mostly in tropical rain forests. Only four species are found to the east of the biogeographical boundary between Borneo and Sulawesi.

Tangkoko Red Knobs. One of the Borneo species of hornbills, the Tangkoko red knobs, is large and loud. These birds weigh more than five pounds and produce a variety of honks, croaks, squawks, and barks, some of which can be heard more than 300 yards away.

Unusual Nesting Behavior. The female nests in a tree cavity or rock crevice and then seals the nest entrance — with mud delivered by the male and her own fecal matter — leaving only a narrow slit for receiving food from the male. This behavior is thought to have evolved from one or more of these reasons:
- protection from predators
- defense against intruding hornbills
- ensurance of mate fidelity (female can't escape to the nest of another; or, variously, male is too exhausted feeding one female and chick to seek an additional mate)

However, the Tangkoko red knobs are bothered by few dangerous predators, so their unusual nesting behavior seems a holdover from earlier times.

The subtopics in each paragraph are labeled with run-in, boldfaced headings. A bulleted list makes reading easier.

FIGURE 11.2   Clearly Chunked Table of Contents[6]

What principles of design do you see at work in this home page?

Not only do you need to chunk small amounts of information (like categories of rivets), but you also need to show the overall organization of information. One of the most efficient ways to inform your audience about the way you've chunked information is in a table of contents. Figure 11.2 shows a clearly chunked home page for Nikon, in which every bulleted item is a link.

White Space to Chunk Information 用空白集中信息

Once you have determined the chunks of information, you can separate these chunks by using white space, and then you can label them with headings. *White space* (or *negative space*) is the part of any page or screen that is blank, without print or visuals. Not only does white space signal chunks of information, it also makes documents more appealing.

No hard and fast rules exist concerning the use of white space. Several conventions, which apply both to print pages and electronic pages, suggest that white space be used for margins, between lines within a paragraph (called *leading* or *line spacing*), between paragraphs and sections of a document, and around visuals. The amount of white space is also affected by the justification and length of the lines of text. The impact of white space on a page is illustrated by the two segments in Figure 11.3a and 11.3b — the first with crowded printing and skimpy margins, the second with wider margins and more space between lines.

FIGURE 11.3A Skimpy White Space	FIGURE 11.3B Appropriate White Space
This paragraph is more difficult to read because little attention is given to physical features of the presentation. Narrow leading and full justification create greater eye strain. The small margins give an impression of crowding. The proportion of text is too great for the amount of space.	This paragraph is easier to read because the physical features consider the reader. The material has sufficient space between the lines and is surrounded by margins. The white space and text are balanced.

Margins. The four margins on a print page, which usually have different widths, are also used to chunk information. The top (head) margin is the narrowest. The inner margins (gutters) are wider to ensure that no words are lost in the binding; the outer margin is wider still. Type that runs nearly to the edge of the paper not only is unattractive but also leads readers' eyes off the page. Sometimes, outside margins are even wider to provide space for note taking or a running gloss, which are marginal notes that emphasize particular points. The widest margin is usually at the bottom of the page. The thumbnail sketches in Figure 11.4 show the flexibility you have in adjusting margins: the typical 1-inch margins in version a, the wide equal margins in version b, the extra-wide left margin in version c.

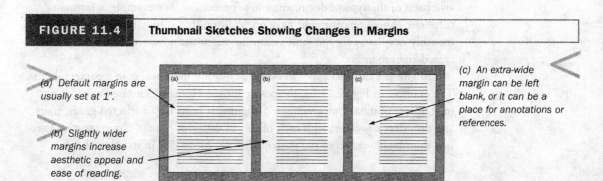

FIGURE 11.4 Thumbnail Sketches Showing Changes in Margins

(a) Default margins are usually set at 1".

(b) Slightly wider margins increase aesthetic appeal and ease of reading.

(c) An extra-wide margin can be left blank, or it can be a place for annotations or references.

> Explain which you think is more important: a neat, clean appearance or an easy-to-read document.

Alignment. Another element that affects chunking and, thus, accessibility/legibility is alignment. If all the lines of type on a page are exactly the same length, the lines have been justified, or adjusted to equal length by proportional spacing between words on each individual line. Fully justified lines give a document a neat, clean appearance, as Figure 11.5a illustrates. If the lines all begin at the same left-hand margin and the right margin is ragged, the right margin is unjustified, as Figure 11.5b shows.

FIGURE 11.5 Thumbnail Sketches Showing Alignment

(a) Fully justified text has a formal, neat look, but reading many pages of fully justified text is difficult, especially if the print is small and the lines are long.

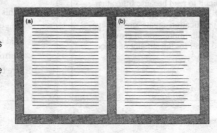

(b) Most ragged-right text (justified only on the left) is easier to read than fully justified text.

Although some editors and designers prefer that both left and right margins be justified, both because of tradition and because more words will fit on a page or screen, fully justified text is not as easy to read as text with a ragged right margin. Because all the lines in a fully justified text are the same length, readers can easily lose their place — and readers lose their place even more easily in on-screen reading than in paper reading. In addition, a long-cited survey in the journal *Technical Communication* indicates that a majority of both managers and nonmanagers prefer documents with ragged-right margins.[7]

Generally, readers find texts with shorter line lengths and ragged-right margins easier to read; however, these generalizations need to be applied with an awareness of the type of document you're producing. For example, a formal corporate annual report might have one column that is fully justified, whereas a monthly newsletter for the same company might use a two-column format with ragged-right margins.

Alignment can also apply to elements beyond lines of text in a paragraph. The example in Figure 11.6a, the poster for the Human Genome Project, is a masterpiece of data compression and alignment in its list of selected genes, traits, and disorders associated with each of the 24 different human chromosomes. Even in a thumbnail version of the poster, which is 24" × 36" in its original size,

FIGURE 11.6 (a) Thumbnail of Human Genome Landmarks Poster; (b) Human Chromosome 5 in Detail[8]

A

B

194 million bases 5

Dopamine transporter
Attention-deficit hyperactivity disorder, susceptibility to
Cri-du-chat syndrome, mental retardation in
Chondrocalcinosis
Taste receptor
Alpha-methylacyl-CoA racemase deficiency
Differentially expressed in ovarian cancer
Ketoacidosis
Leukemia inhibitory factor receptor
Myopathy, distal, with vocal cord and pharyngeal weakness
Molybdenum cofactor deficiency, type B
Endometrial carcinoma
Klippel-Feil syndrome
Anemia, megaloblastic
Sandhoff disease
Spinal muscular atrophy, juvenile
X-ray repair
Convulsions, familial febrile
Adenomatous polyposis coli
Gardner syndrome
Colorectal cancer
Desmoid disease
Turcot syndrome
Ehlers-Danlos syndromes
Neonatal alloimmune thrombocytopenia
Myelodysplastic syndrome
Limb-girdle muscular dystrophy, autosomal dominant
Deafness
Bronchial hyperresponsiveness (bronchial asthma)
Hemangioma, capillary infantile
Spinocerebellar ataxia
Macrocytic anemia
Gastric cancer
Non small-cell lung cancer
Retinitis pigmentosa, autosomal recessive
Charcot-Marie-Tooth neuropathy
Netherton syndrome
Treacher Collins-Franceschetti syndrome
Pituitary tumor-transforming gene
Coagulation factor XII (Hageman factor)
Myeloid malignancy, predisposition to
Craniosynostosis, type 2
Parietal foramina
Leukotriene C4 synthase deficiency
Dopamine receptor
Hermansky-Pudlak syndrome

Homocystinuria-megaloblastic anemia, cbl E type
Craniometaphyseal dysplasia
Leigh syndrome
Polycystic ovary syndrome
Hirschsprung disease
Severe combined immunodeficiency
Dwarfism
Malignant hyperthermia susceptibility
Pituitary hormone deficiency
Cytotoxic T-lymphocyte-associated serine esterase
Hanukah factor serine protease
Maroteaux-Lamy syndrome
Serotonin receptor
Schizophrenia susceptibility locus
Wagner syndrome
Erosive vitreoretinopathy
Basal cell carcinoma
Obesity with impaired prohormone processing
Diphtheria toxin receptor
Contractural arachnodactyly, congenital
Cutis laxa, recessive, type I
Deafness
Cortisol resistance
Corneal dystrophy
Eosinophilia, familial
Serotonin receptor
Schistosoma mansoni infection, susceptibility/resistance to
Natural killer cell stimulatory factor-2
GM2-gangliosidosis, AB variant
Startle disease, autosomal dominant and recessive
Diastrophic dysplasia
Atelosteogenesis
Achondrogenesis
Epiphyseal dysplasia, multiple
Asthma, nocturnal, susceptibility to
Obesity, susceptibility to
Muscular dystrophy, limb-girdle, type 2F
Carnitine deficiency, systemic primary
Atrial septal defect with atrioventricular conduction defects
Arthrogryposis multiplex congenital, neurogenic
Leukemia, acute promyelocytic, NPM/RARA type
Vascular endothelial growth factor receptor
Lymphedema, hereditary
Cockayne syndrome
Pancreatitis, hereditary

the alignment of the chromosomes is remarkably clear. Figure 11.6b shows chromosome 5 and a number of the genes, traits, and disorders associated with it.

WEBLINK

Go to **www.english.wadsworth.com/burnett6e** to find a link to the online chromosome viewer, which gives you an opportunity to click on any chromosome and see selected genes, traits, and genetic disorders associated with each chromosome.
  CLICK ON WEBLINK
    CLICK on Chapter 11/chromosome

Leading and Line Length. The spacing between lines of type (called *leading* in paper documents; more often called *line spacing* in Web documents) is another way of chunking information that improves accessibility/legibility and, thus, increases ease and speed of reading. Generally, text that is easiest to read has line spacing that is one-and-a-half times the letter height. (See Chapter 3 and Chapter 13 for additional discussion about reading electronic documents.)

> How do leading and line length affect accessibility of information for users of online documents?

Lines that are too short annoy readers; lines that are too long are difficult to read. But "short" and "long" are relative, related to font type and size rather than to absolute line length. In general, font size larger than 12 points has a "primer" look and reminds people of their elementary school reading. (Exceptions to this, of course, are materials for readers who are visually impaired.) And a font size smaller than 7 points is usually too tiny to read easily. However, changes in leading and adjustments in justification and line length can have a great impact on ease of reading, as the following two examples show:

8-point Geneva, 8-point leading, full justification, and long lines

The whole world ocean extends over about three-fourths of the surface of the globe. If we subtract the shallow areas of the continental shelves and the scattered banks and shoals, where at least the pale ghost of sunlight moves over the underlying bottom, there still remains about half the earth that is covered by miles-deep, lightless water, that has been dark since the world began. (Rachel Carson, from "The Sunless Sea" in *The Sea Around Us*)

8-point Geneva, 12-point leading, ragged-right margin, and shorter lines

The whole world ocean extends over about three-fourths of the surface of the globe. If we subtract the shallow areas of the continental shelves and the scattered banks and shoals, where at least the pale ghost of sunlight moves over the underlying bottom, there still remains about half the earth that is covered by miles-deep, lightless water, that has been dark since the world began. (Rachel Carson, from "The Sunless Sea" in *The Sea Around Us*)

Does line length really make a difference? Read a short study that shows that line length and margin width interact to affect the ease of reading a document. This is an experiment that you could replicate. To access it, go to **www.english.wadsworth.com/burnett6e** for a link.

   CLICK ON WEBLINK
      CLICK on Chapter 11/line length

WEBLINK

Headings to Label Chunked Information 用标题标注集中的信息

Headings and subheadings can label chunked information and identify the relative importance of these chunks in a document, whether print or online. Headings not only establish the subject of a section; they also give readers a chance to take both a literal and a mental breath while previewing the upcoming content. Some writers try to use a heading or subheading every three to five paragraphs to avoid visual monotony and keep the reader focused. Although you may find such breaks too frequent, the concept is important. As noted in Chapter 10, a well-designed outline can serve as the structure for the table of contents and also provide headings and subheadings that make a document easier to read.

    The thumbnail sketches in Figure 11.7 show various ways you can incorporate headings into your documents. Relative importance is signaled by capitalization, type size, and typeface. When you test the draft of a document with your audience, check that they are helped, not confused, by your titles, headings, and subheadings.

FIGURE 11.7   **Thumbnail Sketches of Heading Placement**

(a) Headings can be pulled out of the text and placed in a separate narrower column used solely for headings and annotations.

(b) Headings can be used to signal a change of topic as well as to reduce visual monotony and create visual interest for the reader.

(c) Headings can partially or fully extend the width of the grid column.

Arranging Related Chunks of Verbal and Visual Information

整理文字和视觉信息

In arranging verbal and visual information, you can draw on design conventions as well as avoid design problems.

Using Design Conventions 使用设计原则

Two practices used by professional designers will help you produce more effective documents:

- Selection of appropriate grids
- Placement of visuals near related text

> *Why should subject matter experts spend time learning about the design of documents?*

The easiest and most efficient way to design a page (or an entire document) is to see the page or a screen as a *grid* — columns and rows that help you organize the textual and visual chunks. In most situations, you will use one-column, two-column, or three-column grids, illustrated in thumbnail sketches in Figure 11.8. For more detailed grids, you'll probably be working with a designer or graphic artist. When you are working independently, you'll be able to create thumbnail sketches of various grids and consider which one is most appropriate.

Different grids are appropriate for different purposes and audiences. Imagine, for example, that the one-column grid in Figure 11.8a is for an in-house technical report about reconfiguring computer workstations; the two-column grid in Figure 11.8b is for an operator's manual for office workers using desktop publishing; the three-column grid in Figure 11.8c is for a corporate newsletter.

Readers of print documents appreciate not having to constantly turn back and forth between the page they're reading and visuals placed in an appendix. A long-accepted survey concerning the format of NASA technical reports indicated that 80 percent of management and nonmanagement engineers and scientists preferred visuals integrated into the text rather than placed in an appendix. The only exceptions noted were if several consecutive pages of visuals interrupted the flow of the text and thus distracted the reader.[9] Figure 11.9 shows several acceptable possibilities for incorporating visuals into your text.

FIGURE 11.8 | **Thumbnail Sketches of Columns for Grids**

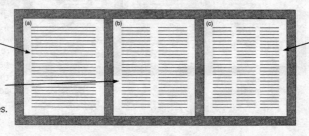

(a) One-column grids are typically used for correspondence and reports.

(b) Two-column grids are typically used for manuals and brochures.

(c) Three-column grids typically are used for newsletters.

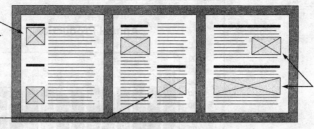

FIGURE 11.9 Thumbnail Sketches Showing Placement of Visuals

Visuals can be pulled out of the text and placed in the margin (or on a separate page).

Visuals can be incorporated in the text, fitting into one column on the grid.

Visuals can also take up more or less space than a grid's column.

Readers of online documents appreciate hyperlinks that allow them to move back and forth between the page they're reading and a linked document or visual. Readers working on a relatively small screen will toggle back and forth; however, as monitor size increases and the price of high-resolution flat-panel screens decreases, users often have access to monitors that can display two full pages at the same time.

Avoiding Problems in Arranging Information 避免信息整理中的问题

Before you design a print or online document, you need to be aware of four potential problems that distract readers:

- Chartjunk
- Tombstoning
- Heading placement
- Widows and orphans

One problem involves the temptation to clutter visuals with unnecessary *chartjunk*, miscellaneous graphic junk that does nothing to help people understand the information. This temptation is multiplied when you are using computer software that entices you to add fancy features to visuals. Figure 11.10 contrasts a graph with unnecessary and distracting chartjunk and one with less chartjunk and more white space. Whatever is included on visuals should contribute to the meaning and make the information more accessible and appealing.

Another problem, called *tombstoning*, involves aligning headings so that readers mistakenly chunk the text when they look at the page. In Figure 11.11a, readers could easily believe that the top half of the page was one section and the bottom half was another. Figure 11.11b shows that you can rearrange the headings to avoid this potential confusion.

A third problem, *heading placement*, comes from leaving too few lines after a heading or subheading at the top or bottom of a column or page. Figure 11.12a shows the problem of not leaving at least three lines in a column or on a page before beginning a new heading or having at least three lines following a new heading at the bottom of a column or page. Figure 11.12b shows the adjustment, which included more lines.

| FIGURE 11.10 | **Chartjunk versus White Space** |

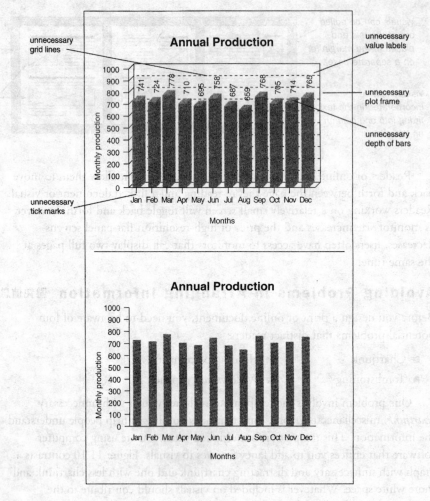

This version has too much chartjunk and too little white space, so the data are obscured.

This version, without the chartjunk, has more white space, so the changes in monthly production are easier to see.

What arguments can you think of for and against using chartjunk?

| FIGURE 11.11 | **Tombstoning** |

(a) Because of the aligned headings (arranged like tombstones), the top two columns could be mistakenly seen as one chunk of the text.

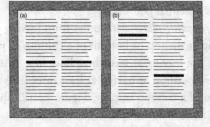

(b) The placement of the headings makes much clearer that readers should move through the first column and onto the second. Any temptation to mischunk the text is lessened.

FIGURE 11.12   Placement of Headings

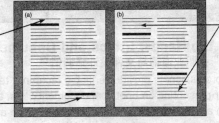

(a) Avoid placing a single line or two at the top of a column or page when followed by a new heading.

Avoid a heading at the bottom of a column or page that has room for only one or two lines of text.

(b) Have several lines of text preceding and following a heading.

A final problem deals with widows and orphans. *Widows* are leftover words — one or two words hanging on awkwardly as the last line of a paragraph. You can avoid them by revising the sentences in the paragraph to add or delete a few words so that one or two are not left on a line alone. *Orphans* occur when a column or page break occurs in a paragraph after the first line of the paragraph (see Figure 11.13). Try to arrange column or page breaks after a few lines rather than at the very beginning or end of a paragraph.

FIGURE 11.13   Widows and Orphans

WIDOWS
Widows occur when one or two words hang on as the last line of a paragraph.

ORPHANS
Orphans occur when a column or page breaks after the first line of the paragraph.

Sometimes problems in arranging information are more serious than simply inconveniencing readers whose time may be wasted or understanding restricted because of careless or inadequate attention to information design. The ethics sidebar on the next page discusses the document design of a government document and the ways that type size, white space, and boldface type potentially can bias readers.

What are some techniques you could use to avoid using font sizes deceptively?

WEBLINK

A short, easy-to-read article summarizing the "seven deadly sins of information design" will help you avoid some basic errors. To access the article, go to **www.english.wadsworth.com/burnett6e** for a link.
CLICK ON WEBLINK
  CLICK on Chapter 11/deadly sins

ETHICS SIDEBAR
职业道德规范知识吧

"A Wound to the Hand": Ethics and Document Design
"手上的伤口"：职业道德与文件设计强调信息

> *Emphasizing information is an important part of document design in technical communication, but technical professionals must be aware of the ethical line between emphasis and deception. Where is this line for you? How much does document design, in elements like type size or spacing, affect how a document is interpreted?*

Can technical professionals provide verifiable facts in a technical document but still be at fault for presenting an unethical document? Yes, they can — if those facts are found in a document that is designed to deceive and mislead the audience. So found researcher TyAnna Herrington in her review of research on the relationship between ethics and document design.[10] Herrington's research indicates the way facts are presented in a document is as important as the facts themselves. Design elements like headings, titles, spacing, and font size guide readers in determining the inherent value of the information and the relative importance of that information when compared to other information inside (and outside) the document. These design elements can intentionally or unintentionally lead readers to interpretations and conclusions that may not be supported by the facts or that hide more credible or relevant explanations.

Herrington believes an example of unethical document design can be found in a government report about the siege at the Branch Davidian compound in Waco, Texas, in 1998. The Branch Davidians, a small religious group, and the U.S. Department of Alcohol, Tobacco, and Firearms (ATF) clashed in February of that year when the ATF attempted to confiscate weapons they believed the Branch Davidians had obtained illegally. The violent confrontation between the ATF agents and the Branch Davidians at the Davidians' housing compound led to multiple deaths on both sides.

Herrington reviewed the tables in the government report and found that type size, white space, and boldfacing emphasized the ATF injuries and de-emphasized the Branch Davidian injuries, even though more Davidians than agents died during the attack. For example, the titles for the ATF tables are in boldface and are a larger type size (14-point vs. 12-point) than the Branch Davidian titles, which are not boldfaced. She also found additional white space around the titles in the ATF tables, which helped these tables stand out more in the overall document. These visual differences, Herrington believes, help accentuate the ATF casualties.

> *What are some techniques you could use to avoid using font sizes deceptively?*

The descriptions in tables listing ATF and Davidian injuries also accentuate the ATF casualties. In the ATF table, the wording of the descriptions is more understandable to the untrained reader than the descriptions in the Davidian tables. For example, the ATF table lists a "gunshot wound to the hand" while the Davidian table lists a "craniocerebral trauma-gunshot wound." Herrington believes these differences are unethical because they may lead to unsupported and misleading interpretations of the events in Waco.

WEBLINK

When you get really involved in the design of information, you often want to read about various practices and issues. For a list of remarkably varied and valuable links, go to **www.english.wadsworth.com/burnett6e**. You'll be able to access one of the special interest groups (SIGs) of the Society for Technical Communication that focuses on information design, as well as access the tables of contents of *Document Design: Journal of Research and Problem Solving in Organizational Communication*.
   CLICK ON WEBLINK
      CLICK on Chapter 11/design references

Emphasizing Information
强调信息

Once information is chunked, labeled, and arranged, you may still need to emphasize selected portions of the text to make the information more accessible, comprehensible, and usable.

On printed pages, chunking, labeling, and arranging are fixed. However, readers can alter the way they view Web pages by changing browser preferences. For example, readers can choose to "view pictures and text," "pictures only," or "text only" by turning graphics on or off. They can choose specific fonts for their browser to use as a default and turn off the fonts specified in the document, disable dynamic fonts, and so on. Readers can also specify link and background colors.

Despite a designer's careful and considered choices, some readers may choose to override the designer's decisions. Most readers, though, do use the design on the Web page; thus, typeface and typographic devices remain important for creating emphasis for both print and Web pages.

> Explain whether knowing a great deal about making documents appealing to readers increases the likelihood that carelessly done work — perhaps inaccurate or unsupported information — could be presented in an effective "package" that might disguise its inadequacies.

WEBLINK

Typography in the Western world dates from the early- to mid-15th century, depending on which historical records you read. To learn more about the history of typography, including examples of how typography evolved, discussions about the politics of typography, and critical features of particular typefaces, go to **www.english.wadsworth.com/burnett6e**.
   CLICK ON WEBLINK
      CLICK on Chapter 11/typographic history

Typefaces 字体与字号

Typeface (also called *font*) affects readers' attitudes and reactions to a print or electronic document, as well as their ability to access, comprehend, and use information easily and quickly. The desktop publishing revolution makes imperative your knowledge of basic characteristics about typefaces:

- Serif or sans serif
- Typeface variations
- Type size
- Style choices

WEBLINK

Skillful designers can distinguish various typefaces and determine which ones are appropriate for various purposes. Part of being able to make informed decisions about typefaces involves learning to recognize the fonts that are available. To access sites illustrating various typefaces, go to **www.english.wadsworth.com/burnett6e** for links.
CLICK ON WEBLINK
    CLICK on Chapter 11/typography

Whether you're selecting typefaces for a print document or for a Web page, you have the same choices, but the constraints are considerably different. For a Web page, follow these general guidelines:

- Select conventional fonts that you can be fairly sure users will have installed on their computer.
- Remember that in print the relationship between typographical elements is fixed on a page. However, on a Web site, users scroll and link in different (and sometimes unanticipated) ways, so reaction to typographical elements is never to a fixed page.
- Web sites can use technology to build in interaction — for example, overlays or pop-ups — to engage users.

Serif or Sans Serif. Most typefaces can be classified as *serif* or *sans serif*. Serifs are tiny fine lines usually at the top or bottom of letters.

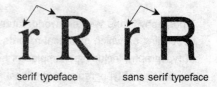

These are examples of lowercase and uppercase versions of the letters *b, p,* and *x* in common serif and sans serif typefaces:

serif: b B (10-point Times Roman)	sans serif: b B (9-point Helvetica)
serif: p P (10-point Palatino)	sans serif: p P (9-point Arial)
serif: x X (10-point New York)	sans serif: x X (9-point Geneva)

Sans serif typefaces have a neat, appealing appearance and are often used for short documents. Because sans serif typefaces are simpler, the letters don't have as many distinguishing features, making them slightly less accessible in print documents for some people; thus, documents for children, the elderly, people with visual impairments or disabilities, and people with learning disabilities are often printed in serif typefaces. Similarly, long documents (for example, long technical reports and journal articles) for all readers often use a serif typeface so that readers won't tire so quickly. These generalizations don't apply, however, to electronic documents, which many people believe are easier to read in sans serif typefaces, especially those designed for on-screen reading.

WEBLINK

The information architecture and typography for Web sites requires special attention to a range of factors ranging from platforms to screen sizes. For useful information about Web design, go to **www.english.wadsworth.com/burnett6e** for links.
  CLICK ON WEBLINK
    CLICK on Chapter 11/web design

Typeface Variations. Your selection of typeface should be influenced both by the kind of document and your sense of how the readers will react. Readers are discouraged if typefaces are inappropriate for the document or situation or are difficult to read.

- *This typeface is called Edwardian Script and is usually used only for social announcements.*
- This typeface is called Helvetica and is often used for standard business letters.
- This typeface is called Adobe Garamond and is often used for typesetting lengthy reports and books, including this one, because it is easy to read.

Figure 11.14 illustrates ways in which typographical conventions, including typeface, are used in a Dell Computer user's manual as visual cues to help readers. Each typeface has a specific meaning. For example, all items on the manual's menu screens are presented in Helvetica; all commands lines are presented in Courier. Associating meaning with various fonts and other typographic cues helps readers because it gives them textual content as well as visual cues to help construct meaning.

Type Size. You can also affect readers by the size of the type. You can discourage, insult, or alienate readers by using an inappropriate type size. For example, although tiny type reduces the number of pages in a user manual, it also makes the manual difficult for readers to use. Unnecessarily large type can make a document seem elementary because many people associate large type with children's books. You generally use 10- or 12-point type for the text of business documents. Headings may use larger type. The type used for PowerPoint

What federal mandates exist for making information accessible to visually impaired readers? What guidelines exist to help design documents for elderly readers?

Chapter 11 Designing Information   397

FIGURE 11.14 Typographical Conventions Used in a Dell Computer User's Manualiv[11]

Bold signals interface components such as menu names.

<Angle brackets> signal keycaps and key combinations.

Lower case bold signals filenames, directory names, information for reference, and commands.

[Brackets] indicate optional information.

`Courier New` signals command lines and text to be typed.

Italics signals variables.

Typographical Conventions

The following list defines (where appropriate) and illustrates typographical conventions used as visual cues for specific elements of text throughout this document:

- *Interface components* are window titles, button and icon names, menu names and selections, and other options that appear on the monitor screen or display. They are presented in bold.

  Example: Click **OK**.

- *Keycaps* are labels that appear on the keys on a keyboard. They are enclosed in angle brackets.

  Example: <Enter>

- *Key combinations* are series of keys to be pressed simultaneously (unless otherwise indicated) to perform a single function.

  Example: <Ctrl><Alt><Enter>

- *Commands* presented in lowercase bold are for reference purposes only and are not intended to be typed when referenced.

  Example: "Use the **format** command to . . . ."

  In contrast, commands presented in the Courier New font are part of an instruction and intended to be typed.

  Example: "Type `format a:` to format the diskette in drive A."

- *Filenames* and *directory names* are presented in lowercase bold.

  Examples: **autoexec.bat** and **c:windows**

- *Syntax lines* consist of a command and all its possible parameters. Commands are presented in lowercase bold; variable parameters (those for which you substitute a value) are presented in lowercase italics; constant parameters are presented in lowercase bold. The brackets indicate items that are optional.

  Example: **del** *[drive:] [path] filename* **[/p]**

- *Command lines* consist of a command and may include one or more of the command's possible parameters. Command lines are presented in the Courier New font.

  Example: `del c:\myfile.doc`

- *Screen text* is a message or text that you are instructed to type as part of a command (referred to as a command line). Screen text is presented in the Courier New font.

  Example: The following message appears on your screen:

  `No boot device available`

  Example: "Type `md c:\programs` and press <Enter>."

- *Variables* are placeholders for which you substitute a value. They are presented in italics.

  Example: DIMM_x (where x represents the DIMM socket designation).

presentations or transparencies (vu-graphs) should be larger (18-point, 24-point, or 32-point type works well for making visuals to accompany oral presentations) so that the information can easily be read from the back of the room.

Variation in type size can also be used to capture your readers' attention. This warning, printed in 20-point Berkeley Old Style, is intended to grab readers.

WARNING! Ingestion of this chemical could be fatal!

However, the warning would not be nearly as effective if it were printed in 8-point type. Reducing the type size reduces the impact.

WARNING! Ingestion of this chemical could be fatal!

Typeface itself influences the size; all 10-point type does not look the same size. Combinations of type size and typeface provide visual appeal and variety. For example, the body of this book is set in 10.5-point Adobe Garamond with 12-point Franklin Gothic Demi main headings; 9-point Franklin Gothic Book is used for the examples. The part headings are in 18-point Franklin Gothic Book, as are the chapter titles.

If particular material must fit into a prescribed and limited amount of space, you can use type size to make minor adjustments. For example, information for a résumé could fit attractively on a single 8½-by-11-inch sheet using a 10-point font, whereas the information might take up one and a quarter sheets using a 12-point font.

Flexibility in type size depends on the equipment you use. Some printers may restrict your choices of typeface and type size. However, most inkjet and laser printers offer tremendous flexibility. Many inkjet printers offer the option of color cartridges so that you can print in color for a relatively low cost. Word-processing packages let you select from 8-point (or smaller) to 72-point (or larger) type in a great variety of fonts.

And what about fonts for Web sites? The same fonts are displayed differently on Macintosh and Windows operating systems. In general, fonts on Windows-based browsers look two to three points larger than the equivalent fonts on Macintosh browsers. The difference in the way fonts are displayed can have a major impact on your page design.[12]

Style Choices. The style of type you select can also influence the audience. Depending on the computer software you're using, you have the capability of using CAPITALIZATION, SMALL CAPS, **boldface,** and *italics,* as well as fancier variations such as shadow or outline.

Using ALL CAPS for occasional emphasis can be effective; however, your use of ALL CAPS should be limited to headings and single words or short phrases in the text. WHEN YOU USE ALL CAPS FOR ENTIRE SECTIONS OF TEXT, THE

READER IS NOT ABLE TO RAPIDLY DIFFERENTIATE THE WORDS BECAUSE ALL THE LETTERS ARE THE SAME HEIGHT. THUS, READING IS SLOWED. YOUR INTENT TO EMPHASIZE A POINT IS LOST IN THE VISUAL MONOTONY OF CONSISTENT CAPITALIZATION.

Visual emphasis can be created by using **boldface** or **BOLD SMALL CAPS** or **BOLD ALL CAPS.** These techniques are usually reserved for signaling warnings, cautions, and dangers and for calling attention to important points and terms. Use all these type variations with restraint. Try to work within a general guideline of using no more than two typefaces and a total of four variations of typeface, type size, or style on a single page or screen.

Typographic Devices 文档符号

Sometimes you need to emphasize information by separating it or visually distinguishing it from the text. Effective devices include numbered lists, bulleted lists, underlining, boxes, shading or tints, and colors. As with any device, their impact diminishes with overuse. Too many visual devices make a page look so cluttered that the reader cannot concentrate on content.

Numbered lists are particularly common elements in sets of instructions, and they also appear frequently in reports and proposals. Numbered lists suggest one of three things to readers:

- Sequence or chronology of items is important.
- Priority of items is important.
- Total count of items is important.

When all items in the list are equivalent, a bulleted list is preferable, as illustrated in the preceding lines. The bullets draw attention to each item in the list but infer no priority to the sequence. You can create bullets with most word-processing software by using one of the option keys or menu items.

Underlining words or phrases is a holdover from typewriters that didn't have italics or boldfacing to create emphasis; instead, underlined text was converted to italics when the material was typeset. A summary of underlining conventions appears in the *Usage Handbook* on the Companion Web site at www.english.wadsworth.com/burnett6e. And, as the preceding sentence illustrates, underlining now has another function: to signal hyperlinks in Web documents. In addition to being convenient for all readers, underlined hyperlinks increase accessibility for colorblind users as well as those with monochrome monitors. Unless you are signaling a hyperlink, avoid underlined text.[13]

Boxed and shaded information is emphasized. Information that is boxed should be surrounded by white space so that the text does not run into the box. Sometimes the boxed material relates directly to the text; other times it is supplemental. Too much shading diminishes its impact. Note particularly the use of shading for boxed figures in this text.

> Boxes are often effective in the following situations:
> - Identify major headings
> - Highlight key terms
> - Emphasize formulas or equations
> - Separate anecdotal material

> Shading highlights and emphasizes material. Sometimes shaded areas are used in conjunction with boxes. Readers are drawn to shaded material because it is differentiated from the rest of the text.

Color is an especially appealing visual device, which often contributes significantly to the effectiveness and clarity of a document. Some technical materials require color. For example, as you'll see in Chapter 12, anatomical diagrams need shading and color. Similarly, color-coded electronic components should be accompanied by color-coded troubleshooting diagrams. In documents with difficult material, color can create visual interest, highlight section headings, identify examples, and emphasize important points. In this text, color is used to help distinguish parts of visuals and to highlight important textual elements more distinctively than if a gray-scale were used.

> Shading highlights and emphasizes material. Sometimes shaded areas are used in conjunction with boxes. Readers are drawn to shaded material because it is differentiated from the rest of the text.

> Using color instead of a gray-scale calls even more attention to the information. The color should not decrease legibility (e.g., blue text on a black background) nor be so flamboyant that the content is ignored.

WEBLINK

> Color is a powerful design element. You can learn a great more about color by going to **www.english.wadsworth.com/burnett6e** for a link to a considerable number of references.
> CLICK ON WEBLINK
>   CLICK on Chapter 11/color portal

Color has a number of specific benefits, as illustrated in the thumbnail sketches in Figure 11.15. (The use of color in specific visuals is discussed in greater detail in Chapter 12.)

FIGURE 11.15 Use of Color for Creating Emphasis in Text

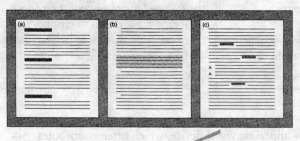

(a) Highlight text hierarchy

(b) Highlight important parts

(c) Signal key terms and cautions

- *Identify text hierarchy.* Color can help readers locate the main sections in a text. For example, Figure 11.13a shows how color can be used to highlight headings, but it can also be used for section dividers.

- *Chunk information.* Color can effectively chunk related information for readers. For example, Figure 11.13b shows how color can be used to highlight an important part of a paragraph.

- *Emphasize key points.* Figure 11.13c shows how color can be used to highlight terms, which helps readers recall and remember that information. Similarly, color can be used to emphasize critical parts of the text — for example, to signal cautions and warnings.

Despite its value, the use of color is often restricted by cost if you are using a commercial printer because a separate print run is needed for each color added to a page. Often, a well-designed document employing a variety of visual devices other than color can be equally effective.

WEBLINK

If you are particularly interested in the theory of design, go to **www.english.wadsworth.com/burnett6e** for a link to an interesting and provocative article.

CLICK ON WEBLINK
CLICK on Chapter 11/design theory

Individual and Collaborative Assignments

个人作业和小组作业

1. **Choose the appropriate format for a document.** Four common presentation formats have been explained in this chapter:

   - textual presentation alone in paragraph format
   - textual presentation with visuals
   - visual presentation with text explanations
   - visual presentation alone

   Choose one of these formats for each of the following situations and explain your choices:

   - Instructions for first-aid emergency
   - Preparation of a car for repainting
   - Explanation of a solution for a manufacturing problem
   - Presentation of computer printer components
   - Application of fertilizer to golf course

2. **Evaluate effective page design in a technical document.** Work with a small group of classmates in your academic discipline or a related one.

   (a) Based on what you have learned in this chapter and your own observations of page design, create a rubric that you can use to evaluate several documents.

   (b) Look for examples of page design in technical documentation and evaluate several.

   (c) Choose a page that is a particularly good example of effective page design and discuss the elements that make the page design effective and appealing.

   (d) Choose a page that is difficult to read because of poor design or poor visuals and redesign its layout.

3. **Use design principles for analysis.** Work with a small group of classmates to carefully study the following page from the quarterly publication *Conservation Frontlines*, published by Conservation International. Identify the design elements and then analyze the design principles that are at work in this page. Specifically, note the way information is chunked and labeled, the way it is arranged, the integration of textual and visual information, and the way information is emphasized.

dispatches

Biological survey uncovers marine marvel

A CI marine Rapid Assessment Program survey of reefs off the northwestern coast of Madagascar uncovered a remarkably diverse ecosystem, recording at least nine coral and three fish species new to science. Researchers documented 304 coral species, one-third of the world's known total and nearly double the number known to exist in Madagascar. CI and local groups are using survey results to help establish protected areas in this extraordinary marine environment.

[LEFT] Resplendent goldie *(Pseudanthias pulcherrimus)*, a species found in Madagascar's diverse coral reefs.

Rangers trained to save imperiled "man of the forest"

CI is providing antipoaching and law enforcement training to park rangers in Sumatra's Gunung Leuser National Park, part of a new program aimed at saving the endangered Sumatran orangutan. The program also is building a cadre of local monitors within the park to enhance protection efforts. The shaggy red orangutan, whose name translates as "man of the forest," is one of the world's most imperiled primates.

[ABOVE] Orangutan, one of the world's most endangered primates.

■ HOTSPOTS
■ MAJOR TROPICAL WILDERNESS AREAS

[LEFT] Nangaritza River, located in Ecuador's newly formed Nangaritza Protected Area.

Brazilian government backs Kayapo accord

In its first-ever agreement with an environmental organization, Brazil's Funai, the government agency responsible for indian affairs, has agreed to partner with CI to help the Kayapo indigenous community safeguard its 25-million-acre ancestral home in the Amazon wilderness area. Under the agreement, CI is providing equipment and training to support Kayapo efforts to protect the reserve.

[RIGHT] Men from the Kayapo reserve in Brazil wearing ceremonial headdress.

Protected area in Ecuador doubles in size

Collaboration among CI, local partners and the government of Ecuador has led to the creation of the 295,000-acre Nangaritza Protected Area adjacent to Podocarpus National Park, doubling the size of the protected region. Nangaritza is located in southeast Ecuador, near the border of Peru and within the biologically important Condor-Cutucú conservation corridor.

4. **Assess the differences between print and electronic journals.** Work with a group of classmates who share your major or a related field of study.

    (a) Locate an academic journal in your field in the library.
    (b) Search the Web for its corresponding electronic version.
    (c) Evaluate the differences between the two versions of the journal. Write your findings in a memo to your instructor.

5. **Transfer a print document to the Web.** Electronic publication of existing print documents involves different design and organizational considerations. Use a print document that you have already completed for this or another class. Change its format, design, and organization and publish it on the Web. Write a memo to your instructor in which you detail the changes that you made in your print document in order to make it Web accessible.

6. **Evaluate the effectiveness of the design of a technical Web site.** Locate several Web sites that deal with technical information in your field of study. Compare the effectiveness of the design of these Web sites.

    (a) Use (and modify) the rubric you created in Assignment 2 or use (and modify) the rubric. Consider the following questions:
    - Which presentation formats are most popular in Web-based documents?
    - Why do you think this is so?
    - What suggestions do you have for technical communicators designing Web-based documents?

    (b) Present your findings and your final rubric in a memo to your classmates.

Chapter 11 Endnotes

[1] Modified from (1) Kostelnick, C. (1989). Visuals rhetoric-oriented approach to graphics and design. *The Technical Writing Teacher, XVI*(1), 77-88; (2) Allen, J. T., & Chance, B. *Formal aspects of design.* Retrieved November 1, 2003, from http://desktoppub.about.com/gi/dynamic/offsite.htm?site=http%3A%2F%2Fs9000.furman.edu%2Fcs16g%2Fresources$2Felements.html

[2] The information about elements of graphic design has been drawn from a variety of print and electronic sources, all of which are worth checking for further details: (1) Bear, J. H. (2004). *What you need to know about desktop publishing* (and the many links available). Retrieved January 20, 2004, from http://desktoppub.about.com/cs/designprinciples/; (2) Goin, L. (2002). *Graphic design basics.* Retrieved November 1, 2003, from http://www.graphicdesignbasics.com/article1043.html/; (3) Jirousek, C. (n.d.). *Art, design, and visual thinking.* Retrieved November 1, 2003, from http://char.txa.cornell.edu/language/principl/rhythm/rhythm.htm; (4) Schriver, K. A. (1997). *Dynamics in document design: Creating text for readers.* New York: John Wiley & Sons. (5) Williams, R. (1994). *The non-designer's design book.* Berkeley, CA: Peachpit Press.

[3] Urquhart, G., Chomentowski, W., Skole, D., & Barber, C. (n.d.). *Tropical deforestation.* Retrieved November 1, 2003, from http://earthobservatory.nasa.gov/Library/Deforestation/

[4] Allen, J. T., & Chance, B. (n.d.). *Formal aspects of design.* Retrieved November 1, 2003, from http://desktoppub.about.com/gi/dynamic/offsite.htm?site=http%3A%2F%2Fs9000.furman.edu%2Fcs16g%2Fresources%2Felements.html

[5] Kinnaird, M. F. (1996, January). Indonesia's hornbill haven. *Natural History, 105*(1), 40–44.

[6] Nikon. (n.d.). Home page. Retrieved November 1, 2003, from http://www.nikonusa.com/home.jsp

[7] Pinelli, T. E., Cordle, V. M., McCullough, R. (1984). Report format preferences of technical managers and nonmanagers. *Technical Communication, 31,* 6–7.

[8] U.S. Department of Energy Human Genome Project Information Web site. (n.d.). *Human genome landmarks poster.* Retrieved November 2, 2003, from http://www.ornl.gov/sci/techresources/Human_Genome/posters/chromosome/index.shtml

and http://www.ornl.gov/sci/techresources/Human_Genome/posters/chromosome/chromo05.shtml

[9] Pinelli, T. E., Cordle, V. M., McCullough, R. (1984). Report format preferences of technical managers and nonmanagers. *Technical Communication, 31,* 6–7.

[10] Herrinton, T. (1995). Ethics and graphic design: A rhetorical analysis of the document design in the "Report of the Department of the Treasury on the Bureau of Alcohol, Tobacco, and Firearms investigation of Vernon Wayne Howell also known as David Koresh." *IEEE Professional Communication, 38*(3), 151–157.

[11] Notational Conventions. (n. d.). *Preface: HP OpenView Network Node Manager Special Edition 1.3 With Dell OpenManage™ HIP 3.3 User's Guide*. Retreived May 12, 2004, from http://support.ap.dell.com/docs/SOFTWARE/smnnmse/nnmse13.preface.htm

[12] Lynch, P. J., & Horton, S. (2002). Type size. In *Web style guide* (2nd ed.). Retrieved November 3, 2003, from http://www.webstyleguide.com/type/size.html

[13] Lynch, P. J., & Horton, S. (2002). Emphasis. In *Web style guide* (2nd ed.). Retrieved November 3, 2003, from http://www.webstyleguide.com/type/size.html

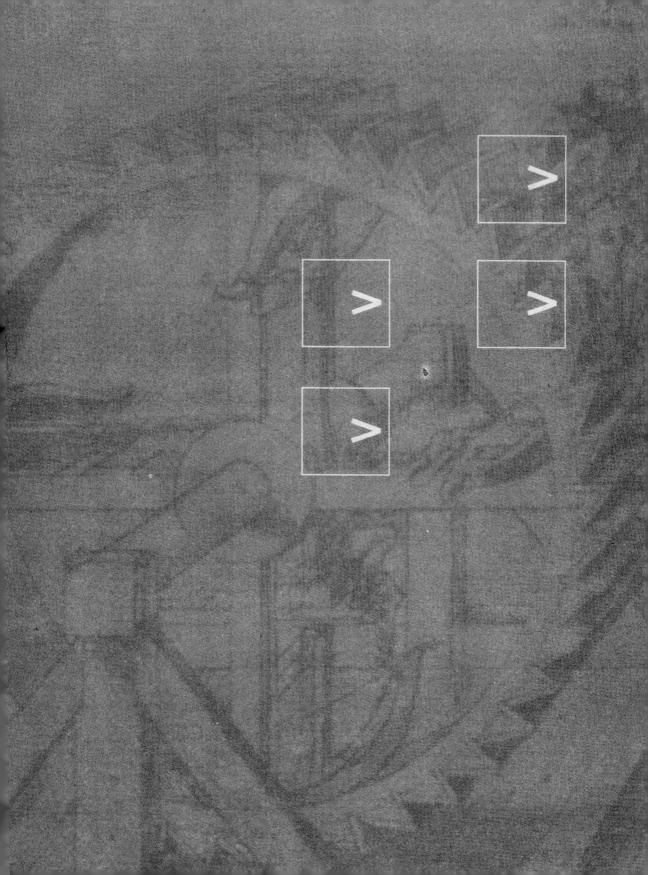

CHAPTER 12

Using Visual Forms
使用视觉形式

视觉手段的应用不仅可以吸引读者的注意力而且有助于读者对信息的理解。本章首先介绍了如何根据不同读者背景和场合情况（如对特定技术的了解、时间），通过变化信息内容的复杂性、呈现方式、颜色及文字大小等调整视觉手段。本章然后介绍了在文本中标注和放置表格的通用规范。本章重点阐述了不同视觉手段（如表格、图表、图画、地图、照片）在呈现信息时的七个作用。

Objectives and Outcomes 学习目标

This chapter will help you accomplish these outcomes:

- Understand that visuals not only attract attention and create appeal but also benefit cognitive processing and learning

- Adapt visuals by varying the complexity of content, presentation, color, and size to different audiences and different situations (limited technical knowledge, limited time)

- Make effective decisions about textual references and labeling and placement of visuals

- Carefully design or select visuals to fulfill specific functions:

- Use color appropriately and productively

Technical visuals are not a recent addition to technical communication. Leonardo da Vinci is only one of many scientific investigators who have produced a wide variety of technical art. His work, some of which is reproduced in chapter dividers of this text, exemplifies the accuracy and attention to detail found in effective technical visuals.

Like Leonardo da Vinci's visuals from the late fifteenth and early sixteenth centuries, visuals in contemporary technical documents should have a specific purpose and convey specific content. Why use visuals instead of or in addition to text? Not only do visuals attract attention and add appeal, they also strengthen documents in other ways.

> In what situations might visuals be distracting or minimally helpful to a reader?

- *Visuals can be more specific than text.* The word *tugboat,* for example, could represent anything from "Tommy Tug" in a children's story to barge tugboats, but a visual of a specific tugboat is easily identifiable.

- *Well-designed visuals can usually be understood more easily than text.* Visuals can be particularly effective when dealing with numeric data. Consider the following text and the corresponding graph. While the text presents precise numbers, the graph makes the overall trend in the figures far easier to understand. Most readers are better able to process and remember trends that are presented in graphs and charts.

Quickly read the following two versions that present the same information. Which one is faster to comprehend?

Verbal Version: Text

Staff growth. In the past four years, our staff size has changed. For full-time staff, numbers have changed from 24 in 2002 to 26 in 2003 to 29 in 2004 to 30 in 2005. For temporary staff, numbers have changed from 5 in 2002 to 6 in 2003 to 8 in 2004 to 7 in 2005.

Visual Version: Graph

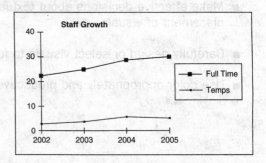

Virtually all readers can comprehend the visual version faster and can recall the visual information more easily. Why?

- *Visuals can be processed more quickly than text.* Visuals can be processed at a glance in as little as one-third of a second (although obviously more time is required to get the full meaning of a complex chart), while text must be consciously scanned.
- *Visuals help readers learn.* Readers who are given documents containing visuals consistently comprehend and retain information better than readers given only text. On average, readers who are given documents containing text and visuals learn 36 percent more than those given text-only documents.

Given these benefits, visuals can be extraordinarily important in increasing the accessibility and usability of your documents. However, you also need to understand the parameters in which you're operating. For example, how much can you alter and adjust a visual in order to make your point, such as changing the color on a photo or shifting the scale on a graph? The ethics sidebar below addresses some of the issues involved in deciding whether manipulation of a visual is ethical or unethical.

Is any alteration an unethical manipulation? Where do you draw the line?

ETHICS SIDEBAR 职业道德规范知识吧

"With no sacrifice to truth": Ethics and Visuals "没有牺牲事实"：职业道德与视觉手段

Consider this scenario:

You are working on a report that includes illustrations and photographs. When reviewing the photographs, you find that certain important details are hard to see. To draw out these details, you use visual design software to alter the intensity and hues, making the colors richer. The revised photos seem more appealing.

After you turn in the report, however, your supervisor calls you, claiming you unethically manipulated the photos. You defend yourself, arguing that the changes were artistic and didn't fundamentally alter the truth of the photographs. But your supervisor's response makes you wonder: Did you create unethical photos?

Are changes in intensity or color hues unethical manipulation of visuals? The editors of *Time* magazine didn't think so, at least not in the summer of 1994. That summer, the nation was captivated by the O. J. Simpson murder trial. After Simpson's arrest in June, both *Time* and *Newsweek* used versions of Simpson's police mug shot on their covers. *Time*'s version, however, drew public criticism because the photo had been altered. The image, referred to by *Time* as a photo-illustration, artificially

How could you alter a visual without deceiving the audience?

> To avoid creating unethical visuals, Kienzler offers some questions we can ask ourselves as we work with documents:
> - What are possible consequences of our visuals?
> - How would we feel if we received the visual?
> - What would the world be like if everyone used these visual techniques?
>
> Do you agree with Kienzler that the altered photo was unethical?

darkened Simpson's face, although it still looked like the official police mug shot.

Critics argued that the altered photo was racist, making Simpson look more menacing, especially when compared to Newsweek's nearly identical but unaltered cover. Time's managing editor, James Gaines, replying to the criticism, argued that the changes "lifted a common police mug shot to the level of art, with no sacrifice to truth." While Gaines recognized that "altering news pictures is a risky practice," he stated that "every major news outfit routinely crops and retouches photos to eliminate minor, extraneous elements, so long as the essential meaning of the picture is left intact."[1]

But was the "essential meaning" intact? Not according to researcher Donna Kienzler, who identifies the altered photo as unethical. Kienzler believes the image is unethical because readers did not immediately know that the image had been altered. Kienzler argues that the altered image should be seen as art, which "filters reality," and not as truth. The acknowledgment that the photo had been altered was not placed on the cover; it was instead placed on the contents page. According to Kienzler, placing the acknowledgment within the magazine violated the "readers' informed consent to be persuaded by art, rather than themselves evaluating a photograph" (180).[2]

Your professional success will be greatly influenced by your ability to understand and use visuals. Among the things you need to learn are factors that affect the way you incorporate visuals into a document, specific functions of visuals in technical documents and oral presentations, and conventions in using color.

Incorporating Visuals
应用视觉手段

> In what situations might visuals be more appropriate and useful than words for conveying technical information?

Your initial decisions about incorporating visuals involve balancing and integrating verbal and visual information, adjusting visuals for different audiences, and knowing when to choose visuals instead of text.

Visual/Verbal Combinations 视图与文字结合

In technical communication, visuals work by themselves and in combination with text to create stories for the audience. While visuals should make sense by themselves, they should also illustrate, explain, demonstrate, verify, or support the text. In deciding about appropriate visual/verbal combinations, you can choose from several choices, displayed in the thumbnail sketches in Figure 12.1.

You need to select visual/verbal combinations that communicate effectively to your audience. In many situations, visuals are more efficient than words. For example, a troubleshooting manual could begin with a verbal table identifying the problems along with analyses and solutions. Such a table would be far more useful

FIGURE 12.1 Various Combinations of Visual/Verbal Integration

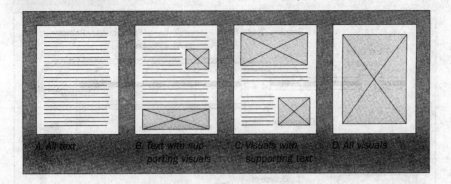

A. All text B. Text with supporting visuals C. Visuals with supporting text D. All visuals

than a series of paragraphs detailing potential problems. You should consider the value of effective, well-designed visuals in the following situations:

- When the audience's understanding of the technical content is limited
- When speed is critical, and reading text would slow the process
- When the process is more clearly illustrated visually

Some concepts or processes are so complex that one visual is insufficient. The three visuals in Figure 12.2, originally published in *NASA Tech Briefs,* all help to illustrate the uses of the Fabry-Perot Fiber-Optic Temperature Sensor. This photonic temperature sensor monitors and controls temperature in highly sensitive areas such as aircraft engines, conventional power plants, and industrial plants, where electronic temperature sensors pose a sparking hazard.

- The top visual in Figure 12.2 shows a cutaway view of the sensor head that is clearly labeled with noun phrases, while arrows point to specific components. Crosshatching distinguishes the nickel-alloy sheath from the Fabry-Perot interferometer that it holds.
- The middle visual in Figure 12.2 diagrams the entire sensor system; the blue arrow indicates the placement of the sensor head. A source of white light flows into one of the pair of optical fibers (represented by black lines) that flow into (and out of) the fiber-optic coupler to the fiber-optic connector and finally to the sensor itself. Shading, spot color, and labels distinguish one component from the other.
- The bottom visual in Figure 12.2 depicts a reflected light spectrum that is characteristic of the temperature in the sensor head. The colored line of this line graph is easily discernible against the white background.

Taken together, this series of visuals tells a story about a particular piece of hardware, the system it connects to, and the work that it does.

FIGURE 12.2   Series of Related Visuals to Tell a Story[3]

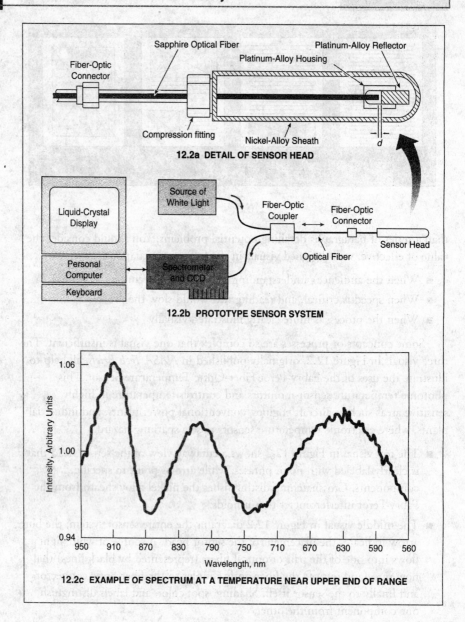

WEBLINK

Various kinds of visuals — for example, graphs, maps, photographs, and drawings — can often be successfully used in combination to tell a story far more effectively than any single kind of visual. For an example of a technical fact sheet that is highly dependent on multiple visuals, go to **www.english.wadsworth .com/burnett6e** for a link.
  CLICK ON WEBLINK
    CLICK on Chapter 12/multiple visuals

Adapting Visuals to Audiences 根据交流对象调整视觉手段

Visuals can be adapted to different audiences by the complexity of content, presentation, and sometimes color and size. Audience members who are not experts need more frequent and simpler visuals than experts. Since nonexperts also may not understand visual conventions that experts readily recognize, they may need additional explanations beyond the standard level of titles, legends, and captions. For example, whereas an expert would know that the bars in a histogram represent ranges of data, nonexperts may need to have that explained.

> What's the difference between "dumbing down" and adapting to the audience?

Figures 12.3 and 12.4 illustrate one way that the same information can be adapted to two very different audiences. Both figures are about the same discoveries and hypotheses in the study of human evolution. Figure 12.3 is more easily understood by educated nonexperts interested in science; Figure 12.4 updates science professionals about new research.

Conventions in Referencing and Placing Visuals 视觉手段参考和放置原则

Virtually all visuals have widely accepted conventions that accompany their use. Although you may sometimes choose to ignore a specific convention for good cause in a particular situation, generally you should follow these guidelines, which will help you to reference, label, and place visuals in ways that will be most useful to readers.

Textual Reference   As a general practice, you should refer to visuals in the text, rather than simply including visuals and expecting the audience to see them and connect them to the appropriate section of the text. Do not assume that the audience will check a visual unless you refer to it. Include adequate information in your text reference such as the figure number and title. Textual references may be embedded references in sentences or parenthetical references:

- "The incision should be made just above a joint with a bud, as illustrated in Figure 2: Grafting."
- "The effectiveness of the antitoxins tested is presented in Figure 4: Antitoxin Response."
- "Table 5 shows the rapid increase of gas prices during a five-year period."
- ". . . (see Table 3)."

| FIGURE 12.3 | **Visual for General Readers**[4] | FIGURE 12.4 | **Visual for Professionals**[5] |

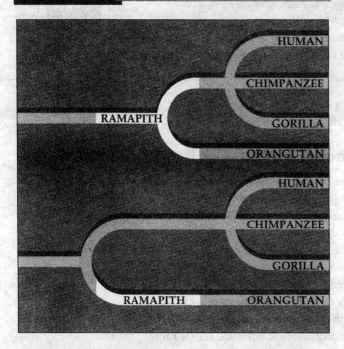

Rival interpretations of the ramapith's role in human evolution: If the top family tree is correct, ramapiths were the common ancestors of orangutans, African apes, and humans. An alternative interpretation, below, has ramapiths ancestral only to orangs. In this view, the common ancestor of humans and African apes remains unknown.

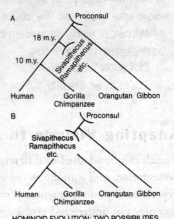

HOMINOID EVOLUTION: TWO POSSIBILITIES

(A) *If the facial features of* Sivapithecus *and* Ramapithecus *are specialized characters shared with the modern orangutan, the group is not ancestral to the later apes and hominids. The dates of the divergences would then be as shown.* (B) *If the* Sivapithecus *orangutan face is primitive, then the group could be the common ancestor to the later hominids.*

In your reference, you can also suggest the particular focus or interpretation you expect the audience to apply when examining a visual. Without an explanation describing its significance, people may not understand a visual's purpose.

> Describe how you would counter this statement: "The visual is right there on the page. I'll insult my readers if I not only tell them to look at the visual but also tell them what to pay attention to."

Labeling   Complete and accurate labeling of visuals makes them much easier to use. Complete labeling includes identification, title, and caption.

            Identification   Title

Table 1: Worker Fatigue Using Wire Cutters   Caption
Worker fatigue was compared using three different
models of ergonomic cutters during a two-week period.

The following conventions are generally followed to help readers locate, interpret, and verify visuals the way you intend:

- If a formal report has more than five visuals or includes visuals that readers would need to access independently from the text, include a list of figures or list of tables at the beginning of the document.

- Include the complete dimensions of objects in each visual, making sure to specify the units of measure or scale.
- Whenever possible, spell out words rather than using abbreviations. If abbreviations are included, use standard ones and include a key.
- Identify the source of the data as well as the graphic designer.

Placement   Generally, place visuals as close as possible following the text reference. Surround visuals with white space to separate them from the text of the document.

If a visual requires an entire page in a document that's printed on both sides of the paper, place the full-page visual on the page facing the text that refers to it. If a visual requires an entire page in a document printed only on one side of the paper, place the visual on the page following the text reference. Visuals that readers need to refer to repeatedly can be placed near the end of the document. For example, they can be located after the final text reference or in the first appendix on a fold-out page, as shown in this thumbnail sketch.

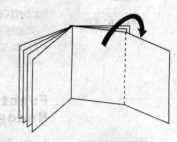

WEBLINK

The National Cancer Institute has published guidelines in both English and Spanish for developing publications that are heavily dependent on visuals for limited-literacy audiences. You can review the entire set of guidelines, or you can go directly to the subsection about integrating visual and verbal information. To access these links, go to www.english.wadsworth.com/burnett6e.
  CLICK ON WEBLINK
    CLICK on Chapter 12/NCI complete guidelines
    CLICK on Chapter 12/NCI visual and verbal integration

Visual Functions
视觉手段的作用

Visuals of different types — tables, graphs, diagrams, charts, drawings, maps, and photographs — all fulfill one or more functions in technical documents. Seven major functions of visuals are the focus of this section:

- Function 1: Provide immediate visual recognition
- Function 2: Organize numeric or textual data (for example, tables and diagrams)
- Function 3: Show relationships among numeric or verbal data (for example, tables, graphs, and diagrams)
- Function 4: Define or explain concepts, objects, and processes (for example, drawings, photographs, and diagrams)
- Function 5: Present chronology, sequence, or process (for example, line graphs, flow charts, organizational charts, and milestone charts)

Locate a figure in this textbook that is particularly useful in helping you understand the information it conveys. Share your preference in class. Note distinct preferences that different readers have.

- Function 6: Illustrate appearance or structure, which may include describing objects or mechanisms (for example, drawings, photographs, maps, and diagrams)
- Function 7: Identify facilities or locations (for example, maps, charts, schematics, and blueprints)

WEBLINK

Visuals are more than decorative. For a useful discussion about the many ways that illustrations can aid comprehension, go to **www.english.wadsworth.com/burnett6e.**
CLICK ON WEBLINK
CLICK on Chapter 12/cognitive benefits

Function 1: Provide Immediate Visual Recognition 作用1：即刻视觉辨认

Some things need rapid visual recognition; they range from the convenient (restrooms) to the critical (radiation). Typically, visual recognition can be provided by symbols that are used by most countries:

- A solid blue circle with a white symbol signals a safety precaution.
- A yellow triangle with a black band and black graphic warns about whatever is displayed in the triangle.
- A red circle with a slash and black graphic prohibits whatever is under the black slash.[6]

Quickly skim the common workplace safety symbols in Figure 12.5 to determine if you know what they mean. They are representative of the dozens of safety symbols used by business and industry around the world. Confirm your opinion by reading the marginal annotations.

All workplace organizations are responsible for educating and training their employees about the meaning of safety symbols. All individual employees have a responsibility to learn the safety symbols associated with their profession or industry.

WEBLINK

Symbols are important on safety labels, though they are more commonly used in Europe than in North America. One manufacturer of safety labels says that "European standards recognize that symbols have the ability to communicate across language barriers."[7] To access a link with more information about using symbols to communicate, go to **www.english.wadsworth.com/burnett6e** for a link.
CLICK ON WEBLINK
CLICK on Chapter 12/ISO safety symbols

FIGURE 12.5 Safety Symbols

Safety Symbols in Figure 12.5
1. ear protection necessary[8]
2. biological hazard[9]
3. low temperatures[10]
4. lasers[11]
5. electrical hazard[12]
6. flammable, combustible[13]
7. crushing or pinch point[14]
8. explosive material[15]
9. hot surface[16]

Symbols designed for immediate recognition can be representational (a symbol that looks similar to the actual object or situation) or abstract (an arbitrary symbol that becomes associated with a particular meaning). Why do these categories exist? What contributes to the effectiveness of each?

Function 2: Organize Numeric or Textual Data   作用2：组织数字或文字数据

Numeric and textual information identifying the characteristics of ideas, objects, or processes can be displayed in tables. The rows and columns of a table provide a system for classifying data and showing relationships that might be confusing if presented only in sentences and paragraphs.

While the information in a table is usually organized in a way that gives readers the sense of reaching their own interpretations, the display itself shapes these interpretations. For example, readers are influenced by the sequence of the rows and columns, by the column and line heads, by the inclusion of footnotes, and so on. The text accompanying a table should discuss the information, providing readers with a further direction for their interpretation.

If the data in a table are self-contained and self-explanatory, they are usually boxed as well as surrounded with white space to set them apart from the text. Such tables are labeled with a number and a title. Established conventions for designing an effective table are listed here and illustrated in Figure 12.6.

- Place columns to be compared next to each other.
- Round numbers if possible.
- Limit numbers to two decimal places.
- Align decimals in a column.
- Label each column and row.
- Use standard symbols and units of measure.
- Use footnotes for headings that are not self-explanatory.
- Present the table on a single page whenever possible.

Tables are often incorrectly seen as simply straightforward presentations of data. How can the design of a table influence the way readers interpret the data?

Chapter 12 Using Visual Forms   419

FIGURE 12.6 Model Format for Tables

Model of an Effective Tabular Format
Subtitle is an Optional Addition

Stub	Multiple Column Head		Single Column Head	Single Column Head
	Subhead[a]	Subhead[b]		
Line Head	ww.w	xxx.x	y.y	zzz.z
Line Head	www.w	x.x	yy.y	zzz.z
Line Head	w.w	xx.x	yyy.y	z.z
Line Head	www.w	xx.x	yy.y	zz.z
Column Average				

[a]Footnote
[b]Footnote

rule — identifies horizontal line of data
rule
rule
rule

Less formal tables are integrated into the text. These shorter tables depend directly on the surrounding text to provide a context for the data. They are not numbered or titled, but they usually do have clear row and column headings.

Numeric Tables That Organize Data   In addition to their obvious organizational benefits, tables can present large amounts of numeric data in an accessible format that takes far less space than the verbal presentation of the same information would. For example, see Figure 12.7, which shows body weight and blood alcohol percentages. The same information presented in a paragraph would be difficult to follow and would force readers to work unnecessarily hard to get the information.

FIGURE 12.7 Table with Visual Cue for Interpreting Data[17]

CHART FOR RESPONSIBLE PEOPLE WHO MAY SOMETIMES DRIVE AFTER DRINKING!

APPROXIMATE BLOOD ALCOHOL PERCENTAGE

Drinks	Body Weight in Pounds								
	100	120	140	160	180	200	220	240	Influenced
1	.04	.03	.03	.02	.02	.02	.02	.02	Rarely
2	.08	.06	.06	.06	.04	.04	.03	.03	
3	.11	.08	.08	.07	.06	.06	.06	.05	
4	.15	.12	.11	.08	.08	.08	.07	.06	
5	.19	.16	.13	.12	.11	.09	.09	.08	Possibly
6	.23	.19	.16	.14	.13	.11	.10	.09	
7	.26	.22	.19	.16	.15	.13	.12	.11	
8	.30	.25	.21	.19	.17	.15	.14	.13	Definitely
9	.34	.28	.24	.21	.19	.17	.15	.14	
10	.38	.31	.27	.23	.21	.19	.17	.16	

Subtract .01% for each 40 minutes of drinking
One drink is 1 oz. of 100 proof liquor, 12 oz. of beer, or 4 oz. of table wine.

SUREST POLICY IS...DON'T DRIVE AFTER DRINKING!

KNOW YOUR LIMITS

> Multiple column heads help readers chunk appropriate information.
>
> Two visual cues — the shading and the right-hand column indicating the level of influence — make the table easier to read.

Tables can use visual cues to help readers understand how to interpret the data. For example, Figure 12.7 effectively uses shading to help readers interpret the connection between alcohol consumption and intoxication and, thus, make an informed decision about safe driving. Originally printed on a business card, this table is designed for people to carry in their wallets or pockets for quick reference.

Textual Tables That Organize Data. Although tables generally present numeric data, the tabular format is also appropriate for some primarily and even completely textual material. Textual tables can be economical and effective. Explaining the information in Figure 12.8 in sentences and paragraphs would be time-consuming, and the resulting text would be difficult to read. The columns in Figure 12.8 are clearly labeled. The rows are presented in alternating shades so that readers can easily see related information.

Function 3: Show Relationships 作用3：展示关系

Visuals can be used to depict relationships in very different ways. First, they can show spatial relationships, such as proportion, proximity, size. Second, they can show quantitative relationships between sets of data.

Spatial Relationships. Spatial relationships are often depicted in various kinds of maps, although drawing and photographs are also frequently used. Typically, a large-scale map, photo, or drawing is presented, with a small area

FIGURE 12.8 Textual Information Organized in a Table[18]

MEET THE BUGS

Name	Possible Symptoms (from most to least common)	Foods that Have Caused Outbreaks	How Soon it Typically Strikes	How Soon it Typically Ends
Campylobacter (bacteria)	diarrhea (can be bloody), fever, abdominal pain, nausea, headache, muscle pain	chicken, raw milk	2 to 5 days	7 to 10 days
Ciguatera (toxin)	numbness, tingling, nausea, vomiting, diarrhea, muscle pain, headache, temperature reversal (hot things feel cold and cold things feel hot), dizziness, muscular weakness, irregular heartbeat	grouper, barracuda, snapper, jack, mackerel, triggerfish	within 6 hours	several days (neurological symptoms can last for weeks or months)
Clostridium botulinum (bacteria)	marked fatigue; weakness; dizziness; double vision; difficulty speaking, swallowing, and breathing; abdominal distention	home-canned foods, sausages, meat products, commercially canned vegetables, seafood products	18 to 36 hours	get treatment immediately
Cyclospora (parasite)	watery diarrhea, loss of appetite, weight loss, cramps, nausea, vomiting, muscle aches, low-grade fever, extreme fatigue	raspberries, lettuce, basil	1 week	a few days to 30 days or more
E. coli O157:H7 (bacteria)	severe abdominal pain, watery (then bloody) diarrhea, occasionally vomiting	ground beef, raw milk, lettuce, sprouts, unpasteurized juices	1 to 8 days	get treatment immediately
Hepatitis A (virus)	fever, malaise, nausea, loss of appetite, abdominal pain, jaundice	shellfish, salads, cold cuts, sandwiches, fruits, vegetables, fruit juices, milk, milk products, infected food handlers	10 to 50 days	1 to 2 weeks

circumscribed; that enclosed area is then enlarged so that it can be shown in greater detail. Each individual map, photo, or drawing must be interpreted in the context of the other(s). The maps in Figure 12.9 depict the May 13, 2002, Gilroy, California, earthquake, which was recorded by Advanced National Seismic System (ANSS) instruments "designed to detect strong ground shaking from urban earthquakes." The small map of California has an area marked in red, which is then enlarged to provide the primary visual focus (map A). Identifying the area where the ANSS instruments recorded the highest ground motion on map A is easy: It's the red bull's eye. Curiously, though, this area is not the earthquake's epicenter, but is about 10 kilometers east-northeast of the epicenter. "The absence of higher ground motion near the epicenter and the portrayal of localized areas of anomalously high or low ground motion marked by bull's eye contour patterns are indicative of too few ANSS stations in the area." This statement is reinforced by map B, an enlargement of the boxed section of map A. Map B shows that a dense array of instruments makes obvious the variability in ground motion. The maps are making a clear argument: "The number of ANSS-quality seismic stations in the San Francisco Bay Area is insufficient to map out the variability in ground motion from earthquakes."[19]

FIGURE 12.9   Spatial Relationship[20]

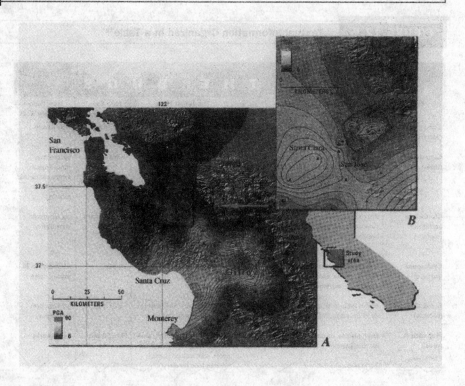

Quantitative Relationships. Relationships between two or more sets of data can be displayed using several types of visuals, but the most frequently used are graphs, including line graphs, scatter graphs, pie graphs, bar graphs, and pictorial graphs.

Line graphs show the relationship between two values, represented by intersecting values projected from the *abscissa* (horizontal) and *ordinate* (vertical) axes on a coordinate grid. They usually plot changes in quantity, showing the exact increases and decreases over a period of time, whether minutes, days, decades, or centuries, or other quantifiable variables. Since line graphs are one of the most commonly used forms of displaying relationships, most readers are familiar with them. In constructing line graphs, these conventions are usually followed:

- Use the horizontal axis to depict time, some event occurring over time, or some other quantifiable variable.
- Limit the number of lines on a graph to those easily interpreted by readers.
- When using more than one line, differentiate the lines by design or color and use a key or label to identify each line.
- Add notes or labels to make information clear to readers.
- Keep the vertical and horizontal axes proportionate.

> What graphs are most commonly used in your discipline or profession? What are ways to distort data with these graphs?

The line graph in Figure 12.10 was produced by an energy company for a major medical center to show its long-term trends in energy use in a new building and factors that affect these trends. The audience can see the beginning of each year (January) and then every other month (March, May, July, September, November) for a 12-year period. Five lines are plotted: current and expected gas use, current and expected electrical use, and square footage of the building. Without any energy conservation, both electric and gas use grew at approximately 3 percent and 5 percent respectively each year. Referred to as "creep," this growth results from increased amounts of medical equipment and the normal deterioration of heating and air conditioning systems.

One of the features that makes this graph particularly useful is that milestones are marked. For example, the very end of 1989 shows a dramatic increase in energy consumption; the callout notes this is when initial occupancy began, with full occupancy a little more than two years later. The text accompanying the graph provides this explanation:

> occupancy is not an instantaneous process. Not every department can move in on the same day and heating and air conditioning systems must be turned on for the whole building even though it is not yet fully occupied, and full "occupancy" is also not immediate in terms of patients, staff and medical and other equipment.[21]

The callouts also note the beginning and termination of an energy conservation program, which may account for otherwise unexplained increases and declines. And finally, the callouts indicate projected trends.

FIGURE 12.10   Multiple Line Graph[22]

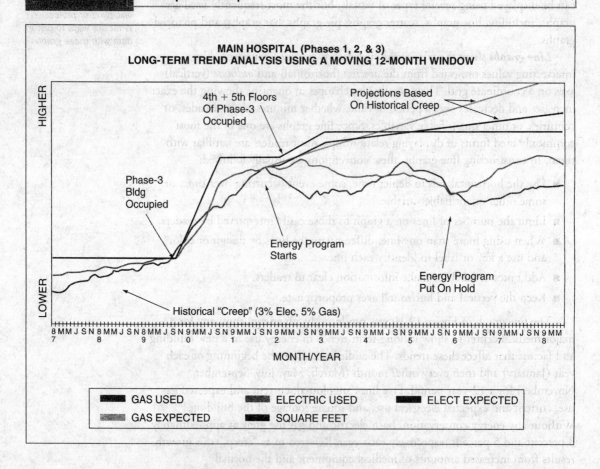

Scatter graphs use single, unconnected dots to plot instances where two variables (one on each axis) meet. Usually, scatter graphs are plotted on graphs where the x-axis (horizontal) and y-axis (vertical) are proportionate. However, if the range of data is very large, the data can be charted logarithmically to show more clearly the direction of the correlation.

The pattern of the dots expresses the relationship between variables, as illustrated in Figure 12.11. If the dots are randomly scattered, the two variables have no correlation. If the dots are primarily on a diagonal running from the lower left to the upper right, the correlation is positive. If the diagonal runs from the upper left toward the lower right, the correlation is negative.

The correlation between the variables is sometimes highlighted by shading an area on the graph. However, the statistical significance of the correlation must also be discussed in the text. Because interpreting scatter graphs is often difficult, their use is generally limited to professional and expert audiences.

FIGURE 12.11 Relationships Displayed in a Scatter Graph[23]

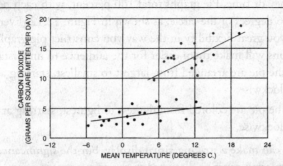

RESPIRATION OF THE FOREST, plotted against temperature, is seen to proceed at a higher rate in summer (colored curve) than in winter (black curve). Annual respiration was calcualted in grams of carbon dioxide, then converted to yield the total respiration, 2,100 grams.

Adding a plot curve and using two colors, one for summer rates and the other for winter rates, helps readers see the relationship between the variables.

The clear caption helps readers interpret the information in the graph

WEBLINK

One kind of distortion and manipulation with graphs can be avoided if you understand the impact of linear and logarithmic scales. For a link to a useful discussion, go to 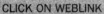 **www.english.wadsworth.com/burnett6e**.
  CLICK ON WEBLINK
   CLICK on Chapter 12/tricky graphs

FIGURE 12.12 Relationships Displayed in a Pie Graph[24]

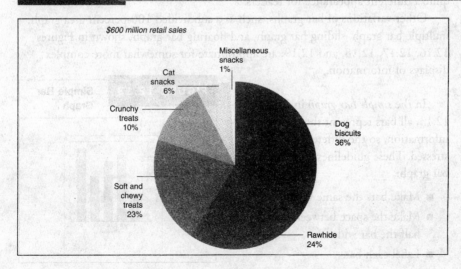

This graph follows conventions:
- *No more than six items are displayed.*
- *Segments move from largest to smallest.*
- *Segments are shaded from darkest to lightest.*

Chapter 12 Using Visual Forms

Pie graphs — also called pie diagrams, pie charts, percent graphs, or divided circle graphs — emphasize the proportionate distribution of something, frequently money or time. Pie graphs total 100 percent, with each percent representing 3.6 degrees of the circle, as shown in Figure 12.12. Even though software gives you great flexibility in the way you construct pie graphs, following these conventions will make them easier for the audience to understand:

- Slices of the pie are arranged from largest to smallest, starting at "noon" and moving clockwise.
- Slices of the pie are colored from darkest to lightest, starting at "noon" and moving clockwise.

Pie graphs can make a striking visual display, but the significance of the presented information must be discussed in the accompanying text. Although they are popular attention-getting devices that focus the reader's attention for examining more detailed data, they are generally unsuitable for the comparison of more than five or six items. The primary problem is the impossibility of comparing areas. Additionally, the visual difference between areas representing similar percentages is minimal.

Bar graphs can show several kinds of relationships, including comparisons, trends, and distributions. Like line graphs, bar graphs are drawn from a series of values plotted on two axes, but the values are represented by vertical or horizontal bars instead of points joined by a line. Because each bar represents a separate quantity, bar graphs are especially appropriate when the data consist of distinct units, such as tons of grain or megawatts of hydroelectric power produced over a specified period.

Commonly used bar graphs include a simple bar graph, subdivided bar graph, and subdivided 100-percent bar graph. Figures 12.13, 12.14, and 12.15 illustrate how the same data plotted on these three kinds of bar graphs can create quite a different appearance for readers.

Other variations of bar graphs, such as a subdivided 100-percent area graph, multiple bar graph, sliding bar graph, and floating bar graph, shown in Figures 12.16, 12.17, 12.18, and 12.19, are appropriate for somewhat more complex displays of information.

In the *simple bar graph* in Figure 12.13, all bars represent the same type of information, so the differences are stressed. These guidelines apply to any bar graph:

- Make bars the same width.
- Make the space between bars one-half the bar width.
- Label each bar.

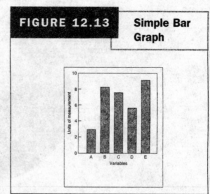

FIGURE 12.13 **Simple Bar Graph**

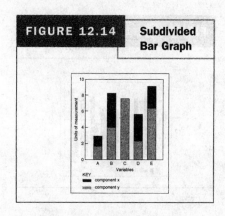

FIGURE 12.14 Subdivided Bar Graph

In the *subdivided bar graph* in Figure 12.14, each bar is subdivided to represent the magnitude of different components. Parts are differentiated by shading or cross-hatching. Although the total magnitude of each bar can be compared, as in a simple bar graph, the individual components are not easily compared.

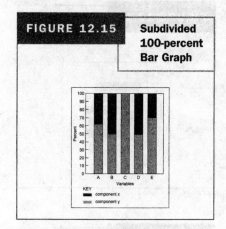

FIGURE 12.15 Subdivided 100-percent Bar Graph

In the *subdivided 100-percent bar graph* in Figure 12.15, each bar extends to 100 percent, and the components of the bar are separated by percentage. Unlike simple bar graphs and subdivided bar graphs that enable you to compare total magnitude, subdivided 100-percent bar graphs enable easy comparison of the individual components.

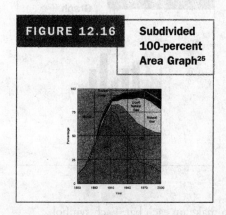

FIGURE 12.16 Subdivided 100-percent Area Graph[25]

Figure 12.16 illustrates a variation of a subdivided 100-percent bar graph — a *subdivided 100-percent area graph*. Imagine a series of 150 bars, each extended to 100 percent and each bar subdivided to show the percentage of, say, types of fuel used during one year. The bars are then pushed together so the overall effect is a continuous line for each category. The area under each bar is shaded to make the distinctions clear.

A *multiple bar graph* groups two or more bars to present the magnitude of related variables. The example in Figure 12.17 compares "Feature X" and "Feature Y" over an eight-year period.

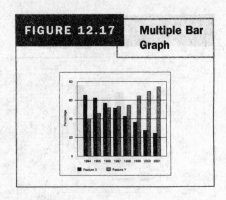

FIGURE 12.17 Multiple Bar Graph

The bars in the *sliding bar graph* in Figure 12.18 move along an axis usually marked in opposing values (active/passive, hot/cold) that extend on either side of a central point, such as values on a temperature scale.

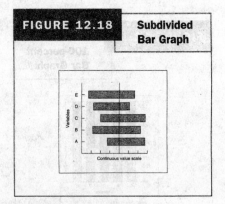

FIGURE 12.18 Subdivided Bar Graph

The *floating bar graph* in Figure 12.19 has bars that "float" in the area above the x-axis, which may extend below zero.

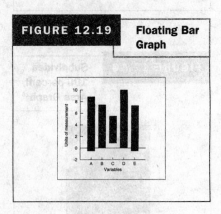

FIGURE 12.19 Floating Bar Graph

Pictorial graphs use actual symbols to make up each bar. Each symbol (*isotype*) represents a specific number of people or objects. Pictorial graphs are very appealing and are widely used with many audiences. Problems arise, however,

FIGURE 12.20 Problems of Pictorial Graphs

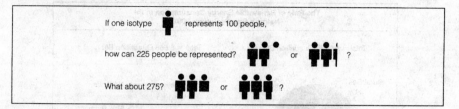

when depicting fractions (see Figure 12.20). Following these guidelines when creating pictorial graphs generally avoids problems:

- Round off numbers to eliminate fractions.
- Make all symbols the same size and space them equally.
- Select symbols that are clearly representative of the object.

Another version of a pictorial graph uses single isotypes of different sizes to represent the quantity or magnitude of each variable, as shown in Figure 12.21. In this graph, the increasing number of children allowed in day care groups is represented by successively larger isotypes representing children in each age group. Such a graph is appropriate for attracting reader attention, but it should not be used to present technical data.

Flouting Graph Conventions. Adhering to conventions for designing graphs is generally a good idea. Flouting those conventions, however, may be done for good cause. For example, Figure 12.22 shows that renewable energy consumption made up six percent of total U.S. energy consumption, a total of 96.6 quadrillion BTUs. If the graph were created conventionally, the pieces of the pie would be in descending order (starting at "noon") from the largest to the smallest. However,

> What's the difference between simply ignoring graph conventions and purposely flouting those conventions in relation to the information being accessible, comprehensible, and usable? How might each approach affect your credibility?

FIGURE 12.21 Relationships Displayed in Pictorial Graphs[26]

> While the isotypes here are proportional, they cannot themselves logically represent group size.
>
> The graph works not because the isotypes represent the size of day care groups but because the isotypes are engaging and encourage readers to look more carefully at the information.

| FIGURE 12.22 | **Purposely Flouting Design Conventions**[27] |

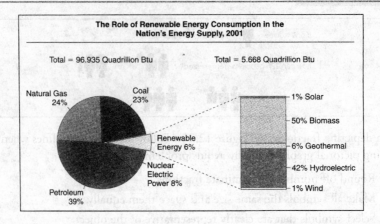

for the overall energy consumption to be connected to the sources of renewable energy, the conventions needed to be flouted, so the pieces of the pie aren't in descending order. Instead, the smallest slice is placed at about 3:00 rather than at about 11:00, where it would be conventionally. As a result, the audience can easily see that of the overall six percent devoted to renewable energy sources, biomass provided 50 percent, hydroelectric energy provided 42 percent, and other sources collectively provided the remaining eight percent.[28]

WEBLINK

One of the most frequent visual forms for professional publication is technical or scientific posters. The primary appeal of posters is their limited text and their dependence on visuals to convey critical information. For a link to several useful sets of guidelines for creating posters, go to www.english.wadsworth.com/burnett6e. (Also see an example of a scientific poster in Chapter 18.)
    CLICK ON WEBLINK
        CLICK on Chapter 12/posters

Function 4: Define Concepts, Objects, and Processes 作用4：定义概念、物体及过程

How does your discipline or profession use visuals for definition?

Visuals can be exceedingly valuable as definitions. The drawings of types of screw heads in Figure 12.23 are more efficient and useful than textual descriptions. Visuals can illustrate details that are difficult to describe, such as the types of heads and slots on the top of screws. Additionally, the angle of a flathead screw is easily depicted in a drawing. Explaining the same information in words would not be nearly as effective.

FIGURE 12.23   Visual Definition of Screws[29]

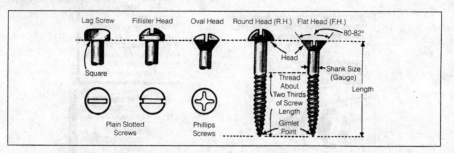

Simply by referring to the visual, readers can correctly identify the various kinds of screws that are illustrated.

The proportions — head, shank, and thread — are easier to display visually than verbally.

Figure 12.24 shows a chromosome with attention in the drawing to the structure of the DNA in one gene. Each chromosome contains many genes, the basic physical and functional units of heredity. Genes include specific sequences of bases that encode instructions about how to make proteins. All the instructions needed to direct their activities are contained within the chemical DNA. In this figure, the structure of the DNA is elegantly and simply communicated through the use of color in the spiraled double helix. This structure determines the exact instructions required to create a particular organism with its own unique traits. The figure clearly defines the DNA sequence through the side-by-side arrangement of bases along the DNA strand (e.g., ATTCCGGA).[30]

Visuals may be more appropriate than text when readers need a definition of an unfamiliar or complex object or process. Figure 12.25 provides a good example. In this visual, the toilet on the space shuttle is explained clearly, with a discrete, non–gender-specific human figure that helps readers understand how the system works. Sufficiently large font and high figure-ground contrast make the

FIGURE 12.24   Chromosome with DNA Structure Defined[31]

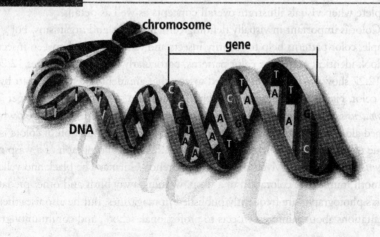

FIGURE 12.25 Visual Definition of NASA Commode[32]

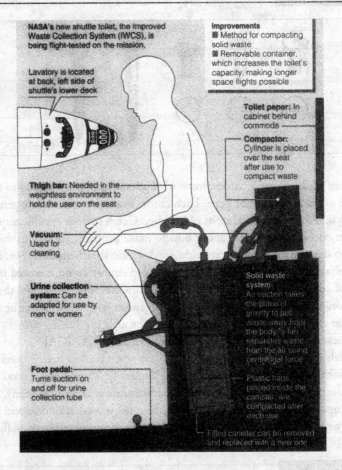

information legible. Readers' comprehension can sometimes be faster and more complete when visuals illustrate overall concepts as well as details.

Color is important in visually defining certain objects and organisms. For example, color patterns help to identify insects and to distinguish between insects that look identical except for color patterns, particularly butterflies. Figures 12.26 and 12.27 show two brilliantly colored insects that are identified in large part by their color. Figure 12.26 is a photograph of a common short-horn grasshopper (*Phymateus saxosus*), which entomologist and photographer Tom Myers took when he stopped along a roadside in Madagascar. The particular combination of colors is unique to grasshoppers in Madagascar. Figure 12.27 is a photograph of a wasp moth (*Orcynia calcarata*) that Myers took while in French Guiana. The black and yellow of this moth mimics the coloration of a wasp, warning away birds and other predators. Myers's photographs are frequently published in magazines, but he also uses them in presentations about rainforest insects to professional, school, and community groups.

| FIGURE 12.26 | Photograph of Short-Horn Grasshopper | FIGURE 12.27 | Photograph of Wasp Moth |

Function 5: Present Action or Process 作用5：展示行动与过程

Visuals are particularly appropriate for action views and processes. While visuals vary widely according to the process being presented, actions are particularly easy to depict in a sequence, and processes are easy to depict in various kinds of charts.

Action Sequences. Figure 12.28 shows the breach of a whale. The sequence of five drawings with arrows to indicate the direction of the movement enables readers to understand the breach without referring to the text. The visual tells a story by itself.

Charts. Charts can represent the components, steps, or chronology of an object, mechanism, organism, or organization. The most common charts are block charts, organizational charts, and flowcharts.

How does your discipline or profession visually present actions or processes?

| FIGURE 12.28 | Drawing Showing Action: Whale Breaching[33] |

Chapter 12 Using Visual Forms

A *block chart* (also called block diagram or classification chart), illustrated in Figure 12.29, uses blocks to represent the components or subdivisions of the whole object, system, or process. This example uses shapes, colors, and arrow placement to increase the likelihood that the audience will access, comprehend, and use the information about the components of Multidisciplinary Design Optimization (MDO), a computer software analysis procedure used to streamline the complicated aircraft design process.

At top, the purple ovals represent the various disciplines necessary to aircraft design, such as aerodynamics and acoustics. At center, the ovals and arrows combine to illustrate the cyclical and complex design process. The MDO networks all of these disciplines throughout each phase of the process. At bottom, the green boxes depict the variety of aircraft products, such as commercial aircraft, launch vehicles, that can be designed, as in Figure 12.31.

Figure 12.29 uses both arrows and color to draw your eyes from the top of the block diagram to the bottom, while the use of a gradient purple color in the

FIGURE 12.29 Block Chart[34]

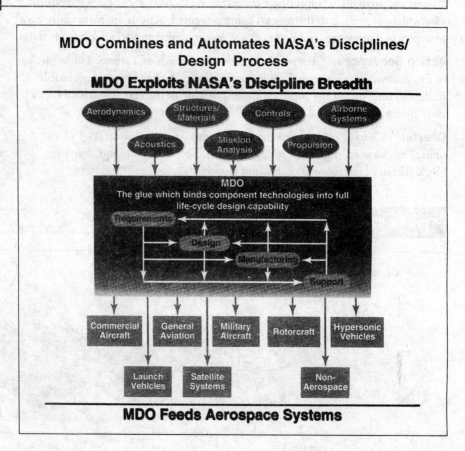

center box also draws your eyes from the top to the bottom. The purple arrows against the white background lead your eye from the purple ovals through the center box to the green "aircraft products" boxes.

An *organizational chart* portrays the hierarchy of an organization by putting each position in a separate block, as in Figure 12.30. This chart shows the vertical and horizontal relationships in the U.S. Department of Energy's Office of Environmental Restoration and Waste Management. In addition to the basic information, the chart also provides icons and brief descriptions of the responsibilities associated with each office.

A *flowchart* (also called a route chart) depicts the sequence of steps in a process. Conventional symbols make flowcharts easy to comprehend. Such charts sometimes also indicate the amount of time each step takes. Conventional flowcharts use standard symbols — for example, ▭ = a step in the process and ◇ = a decision in the process — that make flowcharts easy for professionals to understand regardless of their specialization or language, as in Figure 12.31.

However, some charts designed for general audiences use the principles of flowcharts but substitute small diagrams or drawings for the conventional

FIGURE 12.30   Organizational Chart[35]

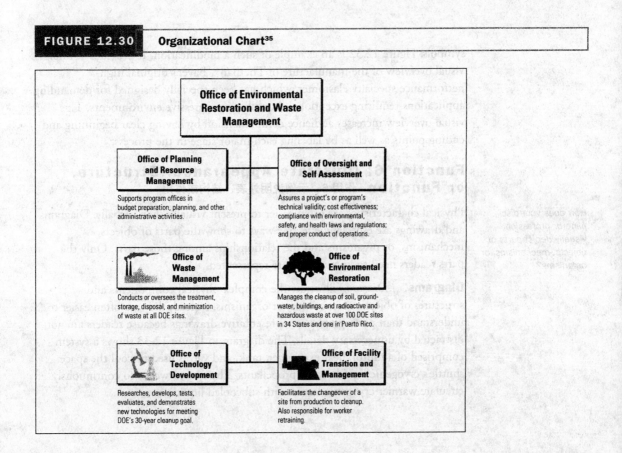

FIGURE 12.31 Flowchart[36]

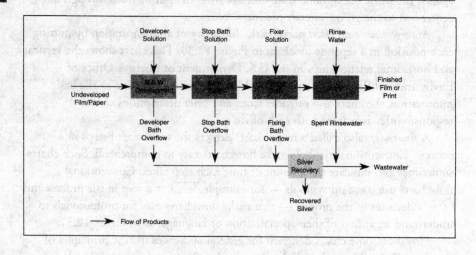

symbols. Figure 12.32 is an example of such a modification. It provides a simple visual overview of the manufacture of Therban®, Bayer's original high-performance specialty elastomer, which has been specially designed for demanding applications requiring exceptional durability in aggressive environments. This visual overview increases audience comprehension by having clear beginning and ending points as well as by labeling each major stage in the process.

Function 6: Illustrate Appearance, Structure, or Function 作用6：示例说明外表、结构或作用

How does your discipline or profession visually depict parts of objects, mechanisms, or organisms?

Physical characteristics are often easier to present visually than verbally. Diagrams and drawings are especially effective ways to show the parts of objects, mechanisms, or organisms and the relationships among those parts. Only the parts readers need to know about are represented.

Diagrams.   *Diagrams* illustrate the complex physical components and structures of objects, mechanisms, or organisms. Indeed, they are often easier to understand than photographs or representative drawings because readers are not distracted by unnecessary details. The diagram in Figure 12.33 shows a system comprised of a motor, heat exchanger, tank, and valves used to cool the space shuttle's cryogenic liquid rocket propellants. The system works to continuously circulate warmer cryogenic liquid with subcooled liquid.

FIGURE 12.32   Visual Overview of Process[37]

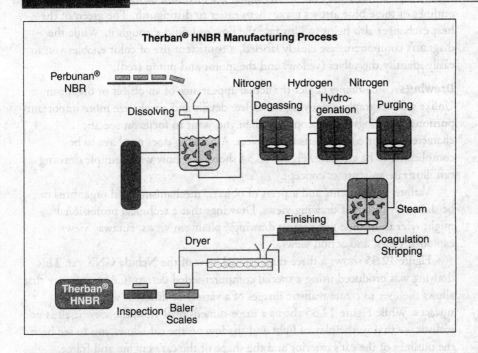

FIGURE 12.33   Diagram[38]

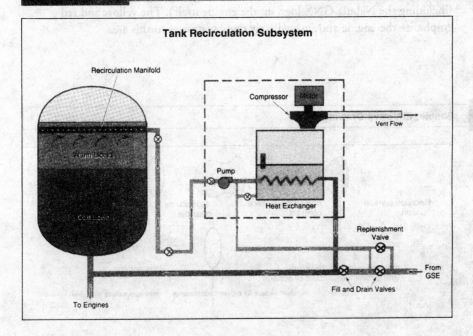

Chapter 12 Using Visual Forms   437

Color distinguishes the warmer liquid (dark purple) from the cooler liquid (light purple), while the blue arrows signal the direction of the flow. The white outlines of these blue arrows make them easier to distinguish. The green of the heat exchanger also helps to illustrate the flow of liquid through it. While the diagram's components are clearly labeled, a consistent use of color enables you to easily identify the valves (yellow) and the motor and pump (red).

Drawings. *Drawings* depict the actual appearance of an object or organism. Unlike a photograph, a drawing can delete details and emphasize more important portions. Drawings are appropriate when you want to focus on specific characteristics or components of a subject. A drawing does not have to be complicated to be effective. Figure 12.34 shows just how well a simple drawing can illustrate an abstract concept.

Various components and aspects of objects, mechanisms, and organisms can be shown by different drawing views. Drawings that a technical professional might refer to include perspective drawings, phantom views, cutaway views, exploded views, and action views.

Figure 12.35 shows a three-dimensional view of the Nebula GNX car. This drawing was produced using a special computer-aided design (CAD) software that allows the user to create realistic images of a variety of different shapes and surfaces. While Figure 12.35 shows a three-dimensional view, the view itself is not realistic — that is, the play of light and shadow on the car allows you to see both the outlines of the car's exterior and the shape of the car's engine and frame.

The car's exterior is deep red, while its interior is a shadowy, gunmetal gray. The car's frame and suspension is yellow, a color picked up in parts of the engine (including the Nebula GNX logo on the engine itself). The yellow and red emphasize the engine and immediately draw your eyes to this area.

FIGURE 12.34 **Simple, Effective Drawing**[39]

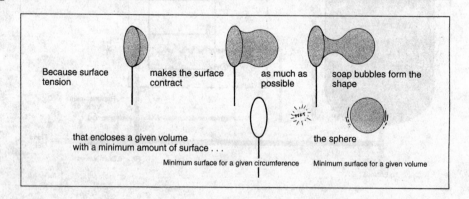

FIGURE 12.35 Three-Dimensional Drawing[40]

What do you see as the benefits and limitations of photographs, drawings, and diagrams of the same object? How would photographs or diagrams of the Nebula GNX respond to the limitations but also have their own limitations?

No one would argue with the idea that visuals often communicate to international audiences when words fail. However, that doesn't mean that visuals (and their related text) are not bound by culture. For several links to Web sites that suggest ways to adapt visuals and text for an international audience, go to www.english.wadsworth.com/burnett6e.
  CLICK ON WEBLINK
    CLICK on Chapter 12/international

WEBLINK

   The versatility of drawings is demonstrated in a book for farriers. The series of three drawings in Figure 12.36 shows an external view — a representational drawing — of a hoof, followed by a phantom view and a cutaway view to reveal the internal structure. Because these drawings have the same scale and are placed close together, you can easily make comparisons.

   Another common type of technical drawing is an exploded view, illustrated in Figure 12.37. An exploded view shows an entire mechanism or organism by separating (exploding) the whole to provide a clear view of each component.

What kinds of problems might occur from errors in proportion and scale in technical drawings?

Chapter 12 Using Visual Forms   439

| FIGURE 12.36 | External View, Phantom View, and Cutaway View[41] |

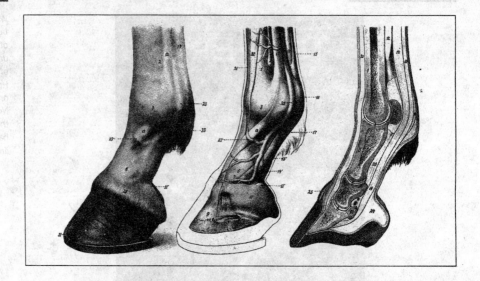

Exploded views are useful as part of an overall description of a mechanism or organism, but they are most frequently used in assembly and repair manuals. Your understanding of the compression faucet in Figure 12.37 is increased by the clear labels next to the appropriate parts and the concise process explanation of the way the faucet works.

| FIGURE 12.37 | Exploded View[42] |

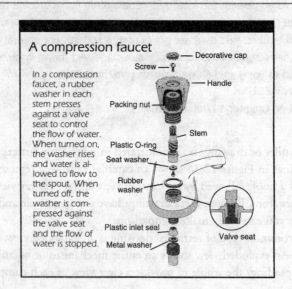

What would be the differences between a drawing like this one designed to show the components and explain the overall operation and a drawing of the same faucet designed to accompany instructions to repair a faucet leak?

440   Part III   Shaping Information

Function 7: Identify Facilities or Locations 作用7：确定设施或地点

Identifying facilities and locations traditionally has meant maps and photographs. Now, however, *map* also refers to a navigational tool used on the Web, and workplace photographs are made as often with digital cameras as with traditional film cameras.

Maps. Geographic information is displayed on maps (called charts, not maps, for air or water). To many people, maps mean road guides. But maps also display topographic, demographic, agricultural, meteorological, and geological data. And now, *maps* also refers to Web sites, providing users with an overview of the electronic terrain.

> How does your discipline or profession use maps?

Maps show features of a particular area, such as land elevation, rock formations, vegetation, animal habitats, crop production, population density, or traffic patterns. Statistical maps can depict quantities at specific points or within specified boundaries. Data can be presented on maps in a number of ways: dots, shading, lines, repetitive symbols, or superimposed graphs. One of the most common maps shows political boundaries, for example, state boundaries in the United States and provincial boundaries in Canada, as shown in Figure 12.38.

FIGURE 12.38 Map Showing Political Boundaries[43]

> In order to use this map productively, what prior knowledge does the audience need about (a) map conventions and (b) markers in the legend?

Chapter 12 Using Visual Forms

Another kind of map is presented in Figure 12.39, which shows a computer model — a map — depicting possible underground paths of water flowing toward the Columbia River in the state of Washington. This groundwater may contain contaminants leaking from tanks at the Hanford Reservation, used to store waste radioactive materials from the manufacture of nuclear weapons. Tracking the groundwater helps the U.S. Department of Energy establish the severity of the problem, determine concentrations and radioactivity of contaminants, and show the feasibility of slowing the movement of the groundwater toward the Columbia River.

The computer model, designed by a geophysicist at Bechtel-Hanford, Inc., in Hanford, Washington, uses color to help viewers interpret the information. The map model shows the bottom and top boundaries of the region being studied and modeled: (1) The purple mountain depicts the impermeable layer of bedrock far underground. (2) The yellow grid (only the top plane of which shows on the model) depicts the actual ground level. Groundwater can flow between purple mountain and yellow grid.

Another way to depict environmental changes is illustrated in Figure 12.40, a map that documents deforestation in Brazil. According to NASA's Earth Observatory, "If the current rate of deforestation continues, the world's rain forests will vanish within 100 years — causing unknown effects on global climate and eliminating the majority of plant and animal species on the planet."[44] Most of the 21,000 square miles deforested annually in South America are in the Amazon Basin. So far, due to the isolation of forest fragments and the increase in forest/clearing boundaries, a total of 16.5% of the Amazon River Basin (an area nearly the size of Texas) has been affected by deforestation. Audiences interpreting Figure 12.40 are helped by a key that shows that the darker the area, the more forest remains.

FIGURE 12.39   **Computer Rendition of an FEM Surface Grid**[45]

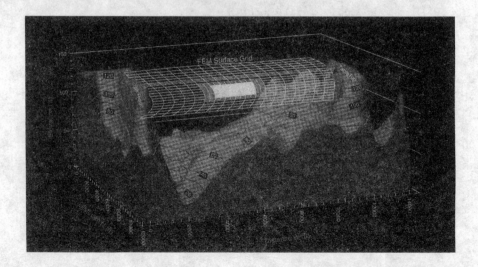

> **FIGURE 12.40** Map Documenting Environmental Changes[46]

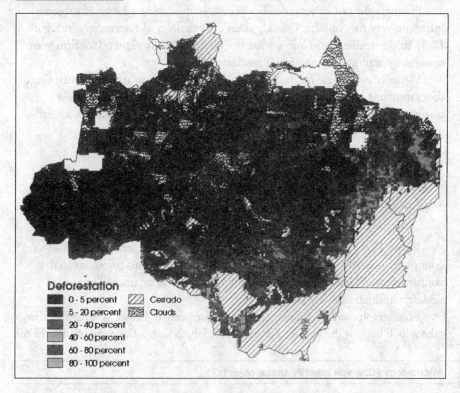

This map shows deforestation at one point in time. How could you effectively display the increasing deforestation over a 20-year period? Over a 50-year period?

WEBLINK

The *Atlas of Cyberspaces* is a collection of cybermaps and graphic representations that help us access, comprehend, and use digital landscapes available in global communication networks and online information resources. Some of the maps are appear familiar, using the cartographic conventions of real-world maps; others are abstract representations of electronic spaces. For a link to these cybermaps, go to **www.english.wadsworth.com/burnett6e**.
   CLICK ON WEBLINK
      CLICK on Chapter 12/cybermaps

Photographs. Because a photograph displays an actual view of a subject, it's appropriate when you want to emphasize realism, particularly the natural features of a setting. However, even though photographs accurately depict locations, they often show too much detail. For this reason, *callout arrows* (small arrows superimposed on a photo) can be used to draw attention to main features.

When a photo is printed, its appearance can be altered so that the primary subject becomes more prominent than the background, thus giving emphasis that

How does your discipline or profession use photographs?

would not be possible if the photo were printed normally. Photos can also be reduced, enlarged, or cropped to emphasize a particular portion of the subject.

Photographs can be remarkably effective in displaying a range of subjects, including very tiny objects. Quickly skim the examples of microscopy in Figure 12.41 to determine if you know what the photos actually depict. Confirm your opinion by reading the marginal annotations.

Virtually every state has both public and private photo archives containing thousands and in some cases millions of aerial photographs that provide a complete record of features in the state. Routinely taken, aerial photos record various kinds of information:

- Agricultural information (crop data, erosion management, forestry management)
- Municipal information (property lines, utilities, streets)
- Transportation information (major and minor roads and highways, bridges, waterways, traffic patterns, railroads, airports)

Figure 12.42 is an aerial photograph. It shows a water treatment facility and county maintenance shed. The hydrogeologist who used this photo wanted confirmation of land features and building locations as he tracked an underground hazardous waste spill.

Photographs can provide an alternative perspective. Before you read further, take a look back at the map in Figure 12.40, which shows the deforestation in the

FIGURE 12.41   **Microscopy (Can you identify these objects?)**

Microscopy subjects
1. Geranium leaf
2. Coral
3. Fruit fly
4. Tomato
5. Mouse embryo
6. Algae diatom

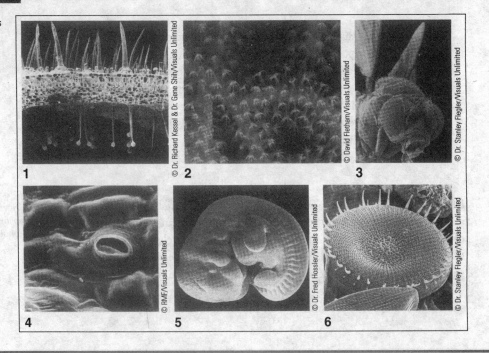

Part III   Shaping Information

| FIGURE 12.42 | Aerial Photograph from Low-Flying Airplane |

| FIGURE 12.43 | Satellite Photo Documenting Environmental Changes[47] |

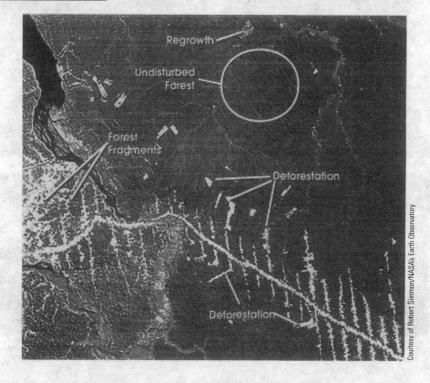

What would be possible different audiences and uses for Figures 12.40 and 12.43?

Chapter 12   Using Visual Forms

Amazon Basin. Now look at Figure 12.43, which is a photograph of the same phenomena. In this satellite image of deforestation in the Brazilian state of Para, the dark areas are forest, the white is deforested areas, and the gray is regrowth. The pattern of deforestation spreading along roads is obvious in the lower half of the image. Scattered larger clearings can be seen near the center of the image.[48]

Another kind of photograph is presented in Figure 12.44, which shows four views of the Long Valley region of California using synthetic aperture radar (SAR) technology. SAR allows all-weather mapping of topographic and geographic features of land surfaces. The four views illustrate different SAR processing steps (clockwise from upper left): the initial SAR image, the interferogram, the perspective view, and the contour map.

Color is important in each of these views. The initial SAR image uses white, black, and gray shadow to illustrate the features of the land; the interferogram uses a range of colors — violet, yellow, blue, and green — to highlight these surface features. The contour map relies on shades of green, yellow, and gray to highlight land surfaces, and black contour lines further distinguish these features. The perspective view relies more heavily on light and shadow rather than contrasting colors — to distinguish the features of the land surface.

FIGURE 12.44 **Satellite Photographs[49]**

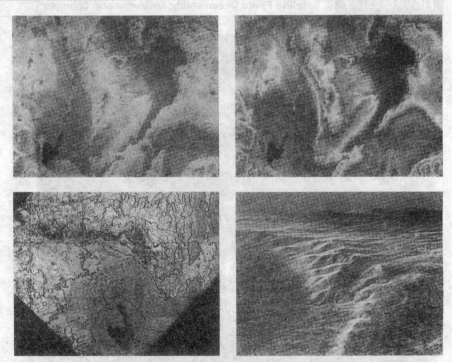

Figure 10-1. Long Valley region of east-central California acquired by SIR-C/X-SAR interferometer, illustrating processing steps from SAR image (upper left) to interferogram (upper right) to contour map (lower left) to perspective view (lower right).

Conventions in Use of Color 颜色使用原则

With the wide availability of relatively inexpensive color printers and color photocopiers, color in technical visuals is commonplace. It can add to the meaning or help interpretation, but it is sometimes unnecessary and too often badly done or inappropriately used. Color can be an extraordinarily powerful tool to help create more effective visuals when the appropriate conventions are followed.

Cautions against Misuse of Color 谨慎使用颜色

Because color is so easy to use, the temptation to overindulge is great. These are some of the problems to avoid:

- *Overuse of decorative color.* Using color simply as decoration contradicts the basic premise that color in technical documents should be functional. It should be associated with meaning or function so that when readers see a color used in a particular document, it triggers appropriate associations:

  The printout of the stress test shows the weak spots in red, the questionable spots in yellow, and the unstressed parts in shades of blue and green.

  or

  The troubleshooting guide for each section is signaled with a red strip on the edge of the page so these pages are immediately identifiable.

- *Too much color.* Using too many colors, too much color, or inappropriate color distracts or annoys readers. Select a few colors rather than trying to pack in as many as possible. Similarly, the intensity of the color should match the context, purpose, or audience. For example, an industrial catalog for laboratory safety supplies can appropriately use seven colors in a table that matches them to OSHA and ANSI color-coded safety guidelines, but in most tables using that many colors would be unnecessary and, therefore, inappropriate.

- *Cultural insensitivity.* Violating cultural expectations can mean that the use of color contradicts the expectations in either the workplace culture or the broader social culture. For example, in industry neon orange is usually used in small triangles to signal warnings, so readers of an instruction manual for a precision lathe might feel disconcerted if all the manual's headings were in bright orange.

In what situations might black-and-white visuals be more appropriate and more useful than ones in color?

Suggestions for Appropriate Use of Color 恰当使用颜色的建议

Used effectively in visuals, color can help readers with issues such as consistency, emphasis, and organization.[50] Most documents are printed in one color — black — on white paper. Some documents have a second color added, which can be printed in a variety of intensities from pale to dark, giving the appearance of a range of colors. In most of the print documents you produce, cost and time will dictate that you use a single color (black) or use black and a second color selected to increase the appeal and accessibility of the document.

Sometimes the content, context, purpose, or audience require that you produce four-color documents. A few documents, this book included, are printed in four colors that combine to create all the rest of the colors in the book. So the rest of the discussion in this section focuses on some of the important uses of four-color visuals.

Whenever color is used in technical documents, it should be an integral part of the information that readers need. Even though the discussion of the following examples emphasizes a particular use of color for each visual, in practice, most well-designed color visuals use color to accomplish multiple purposes. These are among the most important purposes:

- Signal safety
- Attract attention
- Enable accurate identification
- Show structure or organization
- Highlight components and their process or movement
- Aid comprehension
- Influence interpretation

Signal Safety. One of the most important uses of color is to signal safety. The most widespread international agreement about the use of color is probably is with traffic lights: Green = go, yellow = caution, and red = stop, regardless of the country. Additionally, a number of government agencies and international organizations specify the use of particular colors to increase attention to safety: Occupational Safety and Health Administration (OSHA), American National Standards Institute (ANSI), American Public Works Association (APWA), and International Organization for Standardization (ISO) all use color to signal various conditions as well as levels and kinds of dangers. For example, OSHA guidelines indicate that U.S. workplaces should code safety equipment and hazardous areas with specific colors. Similarly, APWA guidelines indicate that U.S. public agencies, utilities, contractors, and others involved in excavation should use color to prevent accidental damage, service interruption, or injury. ANSI provides national standards for U.S. safety signs and labels, while ISO governs international safety labeling requirements.

Some colors such as yellow, orange, and red are mandated by OSHA; other colors such as blue and green are used by common practice but not mandated. Figure 12.45 highlights the colors specified by OSHA to signal various levels of safety or risk in the U.S. workplace and by APWA to label various kinds of cables, wires, and conduits that could be damaged or broken during a construction project.

FIGURE 12.45 OSHA and APWA Safety Colors[51]

OSHA	APWA
Black / White = TRAFFIC MARKINGS, signaling things such as passing and no passing, exit ramps, and shoulder areas.	
Green = SAFETY, signaling instructions about safe work practices, proper safety procedures, safety equipment location (including first aid equipment other than for fire-fighting).	**Green** marks surveying and general construction markings.
Blue = NOTICE, signaling need for attention to safety of personnel or protection of property. Must not used in place of CAUTION, WARNING, or DANGER.	**Blue** marks water, irrigation and slurry lines.
Yellow = CAUTION ▪ Signals a potentially hazardous situation that, if not avoided, may cause minor or moderate injury. ▪ Alerts users to unsafe practices or the potential for property damage.	**Yellow** marks gas, oil, steam, petroleum or gaseous material.
Orange = WARNING ▪ Signals a potentially hazardous situation that, if not avoided, has some probability of death or serious injury.	**Orange** marks telephone, communication, alarm or signal cables or conduit.
Red = DANGER ▪ Red indicates danger or a hazardous situation that, if not avoided, has high probability of death or severe injury. Used in extreme situations. ▪ Indicates STOP (e.g., for emergency bars, buttons, and switches). ▪ Identifies the location of fire protection equipment and apparatus.	**Red** marks electric power lines, cables, conduit and lighting cables.
Fluorescent orange or **orange-red = BIOLOGICAL HAZARD**	
Purple = RADIATION HAZARD	

This orange coupling guard complies with ANSI safety standards.[53]

Documents and signs are not the only places where color plays a critical role in workplace communication. ANSI Standard Z535 specifies that hazardous machinery parts themselves must be marked. For example, protective machine guards covering sections of equipment that have an intermediate level of potential risks that is not self-evident or visible must have a visible, legible, warning-level orange safety label to signal a potentially hazardous situation that, if not avoided, could result in serious injury or death. Beyond the warning label, when a safety color is used to identify hazardous machinery parts having an intermediate level of risk, the machine guards themselves should be safety orange, as shown in the photo here.[52]

Unfortunately, some people are color-blind, which means they need to have compensatory skills. For example, color blindness does not impede safe driving because traffic lights are cued by location as well as color. As long as a person knows that the top light is red, the ability to perceive red the same way that other people do is not necessary. This leads to an important principle when designing visuals: Do not have color be the only distinguishing cue in anything you design.[54] Furthermore, because all organizations are responsible for educating and training their employees about the relationship between colors and various levels of risk, employees need to learn additional ways to identify these risks.

WEBLINK

If you want to know more about color blindness, go to
www.english.wadsworth.com/burnett6e for links.
    CLICK ON WEBLINK
    CLICK on Chapter 12/color blind

Attract Attention. A second use of color is to attract readers so that they are drawn toward the topic. Figures 12.46a and 12.46b show a German brown trout in two versions. The technical illustrator, Dean Biechler, created the color version (Figure 12.46a) for the folder cover for a series of fact sheets produced by the Coldwater Stream Program of the Iowa Natural Heritage Foundation. The strong color drawing on the cover attracts attention. The fact sheets focus on conservation and resource management. Biechler created the black-and-white version (Figure 12.46b) for one of the fact sheets. (This black-and-white version was also used on the Coldwater Stream Program t-shirt.)

| FIGURE 12.46A | Color Drawing of Fish[55] | FIGURE 12.46B | Black-and-White Drawing of Fish[56] |

Enable Accurate Identification. A third purpose for using color is to help readers focus on critical features of the object. Figure 12.47 represents the human lymphoid system. Color is useful in this drawing in several important ways. First, color helps readers to identify key features of the lymphoid system by highlighting two kinds of lymphoid tissues. By drawing the diffuse lymphoid system in green (obviously not the true color of the lymphoid system), the artist immediately draws readers' attention to this key feature. The artist did not select blue or red to represent the lymphoid system because these are colors conventionally used to represent arteries (red) and veins (blue). Despite the fact that the encapsulated organs are also in color, they are de-emphasized when compared to the green diffuse lymphoid system. Second, the artist uses other colors as well as colored arrows to represent the development and maturation of the T lymphocytes and the B lymphocytes in the detail drawing in the lower right-hand corner. Finally, the artist uses the green to highlight the relationship between the primary illustration and the detail drawing. Because green is used to represent the lymph node in the detail drawing, readers are likely to recognize that this information is directly related to the green lymph nodes in the primary drawing.

Color attracts attention, ensures accurate identification, and provides contextual details important to those who are interested in and provide support for the program.

Show Structure or Organization. A fourth purpose for using color is to enable readers to better understand the structure displayed in the visual. It can also organize those parts, chunking them so that readers can more easily see critical relationships. Information of a similar type is presented in the same color so that readers immediately see the likenesses and thus more easily understand and recall information.

Figure 12.48 shows a computer-generated stress analysis of a tooth from the front of a tractor bucket. Test engineers at John Deere first drew the tooth and then used a computer modeling system to apply loads at the positions and from the directions the tooth would be stressed in actual situations. The system then

FIGURE 12.47 Drawing of Lymphoid System[57]

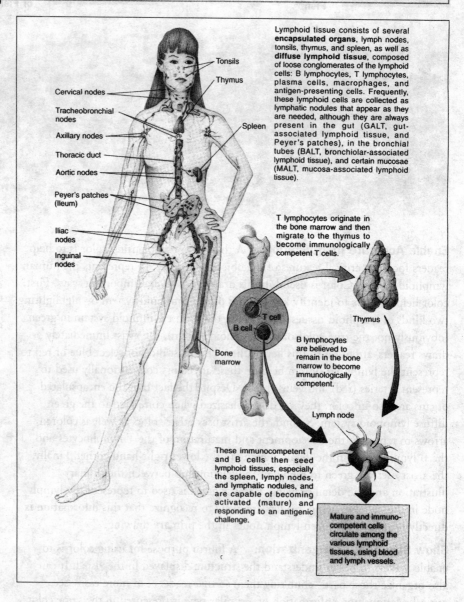

calculated the stresses that would occur on the tooth. Changes in color show regions of stress: dark blue shows the lowest levels of stress, then light blue, green, and orange show successively higher levels of stress. Red shows the highest level.

Highlight Components and Their Function or Movement. A fifth purpose of color is to show readers a path for moving through a visual. Color can signal a change or draw attention to the nature and direction of the change.

| FIGURE 12.48 | Stress Test for Tractor Bucket Tooth[58] |

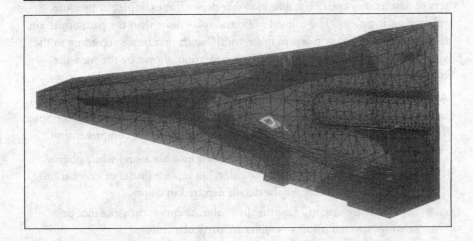

Consistency in the use of color helps readers track the changes an object or organism goes through during a process.

Figure 12.49 shows a computer model created by AmTec Engineering in Bellevue, Washington, using software called TecPlot. The figure is a 3-D depiction of flow over an airfoil (airplane wing), which is useful for aeronautical engineers who want to increase the stability and efficiency of airfoils they are designing or analyzing. The model shows an airfoil, the air flow around the airfoil, and a

| FIGURE 12.49 | Computer Rendition of 3-D Turbulent Flow over a Wing[59] |

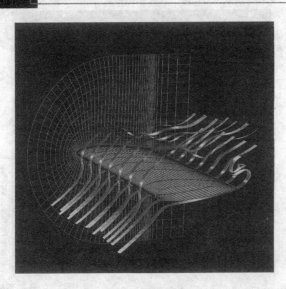

computational grid (only the last plane of this green grid is visible) for analyzing the flow. The model enables aeronautical engineers to collect and analyze huge sets of data as they create visualizations that depict, for example, air pressure, velocity, and vorticity. The colored ribbons display more than the path of the air; they show how the flow twists in finite-width bands that rotate according to the vorticity. In the figure, you can see a flow separation, shown by the ways the ribbons flow up and over the top.

Aid Comprehension. A sixth purpose for color is to make an image easier to understand. For example, the photographs taken by cameras on the Hubble Space Telescope have often been translated into color images to aid comprehension.[60]

- Some Hubble data are originally translated into black-and-white photos. Scientists arbitrarily choose "false colors" to replace shades of gray because people can more easily see the details depicted in color.
- Some data are originally captured in color; scientists then enhance or intensify selected colors to emphasize particular features.
- Some data are captured in true color by taking photographs through separate red, green, and blue filters and then combining the images into a realistic photograph.

The eerie, dark, pillar-like structures in Figure 12.50 are actually columns of cool interstellar hydrogen gas and dust that are incubators for new stars. The pillars protrude from the interior wall of a dark molecular cloud like stalagmites from the floor of a cavern. They are part of the "Eagle Nebula" (also called M16,

FIGURE 12.50   **Pillars of Creation in a Star Forming Region**

Jeff Hester, Paul Scowen/NASA

the sixteenth object in Charles Messier's eighteenth-century catalog of "fuzzy" objects that aren't comets), a relatively close star-forming region 7,000 light years away in the constellation Serpens.

The picture was taken with the Hubble Space Telescope. The color image is constructed from three separate images taken in the light of emissions from different types of atoms. Red shows emission from singly ionized sulfur atoms. Green shows emission from hydrogen. Blue shows light emitted by doubly ionized oxygen atoms.

Influence Interpretation. A final purpose for using color is its ability to influence the way viewers interpret information in visuals such as phase diagrams, which are familiar to chemists, physicists, chemical engineers, and materials scientists.

Phase diagrams are important for the design of chemical separations equipment such as absorbers and distillation columns. These diagrams show the phase behavior of a complex system at a glance and often eliminate the need for in-depth study of detailed, numerical equilibrium data. For example, the phase diagrams in Figure 12.51 were produced at Iowa State University using Animate, an interactive computer graphics program for the study of multicomponent, fluid-phase equilibria.

Phase diagrams for fluid mixtures containing four chemical species (quaternaries) use tetrahedral models to show the results of boiling or condensation. In the computer-generated drawings in Figure 12.51, the pure components A (acetonitrile), B (benzene), C (ethanol), and D (acetone) are designated by the vertexes of the tetrahedron, while all intermediate quaternary mixtures are located in the space within. The compositions of boiling liquids are shown by the red surfaces and those of condensing vapors in green, with the specific, red-green pairs that coexist together (that is, in equilibrium) connected by tie-lines, several of which have been drawn in white.

In the series of images I–IV, the movements of the surfaces, both through the tetrahedron and also relative to one another, show how the equilibrium compositions change in response to increasing fluid pressure while the temperature remains fixed. The rotation of the model itself lets viewers study the diagram from all angles.

WEBLINK

Visuals can be very helpful during preparation for a criminal trial as well as during the trial itself. Visuals can go a long way in aiding comprehension of juries and judges, who must make sense of testimony about complex technical topics. For examples of successful visuals used during trials, go to **www.english.wadsworth.com/burnett6e** for a link.
  CLICK ON WEBLINK
   CLICK on Chapter 12/visuals persuasion

FIGURE 12.51 Composition Tetrahedron for a Quaternary System in Vapor-liquid Equilibrium (Temperature, Pressure Fixed)[61]

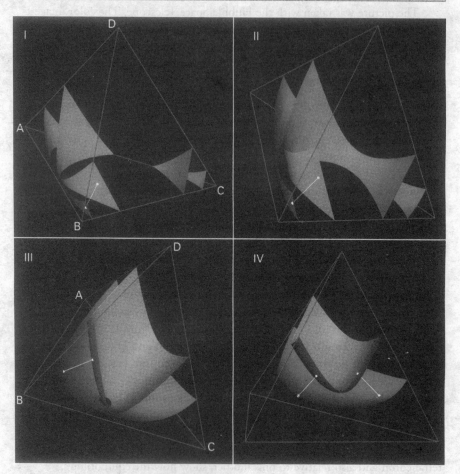

The software was written by Eric Cochran and Professor Kenneth R. Jolls, ISU Chemical Engineering Department, and the sequence was designed by Chad Sanborn, ISU Engineering Publication and Communication Services.

Color in Designing Electronic Documents
设计电子文档时的颜色使用

In print documents, color can be a valuable, or even essential, element. Color is just as important (and is perhaps even expected) in many electronic documents. Because color is produced differently on a screen than it is on paper, technical communicators must think about it differently. On-screen colors, like paper colors, are affected by the environment in which they are viewed — the reflections off the monitor face, the light in the room, and the combinations of colors on the screen all affect the way you see on-screen colors, and the effects work differently than on paper documents.

Because of the variations in the ways viewers interpret on-screen colors, you need to consider color and viewers' reactions to it when you're designing electronic documents.

- Will the document be viewed on a screen of lower or higher resolution than the one you're using? If so, you must consider whether the graphics will look grainy or poorly defined.
- Will the document be viewed in a room with bright lights (such as a fluorescent-lit office) or dim lights (such as a private home)? The reflections from the screen can have a major impact on how color is perceived.
- Will the document be printed? If so, the differences between screen color and paper color must be considered. If readers might print the document without color, you should look at black-and-white hard copy to see if what you thought was functional color becomes a gray blob when viewed in black and white.

What additional questions could be important in your decision about using color in electronic documents?

The issues raised by these questions are discussed in Chapter 13: Designing and Using Electronic Media.

Individual and Collaborative Assignments
个人作业和小组作业

1. **Design a table.** Conduct the appropriate research and then design a speed comparison table that presents the equivalents for kilometers per hour, miles per hour, and knots per hour. For whom would this comparison table be useful?

2. **Transform a pictorial graph.** The following pictorial graph[62] shows the per-capita income disparity for developing, transition, and well-developed countries. Well-developed countries (such as Canada, the United States, Japan, and Israel) show the greatest per-capita income disparity over a 30-year period. That is, over the next 30 years, the rich will become richer while the poor will become poorer. Design another visual depiction of this information. Identify the audience and purpose of your visual.

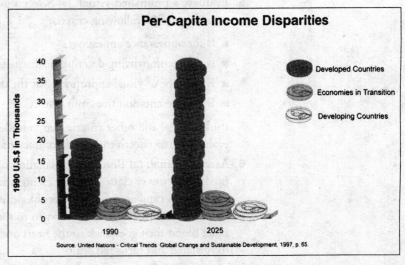

3. **Write a description based on visual information.** Refer to any of the flowcharts or process overviews in this chapter. Write a description of the process based on the information in the visual. Make sure the information is accurate. After you have completed the paragraph, examine it to identify the textual features you used to help readers follow the process. Then decide what's missing from your explanation.

4. **Transform a bar graph.** The following subdivided 100-percent bar graph shows the proportions of saturated, polyunsaturated, and monounsaturated fatty acids in different vegetable oils.[63] All dietary fats comprise mixtures of fatty acids, but lower amounts of saturated fatty acids (like those found in sunflower and safflower oil) are healthier for your body than saturated fatty acids. Develop two additional ways to depict this same information. Identify the audience and purpose of your two new visuals.

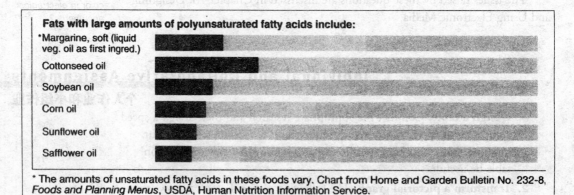

5. **Evaluate a published visual.** (a) Select a published visual and examine it according to the following criteria:
   - Is the appearance appealing?
   - Is the accompanying description/discussion complete?
   - Is the type of visual appropriate for the data and purpose?
   - Is the presentation free from distortion?

   (b) Use these and other criteria that you identify to create a rubric for evaluating the effectiveness and accuracy of visuals.

6. **Assess a visual.** (a) Read this explanation of the following visual:[64] It is used in veterinary classes to show changes to blood as it moves through a capillary. In capillaries (the smallest blood vessels of the body), bright red blood containing oxygen loses oxygen to the tissues and turns slightly blue. Blood then goes back to the heart and on to the lungs where it is oxygenated and turns red again.

(b) Explain whether the use of color is effective. Is it necessary?

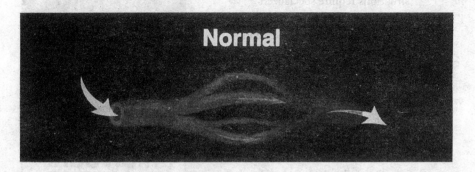

7. **Revise a document by adding visuals.** Select a document that you have previously completed (in this or another course, or in the workplace). Revise it using appropriate visuals to clarify or support the points you made in the document.

8. **Analyze the use of visuals on a Web site.** Visit the following Web sites:

   www.benjerry.com   www.discover.com
   www.dell.com   www.nationalgeographic.com
   www.pbs.org/wgbh/nova   http://cfa-www.harvard.edu
   www.jnj.com   http://natzoo.si.edu/default.cfm

   (a) Evaluate the visuals on two of the above Web sites according to the rubric you developed as well as the following criteria:

   - Do the visuals effectively and accurately explain or enhance the text?
   - Are visuals used for navigational cues? Are they effective?
   - What are some positive attributes of Web site visuals?
   - What are some negative attributes of Web site visuals?
   - What suggestions do you have for Web site technical communicators regarding the use of visuals?

   (b) Prepare your analysis in a five-minute oral presentation in which you display selected screen captures from the Web sites to illustrate your points.

9. **Assess the quality of visuals in a set of guidelines.** Work in a small group to read and then access the visuals in the document *Scientific and Technical Information: Simply Put,* a PDF file that's available at www.cdc.gov/od/oc/simpput.pdf. Use everything you've learned in Chapter 11 and this chapter to assess the visuals. Consider their comprehensibility and usability for the audience and purpose. Consider the image they create. Work with your group to categorize your assessment, using explanations and examples. Present your assessment in a detailed memo to your instructor.

10. **Design a safety sign.** Specialized situations require specialized warnings. For example, the Hawaiian Lifeguard Association includes dramatic visuals on warning signs, as this example illustrates.[65] Such a visual indicates a potentially life-threatening situation, with waves reaching heights of 15 to more than to 25 feet.

Carefully observe your local environment (for example, lab, campus, community, surrounding region) to identify a potentially dangerous situation or area. Use either of the two standard warning templates sketched below to create your own effective sign. You need to decide on an effective signal word, message, and pictorial symbol.

HORIZONTAL LAYOUT　　　　　**VERTICAL LAYOUT**

Chapter 12 Endnotes

1 Gaines, J. R. (1994, July 4). To our readers. *Time, 144*(1).

2 Kienzler, D. (1997). Visual ethics. *Journal of Business Communication, 34*(2), 171–187.

3 (1999, January). *NASA Tech Briefs, 23*(1), 34.

4 Illustration by Ellen Cohen in Hammond, A. L. (1983, November). Tales of an elusive ancestor. *Science 83, 43.*

5 Lewin, R. W. (1983, December). Is the orangutan a living fossil? *Science, 222,* 1223. Copyright © 1983 by the AAAS. Reprinted with permission of the AAAS.

6 Peckham, G. (n.d.). *On your mark: A primer on symbols.* Retrieved November 30, 2003, from http://www.ce-mag.com/archive/02/03/peckham.html

7 HCD safetylabel.com. Are symbols necessary? *Standards FAQ: Symbols.* Retrieved on November 30, 2002, http://www.safetylabel.com/safetylabelstandards/iso-ansi-symbols.php

8 Health and Safety Executive. (n.d.). *Signpost to the health and safety (safety signs and signals) regulations 1996.* Retrieved November 30, 2003, from http://www.hse/gov.uk/pubns/safesign.htm

9 Lehtola, C. T., Brown, C. M., & Becker, W. J. (2000). Biological hazard symbol. Retrieved November 30, 2003, from University of Florida, Institute of Food and Agricultural Sciences Web site: http://edis.ifas.ufl.edu/BODY_OA091

10 EUROport. (n.d.). *International labels, standards, and publications.* Retrieved November 30, 2003, from http://www.europort.com/labels.htm

11 Peckham, G. (n.d.). *On your mark: A primer on symbols.* Retrieved November 30, 2003, from http://www.ce-mag.com/archive/02/03/peckham.html

12 Peckham, G. (2001, January/February). On graphical symbols. *Compliance Engineering.* Retrieved November 30, 2003, from http://www.ce-mag.com/archive/2001/janfeb/Peckham28.html

13 EUROport. (n.d.). *International labels, standards, and publications.* Retrieved November 30, 2003, from http://www.europort.com/labels.htm

14 EUROport. (n.d.). *International labels, standards, and publications.* Retrieved November 30, 2003, from http://www.europort.com/labels.htm

15 Health and Safety Executive. (n.d.). *Signpost to the health and safety (safety signs and signals) regulations 1996.* Retrieved November 30, 2003, from http://www.hse.gov.uk/pubns/safesign.htm

16 EUROport. (n.d.). *International labels, standards, and publications.* Retrieved November 30, 2003, from http://www.europort.com/labels.htm

17 New Hampshire DWI Prevention Council. (n.d.). *Know your limits.* Dover, NH: Author. Reprinted with permission of the New Hampshire DWI Prevention Council.

[18] DeWaal, C. S., Alderton, L., & Liebman, B. Food safety guide. *Nutrition Action Healthletter, 26,* 9.

[19] McCarthy, J., Hartzell, S., & Peterson, M. (n.d.). *ANSS — Reducing the devastating effects of earthquakes* (U.S. Geological Survey Fact Sheet 046-03). Retrieved November 30, 2003, from http://pubs.usgs.gov/fs/fs-046-03/fs-046-03.html

[20] McCarthy, J., Hartzell, S., & Petersen, M. (n.d.). *ANSS — Reducing the devastating effects of earthquakes* (U.S. Geological Survey Fact Sheet 046-03). Retrieved November 30, 2003, from http://pubs.usgs.gov/fs/fs-046-03/fs-046-03.html

[21] Energy Resource Associates. JMMC Energy Analysis Graphs. Retrieved on December 1, 2003, from http://www.eraenergy.com/energy/_graphs.html

[22] Energy Resource Associates. (n.d.). *JMMC energy analysis graphs.* Retrieved December 1, 2003, from http://www.eraenergy.com/energy_graphs.html

[23] Woodwell, G. M. (1970). The energy cycle of the biosphere. In *The biosphere* (p. 72). San Francisco: W. H. Freeman & Company. Copyright © 1970 by Scientific American, Inc. All rights reserved. Reprinted with permission of Scientific American, Inc.

[24] H. J. Heinz Company. (1993, Second Quarter). *Heinz quarterly report of earnings and activities,* 13. Used by permission.

[25] Singer, S. F. (1970). Human production of energy as a process in the biosphere. In *The biosphere* (p. 184). San Francisco: W. H. Freeman & Company. Copyright © 1970 by Scientific American, Inc. All rights reserved. Reprinted with permission of Scientific American, Inc.

[26] MassPIRG. (1985, April). Consumer alert: How to choose day care for your child. *Masscitizen,* 11. Reprinted with permission of the Massachusetts Public Interest Research Group.

[27] U.S. Department of Energy, Energy Information Administration. (n.d.). *Renewable energy annual 2001 highlights.* Retrieved December 1, 2003, from http://www.eia.doe.gov/cneaf/solar.renewables/page/rea_data/rea_sum.html

[28] U.S. Department of Energy, Energy Information Administration. (n.d.). *Renewable energy annual 2001 highlights.* Retrieved December 1, 2003, from http://www.eia.doe.gov/cneaf/solar.renewables/page/rea_data/rea_sum.html

[29] Sears. (1969). Screws. In *Sears Craftsman Master Shop Guide* (sheet 3). Hearst Corporation. Reprinted with permission.

[30] U.S. Department of Energy, Genome Image Gallery. (n.d.). *DNA with features.* Retrieved December 1, 2003, from http://www.ornl.gov/sci/techresources/Human_Genome/graphics/slides/scidnafeature.shtml

[31] U.S. Department of Energy, Genome Image Gallery. (n.d.). *DNA with features.* Retrieved December 1, 2003, from http://www.ornl.gov/sci/techresources/Human_Genome/graphics/slides/scidnafeature.shtml

[32] (1993, January 19). *Des Moines Register,* p. 4A. Reprinted by permission of Tribune Media Services.

33 Whitehead, H. (1985). Why whales leap. *Scientific American, 252*(3), 87. Copyright © 1985 by Scientific American, Inc. All rights reserved. Reprinted with permission of Scientific American, Inc.

34 (1999, August). MDO exploits NASA's discipline breadth. *Insights: High Performance Computing and Communications, 10,* 14. Retrieved 2000 from www.hpcc.nasa.gov

35 U.S. Department of Energy. (1993). *Environmental restoration and waste management: An introduction* (DOE/EM-0104).

36 Environmental Protection Agency. (1991, October). *Guides to pollution prevention: The photoprocessing industry.*

37 Bayer Polymer. (n.d.). *Therban® manufacturing process.* Retrieved November 25, 2003, from http://www.therban.de/intertherban/c1standard_en.nsf/LPSNavigationLUByContentID/CHAR-5C3H4M?OpenDocument&nav=CHAR-5C3H8S

38 (1999, November). *NASA Tech Briefs, 23*(11), 54.

39 Eames, C., & Eames, R. (n.d.). Surface tension. *Mathematics IBM Exhibit Catalog.*

40 (2000, March). *NASA Tech Briefs, 24*(3).

41 Canfield, D. M. (1968). *Elements of farrier science* (2nd ed., p. 10). Albert Lea, MN: Enderes Tool Co. Reprinted with permission of Donald Canfield.

42 (n.a.). (n.d.). *Easy Home Repair, Packet #2* (p. 2). Pittsburgh, PA: International Masters Publishers.

43 Natural Resources Canada. (2001). *The atlas of Canada.* Retrieved November 30, 2003, from http://atlas.gc.ca/rasterimages/english/maps/reference/national/canada_eng.jpg

44 Urquhart, G., Chomentowski, W., Skole, D., & Barber, C. *Tropical deforestation.* NASA Earth Observatory. Retrieved November 30, 2003, from http://earthobservatory.nasa.gov/cgi-bin/texis/webinator/printall?//Library/Deforestation/index.html

45 AmTec. (n.d.). Bellevue, WA.

46 Urquhart, G., Chomentowski, W., Skole, D., & Barber, C. *Tropical deforestation.* NASA Earth Observatory. Retrieved November 30, 2003, from http://earthobservatory.nasa.gov/cgi-bin/texis/webinator/printall?/Library/Deforestation/index.html

47 Urquhart, G., Chomentowski, W., Skole, D., & Barber, C. *Tropical deforestation.* NASA Earth Observatory. Retrieved November 30, 2003, from http://earthobservatory.nasa.gov/cgi-bin/texis/webinator/printall?/Library/Deforestation/index.html

48 Urquhart, G., Chomentowski, W., Skole, D., & Barber, C. *Tropical deforestation.* NASA Earth Observatory. Retrieved November 30, 2003, from http://earthobservatory.nasa.gov/cgi-bin/texis/webinator/printall?/Library/Deforestation/index.html

49 NOAA. (1996, July). Four views of California using computer technology, SAR image, interferogram, contour map, and perspective view. *Operational Use of Civil Space-based Synthetic Aperture Radar (SAR)* 10–8.

50 For additional discussion, see these two standard sources: White, J. V. (1990). *Color for the electric age.* New York: Watson-Guptill Publications; and Keyes, E. (1993, November). Typography, color, and information structure. *Technical Communication, 40,* 638–654.

51 InCom Supply. (n.d.). *OSHA & APWA colors: The right colors for the right reasons.* Retrieved November 30, 2003, from http://www.incomsupply.com/customers/specdata/osha.html

RO-AN Corporation. (n.d.). *OSHA and AWPA safety colors.* Retrieved November 30, 2003, from http://www.roancorp.com/techtips/tisafetycolors.html

Superior Graphix. (n.d.). *OSHA color codes.* Retrieved November 30, 2003, from http://www.superiorgraphix.com/osha.html

52 Doll, R. (2001, September 29). *Avoiding equipment hazards: Ensuring machine-guard safety compliance.* retrieved November 30, 2003, from http://www.chemicalprocessing.com/Web_First/cp.nsf/ArticleID/DPIC-562MWY/

53 Doll, R. (2001, September 29). *Avoiding equipment hazards: Ensuring machine-guard safety compliance.* Retrieved November 30, 2003, from http://www.cehmicalprocessing.com/Web_First/cp.nsf/ArticleID/DPIC-562MWY/

54 Firelily Designs. (n.d.). *Color vision, color deficiency.* Retrieved November 30, 2003, from http://www.firelily.com/opinions/color.html

55 Biechler, D. (n.d.). Chichaqua Bend Studios, Ames, IA.

56 Biechler, D. (n.d.). Chichaqua Bend Studios, Ames, IA.

57 Garter, L.P., & Hiatt, J. L. (Eds). *Color atlas of histology* (graphic 9.1, lymphoid tissues). Baltimore: Williams & Wilkins. Reprinted by permission.

58 John Deere.

59 AmTec. (n.d.). Bellevue, WA.

60 Amazing science of space photography. (1997, October 24–26). *USA Weekend,* p. 14.

61 (1999, October). *Science, 286,* 30.

62 U.S. Commission for National Security in the 21st Century. (1999, September 15). Graph showing per-capita income disparities. *New World Coming: American Security in the 21st Century* (p. 38).

63 U.S. Department of Agriculture Food and Nutrition Service. (1992). Bar graph of a dietary fat chart showing fat and fatty acid proportions. *Building for the Future: Nutrition Guidance for the Child Nutrition Programs* (p. 40). (FMS-279).

64 Tyler, D. E. School of Veterinary Medicine, University of Georgia.

65 *Ocean safety signs.* (n.d.). Retrieved November 30, 2003, from http://www.aloha.com/~lifeguards/bsigns.html#waves

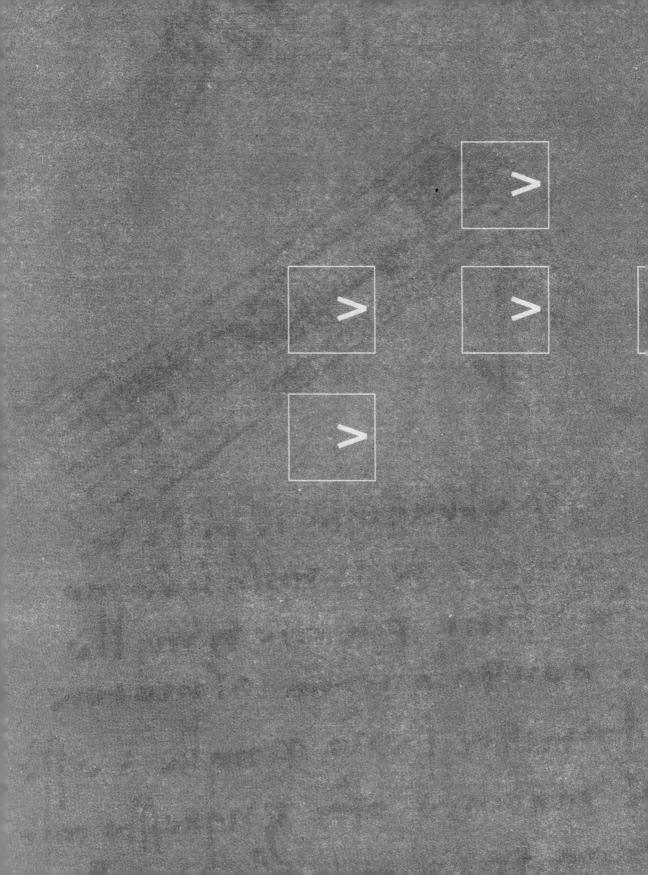

CHAPTER 13

Designing Electronic Communication
设计电子交流

电子交流的各种方式对你的职业生涯的很多方面都影响很大。不论你的职位如何，在进行电子交流时，你都需要考虑股东、开发商、客户的需求。本章注重介绍了通过个人电脑和一些微型电子设备进行的网络电子信息交流。本章首先介绍了有效电子交流的特点，阐释了有效电子交流设计的原则和实践。然后介绍了信息建构的主要构成部分（组织信息、标注信息、查询信息），并指出网页设计的主要原则。最后，本章介绍了电子交流设计的工具、网页设计的过程以及确保网页的可用性和可访问性。

Objectives and Outcomes 学习目标

This chapter will help you accomplish these outcomes:

- Identify the characteristics and features of effective electronic communication
- Understand the principles of effective design for various electronic media
- Analyze key aspects of information architecture: organizing, labeling, and navigating
- Analyze key aspects of effective Web page/screen design: layout, color, graphics
- Understand the standards and tools for designing electronic communication
- Understand the iterative design process
- Assess Web sites for usability and accessibility

Electronic tools and processes that allow people to share information will affect many aspects of your professional success. No matter what role you have, when you contribute to the development of electronic communication, you need to consider the virtual environment from a number of perspectives: stakeholders', developers', and especially users' perspectives.

Because most people using electronic information access the World Wide Web, this chapter focuses on Web-based content accessed from personal computers (PCs) as well as from small-screen devices such as personal digital assistants (PDAs) and cellular telephones. The nature, types, and functions of electronic communication affect the ways you read and construct information on the Web. You need to understand the principles and practices for effective site, page, and content design; important aspects of developing usable content for delivery via a range of technologies; and the iterative design process used for that development.

Characterizing Electronic Communication
电子交流特点

Users and designers often have different perspectives about electronic communication. Users tend to think about tasks they want to accomplish, such as finding information, purchasing a product, or playing a game. Designers tend to think in terms of design and functionality.

Despite these different perspectives, both users and designers see electronic communication as interactive and nonlinear, virtual and open, complex and dynamic:

> In what ways do the electronic tools and processes you have used exemplify the characteristics in this list?

- ***Interactive and nonlinear.*** Electronic communication environments are interactive and nonlinear, established by multiple possibilities for interactions among users, computers, software, interface components, and developers. The goal of electronic communication is for users to accomplish tasks, sometimes something as simple as accessing information on static Web pages.
- ***Virtual and open.*** Electronic communication environments are virtual and open spaces. Virtual spaces do not have a material, face-to-face reality. "Open" means two things, both related to consistency and user expectations: (1) The virtual spaces allow users to move beyond boundaries at will. (2) Standards and conventions are fluid, leading to varied designs and functionality, and often uneven experiences for users.
- ***Complex and dynamic.*** Electronic communication environments are complex and dynamic development efforts that integrate diverse components. Complex development efforts include managing both static and dynamic content, hundreds of individual text and graphic files, multimedia components, and databases. Because development technology changes rapidly, becoming more dynamic and multidimensional, designers must plan for differences in users' available technology.

While these characteristics of electronic communication pose challenges for information designers, people who regularly use electronic communication take its availability for granted, at least until they run into difficulty accomplishing their goals or completing their activities. That's why companies and organizations commit significant resources to create and maintain environments and capabilities for electronic communication, which usually require the collaboration of people with different sets of skills.

Types of Electronic Communication 电子交流种类

The chances are high that you are one of the millions of people who access electronic information and services via the Internet and World Wide Web using a variety of PCs, a vast array of software, and different types of Internet service providers. People visit Web sites using browsers. People search libraries online to locate and read articles and books from the comfort of dorm rooms and offices. People use computers to check weather and bank balances, to make airline reservations and order flowers, even to take courses. People send e-mail messages and documents and share music and graphics. People instant message, blog, participate in synchronous and asynchronous chats, and participate in virtual conferences.

What different types of electronic devices do you currently use? What kinds of activities do you engage in with each? What differences have you noticed about the design of information for each?

In recent years, the capabilities of Web resources and PCs have changed dramatically. In addition, people are now using handheld devices, such as PDAs and cell phones, to access Web-based resources and engage in tasks that they once could only accomplish with desktop computers. People can now use cell phones, paging devices, and PDAs to communicate, store addresses, browse headlines, and keep calendars.

Each of these examples of electronic communication results from the convergence of hardware and software, engineering and programming, connectivity and content. Each type of device places different demands on both technology users and information designers. One obvious example of difference is screen size. The monitor of a desktop or laptop computer obviously displays more information at once than the display screen on a PDA or cell phone. Other less immediately visible differences include memory, bandwidth, connectivity, and the types of standards and protocols required to display information. Designers must account for such differences in designing and developing electronic communication, including handheld and wireless devices.

Chapter 13 Designing Electronic Communication

FIGURE 13.1 Current and Projected Statistics on Web Access by Various Media[1]

Web Access via PCs and Wireless Devices, 2000, 2002, and 2005

Year-end	2000	2002	2005
USA (in millions)			
Web appliances in use	3.2	23.6	115.4
Web appliance share of Internet users	2.3%	14.2%	55.4%
PCs in use	153.2	178.9	221.9
Internet users	135.7	165.7	208.3

Global Internet and Wireless Users, 2001, 2004 and 2007

Subscribers	2001	2004	2007
Internet users (in millions)	533	945	1,460
Wireless Internet users as a percentage of all Internet users	16	41.5	56.8

The use of all electronic devices has increased dramatically in a short time (see Figure 13.1). This rapid expansion of electronic resources and environments means that we need to be concerned with security, especially protecting personal information. How much of a concern this should be is the subject of the ethics sidebar on the next page.

WEBLINK

The statistics show that mobile commerce is booming, especially in Europe, Japan, and the United States. The data in Figure 13.1 are just a hint of its enormous activity. For more details, go to **www.english.wadsworth.com/ burnett6e** for a link. Select what for you is the most surprising statistic in the information presented. Compare your opinion with others in your class.
CLICK ON WEBLINK
CLICK on Chapter 13/mCommerce

We Know Who You Are and Where You've Been 我们知道你是谁和去过哪里

Imagine it's Saturday afternoon and you're browsing at your local bookstore. A salesperson approaches you:

"Can I help you? I noticed that you came in at 1:14 pm through the Main Street entrance, which makes sense since you were just shopping in Baskets and Bows next door. You went right to the bestsellers and considered the latest romance for 56 seconds and then the top-rated mystery for 32 seconds. Now you're browsing self-help books related to depression. Are you depressed? If so, we have several other titles that might interest you. We're also providing information about you to some other businesses with whom we share information — they'll get in touch with you soon. By the way, Jane — your name is Jane Smith, isn't it? — we could have your selections sent right to your home at 123 Elm Street, if you prefer. And, since today is the twentieth time you've been in the store, we have some specials that might interest you. . . ."

Hard to imagine? Not on the Web. Many Web sites collect information about users. Existing technologies for tracking visitors allow Web administrators to collect various kinds of information:

- IP addresses
- Information about operating systems and web browsers
- Time and duration of site visits
- Individual pages accessed, order in which users access them, and amount of time on each
- Other sites users visited, including the link from which a user was referred
- Where users go after their visit

Information about visitors to Web sites is collected a number of ways:

- **Cookies,** small files that servers place on computers, contain information, such as passwords, which frequently makes visiting sites more convenient. Cookies can also track user movements. Session cookies are only used during visits, and then they terminate. Persistent cookies remain on computers until removed or until they expire at a preset time. Cookies are the most common way to collect and use information about users.[2]
- **Forms** users fill out voluntarily ask for personal information that could not otherwise be collected, for example, sex, nationality, age, and e-mail address. The information, often stored in cookies, can assist the site in providing services and offers for users. Some companies sell this information to others.

> How can users become better informed about issues of security and privacy?
> What responsibilities do schools have to protect the privacy of their students?
> What responsibilities do organizations have to protect the privacy of their employees?

- **Hit counters** collect information about visiting IP addresses, users' computers, and the pages users access in a site. Web managers use this information to determine how often their sites are visited, by whom, and for what information.
- **Spyware** (and adware) programs can be placed on users' computers deceptively. While these programs are not illegal, they should cause concern because users often don't know these programs have been installed. Some spyware can track every keystroke that a user makes. Collected information can be sent to a server while the user is online and sold to marketers.[3]

Many companies collect information to make their sites more useful to users. For example, by tracking the most visited pages, companies can provide more of the information users want. Some collected information helps users. For instance, when users check airline flights, they go through several screens of information and make a number of choices that the site server must record to return flight data. Unfortunately, not all data collection is so benign.

If you are developing a Web site that will collect information about users, you should create clear privacy policies and post them on your site. At a minimum your policy should do these things:

- Inform people about the information you collect and the ways you collect it
- Explain the purposes for information collection
- Disclose any information you share and with whom you share it
- Allow users to "opt out" of information collection
- Provide contact information so that users can register any complaints or concerns about your policy

Information collection is a concern to many people including the World Wide Web Consortium,[4] which is drafting policies aimed at making privacy statements on Web sites more thorough, clear, and consistent for users.

Web Sites and Web-Enabled Environments
网站和网络支持环境

The World Wide Web is the largest part of the Internet, a huge network comprised of other networks and millions of individual computers. Internet traffic is routed along a number of *backbones,* which are primary networks owned by organizations and companies. These backbones are connected by *hubs* that can move traffic from one backbone to another. The Internet uses a variety of *protocols,* rules and standards that people have agreed to use when developing for the Internet and the Web. For instance, Internet participants use a protocol called TCP/IP (Transmission Control Protocol/Internet Protocol) that allows computers to locate and communicate with each other. This cooperation is essential to keep traffic on the Internet moving and to provide relatively unlimited access to Internet resources. Various organizations and consortiums develop and maintain the shared protocols.

The Web itself is comprised of networks of servers and users' computers that exchange Internet resources using Internet protocols. Hypertext transfer protocol (HTTP), the primary protocol of the Web, facilitates the exchange of hypertext documents. Hypertext documents are plain-text documents that contain hypertext markup language (HTML), a system of tags placed within the documents that are interpreted and implemented by *browsers,* programs that allow users to interact with servers to request, view, and use Web pages. At the most basic level, HTML tags control the appearance of documents in browsers and allow pages to be linked to other pages.

What do you capitalize? When "web" refers to the World Wide Web, it's a proper noun, so it's capitalized. "Internet" is also a proper noun, so it is capitalized as well.

WEBLINK

> Lots of people use computer terms carelessly or inaccurately. You have easy access to a number of online resources to help you, from the very simple (TekMom with simple example sentences) to the carefully illustrated (TechEncyclopedia). Go to **www.english.wadsworth.com/burnett6e** for links.
>   CLICK ON WEBLINK
>   CLICK on Chapter 13/definition of terms

The individual Web sites that comprise the Web are collections of files that include individual Web pages and graphics and sometimes databases and programs that facilitate sophisticated interactivity, such as searching, placing orders, and playing games. Basically, all the files for a site are stored on a computer with special software that allows the computer to act as a *server.* As the name suggests, what a server does is "serve" users by providing resources that they request by interacting with their browsers. Users' computers are referred to as *clients.*

The relationship between servers and users' computers is called a *client/server relationship.* The concept of a client/server relationship is important to understand because some functions of Web-based materials are performed by the client, and others can only be performed by the server. For example, when you mouse over a menu link on a Web page, the link may change appearance. A small script in the HTML page that is read and acted upon by the client's browser triggers this change in appearance on your computer. On the other hand, when you fill out an online form on a Web site, the information you provide must be handled by a program on the server.

To use Internet resources, people must have access to one of the networks on the Internet. This is generally accomplished by establishing a connection from the client computer and a modem to an Internet service provider (ISP) server that is connected to a network. Examples of ISPs include America Online (AOL), Earthlink, or a point-to-point (PPP) dial-up connection provided through an organization or company. Clients can then request Web pages by accessing the uniform resource locator (URL) of Web pages via browser programs, such as Netscape Navigator, Mozilla, Microsoft Internet Explorer, Mosaic, Opera, and Lynx (which is a text-only browser). Figure 13.2 explains how to interpret a URL.

> **FIGURE 13.2** **Understanding URLs**
>
> The names and locations, or more simply, the addresses, of electronic resources that you visit or create are referred to as URLs, Uniform Resource Locators. A typical URL looks like this Web address:
>
> http://www.agency.gov/news/archives/project087690.html#participants
>
> Each part of this fictional Web page address, which is highlighted and explained below, contains a considerable amount of information that allows users to find and access resources on the Internet and Web.
>
> http://www.agency.gov/news/archives/project087690.html#participants
>
> The first part of the URL is called the *scheme*, which contains information about the protocol that the computers and servers need to use to interact. These are other familiar schemes:
>
> - https:// (secure http server)
> - ftp:// (file transfer protocol)
> - mailto: (e-mail address)
>
> http://www.agency.gov/news/archives/project087690.html#participants
>
> The second part of the URL is the actual address or *domain name* of the server on which the Web page is located. URL names correspond to numeric IP addresses assigned to every computer using the Internet (for example, http://128.10.004.1) but are much easier for people to remember and use.
>
> - *WWW* indicates that the resource type is a Web site.
> - "agency" is the domain name of the specific Web site. Domain names must be registered so that duplications in names are avoided.
> - *.gov* designates the top-level domain in which the resource is included; in this case .gov indicates a government agency. Top-level domains are based on the type and geographical location of the resource. The most prevalent top-level domain is *.com*. These are some of the other top-level domains:
> - .net (provides Internet services)
> - .org (organization)
> - .uk (United Kingdom)
> - .ca (Canada)
>
> http://www.agency.gov/news/archives/project087690.html#participants
>
> The third part of the URL indicates the folders or *directories* in which the Web page resides on the server. Directory locations are important for providing a complete path to an individual page or resource.
>
> http://www.agency.gov/news/archives/project087690.html#participants
>
> The fourth part of the URL is the *file name*, or the individual Web page or other resource. The *file extension*, in this case *.html* for hypertext mark-up language, indicates the type of document that the user is accessing. These are other common file types:
>
> - asp (active server page)
> - .pdf (Adobe portable document file)
> - .wml (wireless mark-up language, used by PDAs and cell phones)
>
> http://www.agency.gov/news/archives/project087690.html#participants
>
> The final part of the URL locates a specific place on a Web page. The pound sign in this example signifies a *named anchor* that is identified by the word "participants."
>
> - When an anchor is included in a URL, users' browsers will take them to a specific spot on a page.
> - Anchors are particularly helpful on pages that contain a lot of text that users would otherwise need to scroll through.

Audiences and Electronic Communication 交流对象与电子交流

Meeting the needs of audiences should be a primary goal of writers and designers of electronic communication. Unlike other types of professional communication, however, electronic environments offer audiences unique opportunities to co-construct the environment and information each time they enter it. For example, because of the Web's hypertext nature, individual users can create unique sequences of information as they move around a Web site or among different Web sites. At a minimum, the sequence of links that users select leads to individual interpretations of information.

Reading and Navigating Electronic Communication. Reading in electronic communication environments is different from reading on paper because it involves an *interface*. In other words, reading electronic media is not simply reading an electronic display of information; instead, it is interactive and brings with it a number of complications. A number of researchers, including Christina Haas at Kent State University,[5] Karen McGrane at Razorfish,[6] and Jakob Nielsen at useit.com,[7] have identified factors that are particularly important in online reading:

- **Screen and page size.** How much text can a reader see at one time? Larger screens (and larger windows on those screens) enable readers to see more. But readers sometimes have difficulty even with large screens, because reading on a computer monitor reduces their awareness of where they are in relation to the whole document.
- **Legibility.** How easy is it to read what's on the screen? Factors such as screen flicker, spacing, and background and text color affect legibility. Readers also sometimes have difficulty because visual cues such as boldface and italics may not show on the screen (as in some e-mail systems), and spacing is sometimes difficult to judge; thus, proofreading is often more difficult to do on a monitor.
- **Responsiveness.** How quickly should a system respond to users' actions? Human factors research shows that users believe a system is reacting instantaneously if the response time is about 0.1 second or less. Users will stay focused and on task if the response time is no more than about 1.0 second, but that's usually not possible on the Web. If the response time is more than ten seconds, people typically lose attention and wander to other tasks.[8]
- **Navigation.** How easily can readers navigate the Web site — that is, how easily can readers move through and locate places in the text? Web readers/users are influenced by images and icons that affect their ability to navigate on the Web, by color, links and backgrounds, and, of course, by typography and layout. But even with navigational aids, it's easier to get lost in an electronic document than in a paper document.
- **Equipment and service.** How much are readers constrained by physical realities? Research at Georgia Tech suggests that even though fast modems and higher bandwidths are available, the modems and lines used by most people are too slow for decent Web response times.[9]

Which of these factors are important to you when reading in an electronic environment? Are some of these factors more important to you than others? Does the purpose or situation change what's more important?

Navigating Electronic Communication. When electronic communication is audience-focused, readers can easily construct paths through resources by choosing their own sequence of links. Researcher Paul Levinson calls this "empowerment of the author through the empowerment of readers."[10] Simply put, hypertext documents allow writers and audiences to link related concepts and restructure knowledge. Different readers can arrive at the same point in a document having discovered different things along the way, either because they activated different links or because they activated the same links but in a different sequence. A document that is read interactively is rarely experienced the same way twice. Electronic communication environments that offer readers this empowerment respect audience needs.

Figures 13.3 through 13.5 show pages from the Food Safety Project Web site. Depending on a user's prior knowledge, needs, and interests, this site could be interpreted in a number of different ways. Visitors to the Food Safety Project Web site can select their own sequence of information.

When readers arrive at the Project's home page, they find that the menu on the left side gives them choices for linking to information about consumer issues, food safety education, foodborne pathogens, and other relevant topics. To the right

FIGURE 13.3 Food Safety Project Home Page[11]

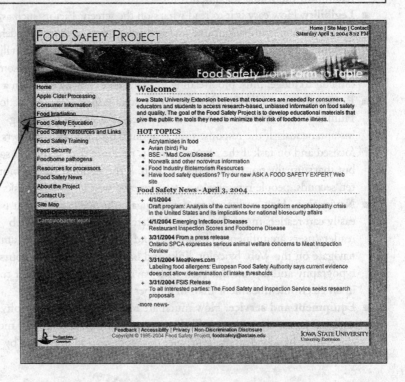

Clicking on the link to Food Safety Education brings users to several additional content choices. They can get lessons about food safety and pointers about kitchen safety.

Menus and links allow users choose their own paths through a Web site. For instance, they might be interested in food safety education.

FIGURE 13.4 Food Safety Project Consumer Control Point Kitchen[12]

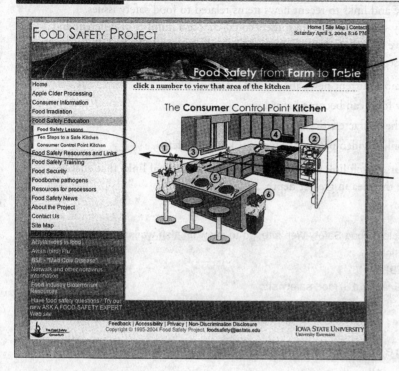

A simple instruction above the kitchen graphic informs users about how to access information.

Users can refine their path by selecting from additional menu choices. What is the Consumer Control Point Kitchen?

The Consumer Control Point Kitchen is a Flash presentation that includes hotspots allowing users to further explore the page's content. Users can click on the numbered items in the kitchen in any order in order to receive safety information specific to that kitchen, or topic, area.

FIGURE 13.5 Food Safety Project Consumer Control Point Kitchen Hotspot[13]

Clicking on Item 1 in the kitchen graphic (shown in Figure 13.4, above) allows users to access information about safe food storage.

Clicking a number triggers a simple animation that provides a close-up of the section of the kitchen that users want to learn about and a text dialog box with specific related information. Users can return to the kitchen for additional information by clicking on "Back to Kitchen."

If users don't find the information they want in the kitchen, they can quickly and easily change their paths through the site because the navigational menu is continuously available. One user may leave the kitchen and visit Food Safety News; another may look for resources under Food Security. In this way, users create their own individual paths through the information.

of the menu, the main section of the home page provides a very brief overview of the site's purpose and links to recent news items related to food safety issues.

After quickly scanning these links, users could choose a number of different and equally productive directions depending on their needs. For example, by following different links, users could do any of these things in whatever order they choose:

- Read the most current news about food safety.
- Learn how food can become hazardous
- Discover the characteristics of a specific pathogen
- View an online video presentation about kitchen safety

And, of course, each link they go to might have additional links that enable them to explore the idea in greater depth.

WEBLINK

To view the complete Food Safety Web site, go to **www.english.wadsworth.com/ burnett6e** for a link.
CLICK ON WEBLINK
   CLICK on Chapter 13/food safety site

Principles and Practices of Effective Design
有效设计的原则与实践

Anyone with time, knowledge, and resources can create a Web site. But designing and developing Web sites that function well for a variety of audiences and a range of technologies requires understanding of users' needs, careful planning, thorough testing, and coordinated design activities. Designers need to consider three important factors:

- *Information architecture* is the framework that structures content. The structure should meet the goals and expectations of the user. Structure can be *sequential* (for example, Web pages that link to the next in a linear style), *hierarchical* (outline format), or *interlinked* (less structured, liberally linked).
- *Page/screen design* is the look and feel of the information in the space on the screen, another mechanism to help users understand information organization and context.
- *Content* is organized and written differently for electronic communication than for traditional print documents. The style of content should match users' ways of finding and reading information using electronic devices.

As you read about the specifics of each factor, remember that the relationships among them determine the degree to which your communication will be usable. For example, you can create beautifully designed Web pages, but if the navigation of the site is poor, your audience will quickly go somewhere else.

WEBLINK

Designing Web sites for international audiences brings additional challenges in areas including language, conventions in graphics and design, and expectations about the organization of information. Go to **www.english.wadsworth.com/ burnett6e** for links to interesting discussions about a range of related issues.
CLICK ON WEBLINK
　　CLICK on Chapter 13/international Web issues

Information Architecture 信息建构

Two of the most significant factors of context creation in electronic communication are the design of information that users access directly through sight, touch, and hearing and the design of the components and pathways that allow user access and navigation. Together, these design factors contribute to the architecture of information — the visible areas, the structures beneath, and the design, engineering, programming and electronic media used to create them. This section focuses on three factors of information architecture common in all types of electronic communication: organizing, labeling, and navigating information.

Organizing Information. You can think of information architecture as the relationships between the content pages and the other components comprising an electronic communication environment. A site map is like a blueprint that shows the site architecture. The site map shown in Figure 13.6 depicts the architecture for a corporate intranet, which is a Web site that provides information to individuals in an organization. Generally, Internet users outside the organization cannot access a company's intranet.

In the site map in Figure 13.6, the blue rectangle in the lower left corner represents the intranet home page. Each rectangle in the rest of the figure represents an HTML page that is linked to the home page via one or more hyperlinks. Boxes and cylinders represent Web-enabled software applications (e.g., billing software) and databases (e.g., personnel information), respectively.

As the example illustrates, organizing the components of an electronic communication environment structures information in several ways that affect users:

- Categories of information available to users are determined.
- Relationships of categories of information are established.
- Pathways through information are created based on judgments about the relationships among categories by the designers (and based on user testing as well).
- Points of interaction are established, for example, where certain functions such as forms are included.

FIGURE 13.6 Intranet Architecture[14]

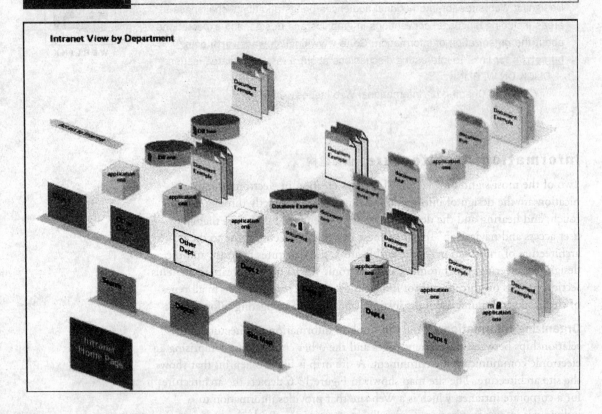

Ultimately, organizing information is a negotiation among users' needs, stakeholders' purposes, the types of media used to provide information, and the capability of the systems supporting the media.

Each of these factors must be carefully considered when organizing information. While no hard and fast rules exist about the best way to organize information, you can begin to think about organizing it by considering several general organizational schemes, illustrated in Figure 13.7, that are frequently used.

WEBLINK

Maps of cyberspaces are often remarkably innovative, much different from the maps you're accustomed to using because the spaces are virtual, not geographic. Go to www.english.wadsworth.com/burnett6e for links to interesting examples.
    CLICK ON WEBLINK
        CLICK on Chapter 13/maps of cyberspaces

| FIGURE 13.7 | **Generic Organizational Schemes** |

Hierarchical structures are frequently used on the Web. A main entry point, such as a homepage, provides access to sections of related information. Sections serve as discreet collections of content and lower-level pages may only be accessible from other pages within the same section.

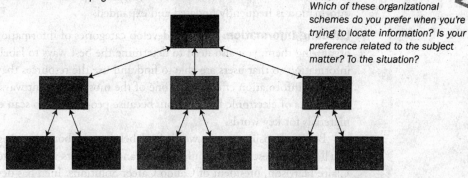

Which of these organizational schemes do you prefer when you're trying to locate information? Is your preference related to the subject matter? To the situation?

Sequential structures exert more control over paths the users can take through pages by providing minimal navigation through content. For example, a multi-page document may provide only sequential links in a prescribed order.

Interlinked structures create multiple relationships among various pages of information and allow significant flexibility for users to choose paths. This type of structure is often used for parts of sites in conjunction with hierarchical structures.

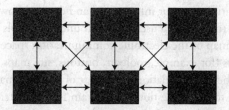

What advantages do Web pages have in comparison to print documents? What disadvantages?

Structure on demand is becoming more prevalent, particularly in e-commerce. These structures are often parts of sites that contain some static elements. Forms for user input are linked to programs and databases that allow people to create information unique to their needs. For example, when you use a search engine to locate particular information, the page of links you receive in response to your query is unique, based on your request and the information available. However, the appearance of the information usually predetermined by the designers, may also be changed by users on some sites.

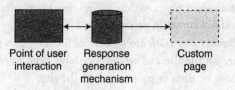

Point of user interaction   Response generation mechanism   Custom page

Chapter 13   Designing Electronic Communication

Organizing information and creating a structure for its use are the first steps in developing an environment for electronic communication. As you work on organizing information for electronic environments, you may not know all the individual pieces of information that your text will include, so plan for flexibility so that information can be added. Flexibility is important because electronic information is frequently updated and expanded.

Labeling Information. As you develop categories of information and begin organizing them, you also need to determine the best ways to label the information so that users are able to find and use the resources they need. Labeling information effectively is one of the most important ways that you can assist users of electronic information, because people tend to scan electronic materials for key words.

Before choosing specific words for labels, think about the categories of labels you'll need to describe your information and that users will need to identify it. Claire Harrison, president of Cando Career Solutions, Inc., has developed one effective classification system for the types of links that are often used on Web sites, as shown in Figure 13.8.

> Think about your department's Web site. Make a list of the category labels that users might expect/want/need. Then check the site to see if your expectations match what's actually on the site.

Labels are pervasive in electronic communication. Labels appear as page titles, menu items, links, headings within electronic documents, buttons and controls on forms, and other functions features. Because labels are necessary for identifying information and the users' location within the information, labeling is a significant aspect of information architecture.

Navigating Information. Another important factor in information architecture is navigation. As the name suggests, navigation concerns ways that users move through electronic information. Once you have determined the organization for your information and decided how to label it, you need to provide tools to help users move around. The tools should help users develop a mental map of the electronic communication space. Consistent navigational elements (for example, toolbars, buttons, site maps, arrows, menus) let users know where they are in relation to the rest of the information. Users consistently want answers to these questions: Where am I on the site? Where have I been on the site? Where else can I go on the site?

> Look at your department's Web site. What navigational elements let you answer these three questions?

How you navigate information depends considerably on your purposes and audiences. For example, why do people visit a particular Web site? What will they look for, and how will they find it? Your navigation strategy also depends on the size and scope of your information. Navigation is usually managed several ways:

- *Menus* are generally horizontal or vertical lists of links to sections or individual pages within a Web site. Users often prefer menus that look like indexes or are in vertical lists.[15]
- *Breadcrumb trails* are sequential lists of pages that let users know where they are on the site and where they have been in relation to either the site's home page or their entry point onto the site.

FIGURE 13.8 A Classification of Links According to Primary Function[16]

Link	Primary Function	Examples on Web Sites
Authorizing	Authenticates the site and its content by describing the organization's legal status, its formal policies, contact information, and so on.	■ About Us ■ Customer Service Policies ■ Archives
Commenting	Provides opinions about the site and/or its content.	■ Press Releases ■ Testimonials ■ Links to reviews
Enhancing	Provides factual information about site content by offering more details or painting a bigger picture.	■ Site Map ■ Guidelines for Membership ■ Site Index; Site Help
Exemplifying	Provides specific examples of content within a broader category.	■ Future Events ■ Job Postings ■ Available Products/Services
Mode-Changing	Moves users from reading to some kind of interaction: an activity or decision making.	■ Online Survey ■ Shopping Cart ■ Taking a Quiz
Referencing/Citing	Provides background or supplemental information about the site's content.	■ Bibliography ■ Related Links ■ Useful References
Self-Selecting	Allows users to narrow searches based on age, sex, geographical location, life situation, personal interests, and so on.	■ E-commerce Sites ■ Your Local Chapter ■ Professional Associations

- *Embedded links* are links within text that take users to another page or site. Be judicious about including links within text. Too many embedded links make reading more difficult.

WEBLINK

The EServerTC Library has a remarkably useful collection of links to articles about information architecture, ranging from usability guidelines to tutorials, from research studies to detailed descriptions of design and development processes. Go to **www.english.wadsworth.com/burnett6e** for a link.
  CLICK ON WEBLINK
    CLICK on Chapter 13/EServer TC Library information architecture

You can help visitors navigate information by taking a few other simple steps that typically make the site more accessible, understandable, and usable:

- Put the organization logo, name, or other identifying information on every page of information. This helps users know where they are relative to the Web as a whole by letting them know when they've left your site and entered another one.
- Include a site map, index, and/or search function so that users can navigate directly to information they want.
- Use the same types of menus, buttons, links, and other navigational elements for all of your information. For example, if you include a back button to return users to the previous page, every page should contain a back button that looks and operates the same way. The colors, sizes, and metaphors of icons, graphics, and text features (such as underlined links) used for navigation should provide a scheme that users can follow.
- Provide dialog boxes and other forms that are similar in appearance and function. Make sure that the location of interactive features makes sense in the overall scheme of the site.

Organizing, labeling, and navigating are critical factors in information architecture. Well-designed electronic information has clues about the architecture built into each screen. For example, the redesigned Fermi Web site in Figure 13.9 contains several embedded clues about site architecture.

Was the redesign a big change? Yes. Figure 13.10 shows what the Fermi site looked like before the 2001 redesign. The 2001 site redesign was a response to the accumulation of electronic documents that the Fermi National Accelerator Laboratory had collected over the time they had been maintaining a Web site. The information needed to be reorganized to provide better access for users. In addition, developing Web technologies made new strategies available for creating content quickly and for providing additional navigational elements, such as the pop-out submenus on the main page links to information hubs.

The Fermi Lab has maintained a site on the Internet since the days of text-only document posting in the early 1990s, when the Internet served scientists who wanted to share information quickly. The Fermi Lab's original site is shown in Figure 13.11. Though the site might look arcane on the modern Web, its simplicity would not be out of place on some PDA or cell phone screens today.

WEBLINK

Based on the information you've read about Fermi National Accelerator Laboratory, you might find viewing the entire site interesting. For a link, go to www.english.wadsworth.com/burnett6e.
CLICK ON WEBLINK
CLICK on Chapter 13/Fermi Lab

FIGURE 13.9 The Old Home Page of the Fermi Lab Web Site[17]

In 2001, the Fermi National Accelerator Laboratory revised its Web site. As part of their effort, the designers created "information 'hubs.' Each current public page has a spot in one of these hubs and new content pages will join one of these hubs."

The "hubs" into which information is organized are listed on the main page and include sub-menus.

The Fermi designers note that, "Each hub has a unique page header that may be included on pages within the hub. This header includes navigation buttons to each of the other hubs."

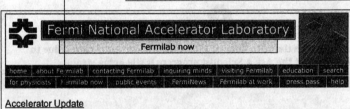

Accelerator Update
Updates on accelerator operations over the last few days and plans for the future.

Accelerator Update Archive
An archive of the past accelerator updates.

Live Tevatron Status
Shows the current status of Fermilab's Tevatron, the world's highest energy particle accelerator, and is updated every 10 seconds. Click on highlighted text for explanations.

Tevatron Luminosity Charts
Luminosity is a measure of particle interaction.

One of the primary purposes of the Fermi site is to distribute news from this national lab, which the designers have made a focus of the site.

The Fermi Web designers point out that, "A news box is prominently featured on the home page. Headlines link directly to the featured news, sections, articles or releases. Members of the Fermi lab community are encouraged to submit news items here. Simply click 'Got news?' from the news box."

Chapter 13 Designing Electronic Communication

| FIGURE 13.10 | The Old Home Page of the Fermi Lab Web Site[18] |

Consider the information categories and labeling of the Fermi Lab's previous site. How would you characterize the organization, labeling, and navigation?

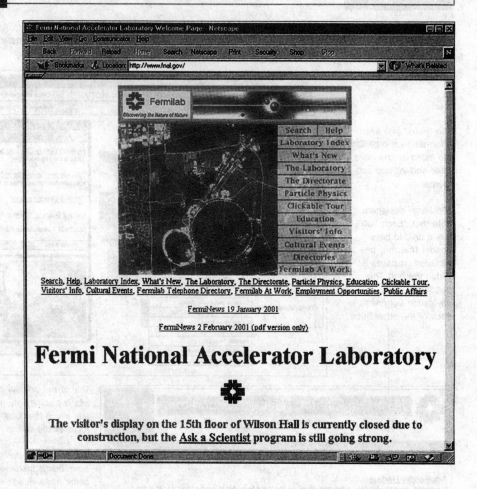

| FIGURE 13.11 | Fermi's First Web Site[19] |

How new is the Web? The World Wide Web was born at CERN in Europe in 1991 as a tool for exchanging particle physics data. When the Fermi Lab Web site was established in June 1992, it was either the second or third Web site in the United States; one at MIT was established at about the same time as Fermi. The first U.S. Web server was created at Stanford Linear Accelerator Center in December 1991.

FERMILAB COMPUTING DIVISION	
Computing[1]	Documentation: General[2], Offline Products[3], Online (DOCDB)[4]
INFO[5]	Access to Fermilab and Computing Division announcements.
H E P[6]	World Wide Web services provided by other High Energy Physics Laboratories, CERN[7], SLAC[8]
Spires[9]	Access to Spires preprint database.
Help[10]	Fermilab Help Page for WWW
WWW[11].	Information on the World-Wide Web project.

Page/Screen Design 页面或屏幕设计

The aspects of information architecture — organizing, labeling, and navigating — come together in the display of electronic information. Pages and screens are the visible means by which users access content. To bring information architecture to users, you'll need to consider several aspects of screen and page design including layout, color, and graphics.

Layout. The layout of screens and pages is an important aspect of designing electronic information. Electronic materials and the ways people use them are different from print pages and their use. Screen displays combine interface elements that people click, mouse over, scroll, type into, and otherwise manipulate with navigation, written content, graphics, and other elements so that users can easily access resources.

You can get a good start on screen and page design by choosing not to move texts formatted for print directly into an electronic environment. Instead be guided by the architecture of your information and apply a consistent grid when deciding how information should be displayed on the screen. Though one set of rules about page layout does not exist, using an established grid may be helpful to beginning designers. Established grids rely on what is known about the ways people look for information and the types of design conventions with which users are already familiar. On the Web, for example, people have become used to navigation menus at the top and sides of the screen. However, conventions are like habits, which can be good or bad, and decisions about information design should be driven by the types of information and user needs within a specific communication context.

Figures 13.12 through 13.16 illustrate the screen/page designs of the current NASA Web site. The pages reflect the complex architecture and variety of user interests that an organization such as NASA must take into account when creating a design. The grids for the information are tailored for NASA's specific goals, but also incorporate some conventional choices.

The content for each type of page on the NASA site is adapted to enhance the information and the users' experiences with the site. Despite the remarkable amount of information available, the NASA site maintains a high level of consistency in the layout of the main site components across all types of pages. When the grids of various page types are stacked on top of each other, a basic pattern emerges. This grid is illustrated and explained in Figure 13.16. The consistency provided by grids is essential for learnability and memorability — two important usability principles discussed in Chapter 9.

Sizing and positioning content on the page are also important considerations of page and screen design because of variations in display sizes. Small PC monitors can generally display information that is 640 pixels wide by 480 pixels high on one screen, for a total of 307,200 pixels. (A "pixel," short for picture elements, is the unit of measurement for Web page elements and monitor screen

| FIGURE 13.12 | **NASA Site Home Page**[20] |

Carefully study this home page for the NASA Web site. What can you tell from this page about the organization, labeling, and navigation of the site? What can you tell about the layout, color, and graphics?

What resolution do you typically use on your computer monitor? What is the range of possible resolutions?

size. The number of pixels affects resolution; the higher the number of pixels, the higher the screen resolution.) Larger monitors can display 800 by 600 pixels or more. Cell phones, PDAs, and other handheld devices typically have much smaller displays. In addition, the way that users set the preferences for their browsers can change the display.

Browsers, by default, display Web page content horizontally to fit within browser windows. The length of a Web page, or the number of screens that you need to scroll down to reach to bottom of the page, is determined by the amount of content that fits on a screen.

You cannot control all the variations in users' hardware and software. If you're designing primarily for the Web, consider designing for small displays or designing pages that display correctly regardless of the way they are resized by browsers. This type of design is called *resolution independent,* which allows the users' browsers to manage the screen space. If you choose this option, make sure

FIGURE 13.13 NASA Home Page with Grid Overlay[21]

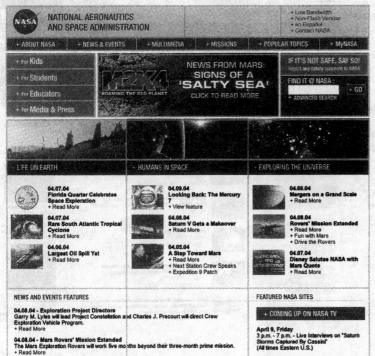

NASA's site uses top navigation to main sections of the site. Top navigation has become a popular choice. The top of the site is also used for identification. Content is displayed below the navigation.

Be careful that your page doesn't become top heavy, with excessive graphics at the top that do little to help the reader situate themselves, navigate, or receive information. Top heavy banners often push important content too far down the page, below the visible screen. If users don't scroll down, they may miss important information.

The green lines on the image of the Web site here and in Figures 13.14, 13.15, and 13.16 show the grid for each page. The thumbnail sketch for each figure highlights the grid for that particular page.

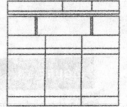

your design organizes the space in such a way that long lines of text don't stretch across the width of large monitors. If you are designing for a variety of information devices, for instance, Web materials that will also be displayed on PDAs, tools are available to help manage and adjust the same information for different modes of delivery. The amount and complexity of information often makes preparing and maintaining separate sets of materials for different systems costly and time consuming.

The following general guidelines will help you design (or revise) usable Web pages:

- ***Content.*** Provide more content than navigation on each page. Users come to your site for the content, so at least 75 percent of your pages beyond the home page should be content.
- ***Identification.*** Include critical information and site identification at or near the top of each page. The top left of a page is an important focal area of Web pages as well as print pages.
- ***White space.*** Don't fill every pixel of your page. White space is important to help guide the user's eye around the page. Leaving space is often preferable to creating divisions with graphics or color bars that detract from your

FIGURE 13.14 NASA News and Events Section Home Page with Grid Overlay[22]

Some pages include navigation and other elements on the left or right sides of the page (and occasionally on the top and both sides, as with a number of the search engine and news sites). The NASA site includes right-side navigation for second-level content within sections of the site.

When you provide navigation and other elements in various locations on the page, it's important to be consistent about the type of information you include in those areas.

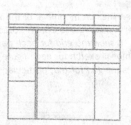

FIGURE 13.15 NASA MyNASA Utility Page with Grid Overlay[23]

The NASA site provides a number of utilities to enhance users' experience of the site. These include links to tools that adjust delivery of the site depending on users' bandwidth, a search engine, and — as illustrated to the right — the opportunity to customize the site.

This screenshot also includes the footer, which appears on every NASA page. Footers can be used to repeat site identification and mirror site navigation at the bottom of pages. Other information commonly found at the bottom of pages includes the site author's name, Web manager's name, last date updated, and/or contact information.

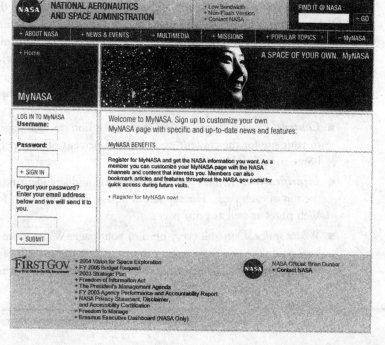

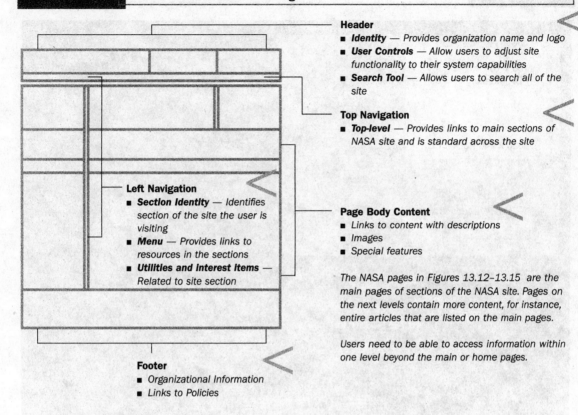

FIGURE 13.16 Basic Grid for NASA Web Pages

content and navigation. ("White space," of course, may not be white on the Web but will be your background color.)

- **Scrolling.** Prevent horizontal scrolling. General consensus among user-testing experts is that people accept a reasonable amount of top-to-bottom page scrolling, which is actually preferable to excessive "click through." Left-to-right scrolling in almost all cases is not tolerated well at all.

Figure 13.17 illustrates the differences in screen real estate for various monitors and devices.

Color. Use color both to highlight different areas of screen displays and to unify the site. Generally, designers choose a palette of a few colors for an individual site. Color can orient users on the site, identify navigation, and signal types of content.

Color should do more than just create interest; it should function as an integral part of the information that users need. Color lets users know where they are on your site and differentiates functions or elements on pages. For instance, in-text links on Web pages are generally all the same color so that people can recognize what text contains links.

FIGURE 13.17 Display Sizes

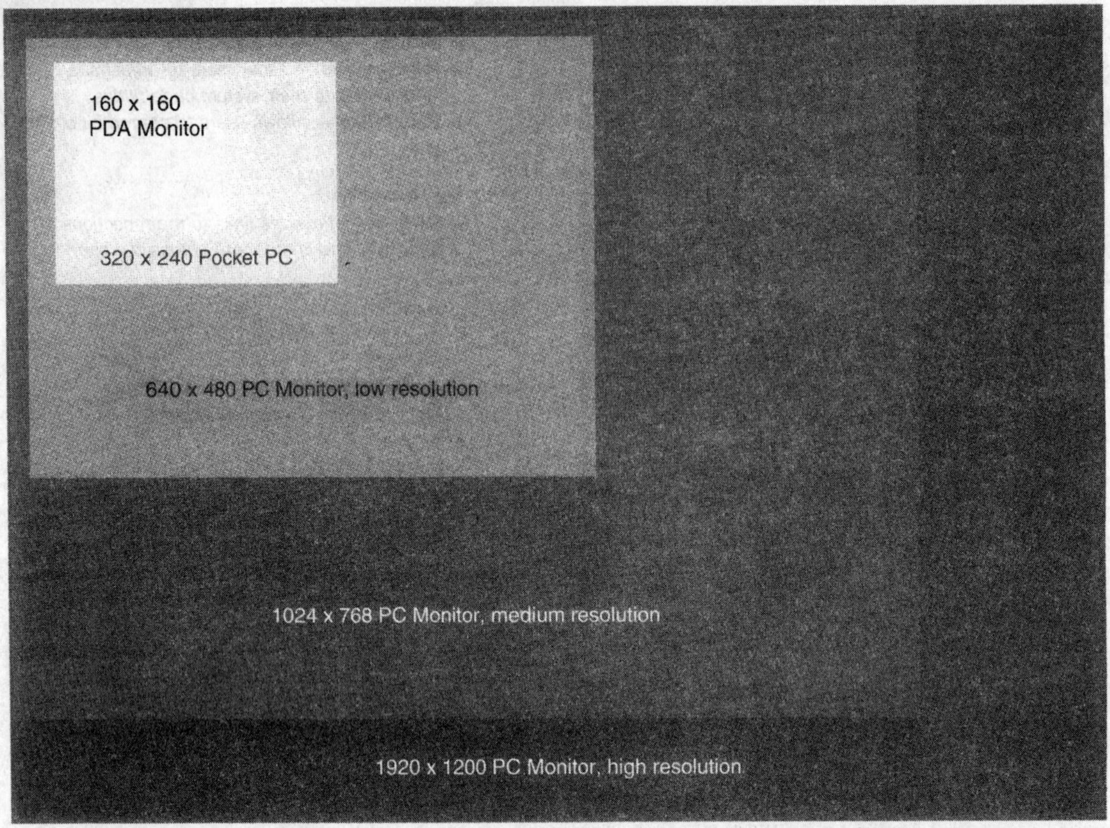

160 x 160 PDA Monitor

320 x 240 Pocket PC

640 x 480 PC Monitor, low resolution

1024 x 768 PC Monitor, medium resolution

1920 x 1200 PC Monitor, high resolution

Think about color as you are planning your development project. Establish a coordinated color palette before putting your site together so that the colors are consistent throughout and complement the purpose of your site. The palette should include background colors for various elements of the site (for instance, navigation areas and text areas), text colors (for body text, heading texts, links, and other types of text), and accent colors (for arrows, buttons, dividers, etc.). Coordinate your palette with the site's graphics. If you are unfamiliar with color coordination, get advice from someone with graphic design experience. If you are designing for a company or organization, follow its identity guidelines, which typically include the use of specific colors.

In choosing background and text color, ensure high contrast between your background color and text color so that the text is easy to read. Although black text on a pale background may not seem exciting, it is still the most readable choice for large areas of text. Avoid backgrounds containing patterns, designs, or images that reduce the legibility or obscure your text and compete with other graphics.

> Avoid problem color combinations. Red on green, for instance, causes difficulty for people with some types of color blindness and makes reading more difficult in general.

> Avoid placing text over patterned backgrounds. Reading information on computer screens is more difficult than reading in print because of the lower screen resolution. Busy backgrounds place additional demands on readers.

Color on a computer screen is produced by combining three colors (red, green, and blue). These three colors make up all colors viewable on a computer monitor. All three colors at 100 percent of their value make white, and the complete absence of all three makes black. Various percentages of each make up 16.7 million colors. Until a few years ago, computers were very restricted in the number of colors they could display. In addition, different computer platforms also used different color palettes; both Macs and PCs had 256 colors in their system palettes, but only 216 of them were the same. To ensure that colors displayed the same way across platforms, Web designers generally restricted themselves to using a Web-safe color palette of 216 colors common to both Windows and Mac computers.

By 1999, however, almost 90 percent of computers that were in use could display colors into the thousands.[24] Even now, though, because the problem of browser compatibility persists to some degree and because Web pages are being served to handheld devices, WebTV, and other platforms, you will get consistent results by continuing to use a Web-safe browser palette. Colors are associated with codes made up of combinations of 6 letters and numbers. For instance, the code for white is #FFFFFF, and the code for black is #000000. Codes are important because they tell the browsers what colors to display. You should use color numbers in your HTML documents to indicate where you want specific colors to appear. Keep a list handy of the color numbers you are using for each project.

> Selecting Web-safe colors is easy. Many sites provide the hex/decimal codes. To see variations of these sites, including one that automatically identifies the code when you mouse over a color, go to **www.english.wadsworth.com/burnett6e** for links.
>
> CLICK ON WEBLINK
> CLICK on Chapter 13/Web colors

WEBLINK

Graphics. People include graphics on Web sites for several reasons:

- Enhance the design and usability of the information
- Help establish identities for Web sites and create excitement and interest
- Help users navigate by calling attention to links, sections of sites, special features, and different areas of pages
- Provide information to illustrate products to consumers or as integral parts of Web-based articles, reports, or other documents

However, you should not rely only on graphics to convey information about your site because that may affect usability. Browsers can be set to display text only, a feature that some people use to lower the load time of pages. Some browsers do not display graphics at all, and people who use screen readers because of a visual disability do not benefit from graphics unless additional information is provided.

The size of graphic files is an important consideration for consistency because large graphics can slow the load time of information. The larger the file, the longer it takes to load into the browser window. Graphic files can be large, and most of the time are larger than the file for the page that contains the text information. File size doesn't necessarily indicate big images, but rather large files sizes (indicated by the number of kilobytes (K), or computer space they use). In general, you should reduce the file size of graphics as much as possible, balancing the quality loss against the load time.

You can control the size of graphics files through your choice of image format. Graphics for electronic display come in a wide variety of file types for different purposes. Three types of image formats are especially useful for display on monitors:

- **JPG image (pronounced "j-peg")** — named for the Joint Photographic Experts Group that created the type — works well for photographic images, images with a high number of colors (above 265), and images with graduated color.
- **GIF image (pronounced "gif" or "jif")** — short for Graphics Interchange Format developed by Compuserve — works well for images with "flat" color areas, transparent images (when you want to have the background of your site show through part of the image), and for small images such as icons. Gifs manage up to 256 colors.
- **PNG image (pronounced "ping")** — for Portable Network Graphics — is a new graphics type that promises to offer qualities of both .jpgs and .gifs with smaller file sizes. However, older browsers do not support this image type, and some graphic production software packages do not include the capability of saving images in the .png format.

The examples on the next page illustrate some of the qualities of .jpgs and .gifs, the two most used types of graphics.

FIGURE 13.18   Web Graphic Examples[25]

(rubber duck photo)	(rubber duck photo)	(big masks image)	(big masks image)
Ducky	Ducky	(small masks image)	(small masks image)
The photo of the rubber duck **(9 KB)** and the word "Ducky" **(2 KB)** are .jpg images.	The photo of the rubber duck **(5 KB)** and the word "Ducky" **(1 KB)** are .gif images.	The big masks **(25 KB)** and the small masks **(7 KB)** are .jpg images.	The big masks **(5 KB)** and small mask **(2 KB)**, are .gif images.
The .jpg files render photographic images more smoothly. However, the file sizes of the .jpg images are larger. You need to decide when you can sacrifice load time for clarity in photographic images. Small pictures of people, for instance, might be worth the extra wait.		Here, large .jpg image file size is quite large compared to .gif image file size — five times larger. However, in the case of flat colors, the .gif is just as clear as the .jpg, so the extra size of the .gif image is not worth the space.	

Graphics files, particularly .jpg files, can be optimized for the Web, which means reducing the file size and, thus, the quality. Generally, programs for creating and adjusting graphics, such as Adobe Photoshop, have tools for optimizing graphics. For graphics that enhance the design and usability of Web sites, follow several useful rules of thumb:

- *Balance graphics and text on a page.* Graphics should not overwhelm your text.
- *Coordinate graphics throughout a site.* Too many different types of graphics confuse rather than help users.
- *Keep size of image files as small as possible to reduce load time.* The size of image files (the K) depends on the type of image used and the procedures to create and save the image.
- *Notify users when you must include a slow-loading graphic.* A message such as "Please wait for image to load" tells users that you are sensitive to users' needs and that the image may be worth waiting for.

- ***Use larger images on lower-level pages.*** If people are satisfied with the design and navigation of your home page, they are more likely to tolerate additional load times on lower-level pages if the graphics are informative and useful.

- ***Don't rely on images alone to convey information.*** People sometimes set browsers to display text only because of excessive load times. Some people use text-only browsers, like Lynx, and people with visual disabilities may use screen readers that rely on text information only. These users rely on alternate text information to be included with graphics.

You can obtain graphics by using software to create your own or by converting them from images you draw or photos you take. Software packages often include generic graphics (clip art) that you can use, although clip art is generally overused and often becomes a visual cliche. A number of sites on the Web also offer free images that you can download and use. When you use graphics from clip art files or from Web sites, read any rules of use or permissions that protect the images. For instance, some permissions allow you to use graphics if you credit the creators on your site. Others allow you to use graphics for nonprofit reasons but not to resell or to use on an e-commerce site. You may not just take graphics from sites and use them on your own. That is copyright infringement.

When designing information for small-screen devices such as PDAs and cell phones, consider that the graphic capabilities for these devices are more limited than PCs and laptops. Small-screen device displays have a much lower resolution and fewer colors. When — and if — you use graphics in content targeted for these devices, use simple graphics that contain only a few basic colors and ensure that the graphics are necessary.

Developing Effective Content 建立有效內容

People must sift through massive amounts of information daily, particularly on the Internet, which means that writing and managing content are critical to the usefulness and usability of electronic information. The best screen layout in the world and the most interesting bells and whistles are useless if content is missing, inaccurate, inadequate, poorly written, or hard to use. Two aspects of content to consider when developing for electronic communication include writing effectively and ensuring credibility.

Writing for Electronic Communication. Writing for electronic media is different than writing for print. People read less and skim more online. Because of the possibilities offered by hyperlinking, people also move quickly among various pages and sites. Your content should facilitate the ways that users locate and read electronic information. Author Steve Outing, writing in the online publication *Editor & Publisher Interactive,* summarizes some of the advice given by Crawford Kilian in his book, *Writing for the Web.*[26]

- **Be concise.** Low-resolution computer screens make reading from a monitor more difficult than reading on paper. Reading from a monitor can be 25 percent slower than reading on paper.
- **Keep chunks of text short.** Readers of electronic documents need minimal text. Write chunks of text between 150 and 200 words, then edit so you get each chunk to about 60 words. Kilian advises that writers "pack the maximum meaning into the minimum text, so your readers will get the message in the shortest possible time."
- **Use headings and bulleted lists.** Long paragraphs don't work well on computer screens. Instead, use headings and bulleted lists so users can scan the text easily.
- **Use active voice.** Active voice identifies the doer of the action, so the action is clearer and readers are more engaged. Say "You need to review the budget" or "The committee needs to review the budget" rather than "The budget needs to be reviewed."
- **Consider international readers.** The whole world may read your message. Your text may be read in Australia, Germany, Israel, Japan, Saudi Arabia, South Africa, and Venezuela; therefore, avoid culture-specific idioms and metaphors.
- **Use an "inverted pyramid" structure for organizing information.** Similar to news reporting, your text should include the important information up front, followed by the details. People are going to scan your text, so make the critical information easy to find.
- **Limit in-text links to other sites and provide information about the links you do include.** Content on the Web is sometimes littered with links and long "hotlists" that contain links with no explanation of what users can expect on the other end. Many users find themselves linking from a page of links with little content to other pages of links with little content.

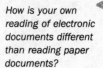

How is your own reading of electronic documents different than reading paper documents?

What ways of presenting information do you prefer when you're reading electronic documents?

Sites often contain reports, white papers, and articles that are essential for users of information. Consider archiving longer documents for download in .pdf or other formats and providing brief summaries of these materials, using guidelines for Web writing.

If you're interested in how people read on the Web, go to **www.english.wadsworth.com/burnett6e** for a link to what usability expert Jakob Nielsen has to say.
  CLICK ON WEBLINK
    CLICK on Chapter 13/reading electronic documents

WEBLINK

The need for extreme brevity is essential for information accessed via handheld devices. Web expert Mark Pearrow explains that the content for many types of PDAs "is based on decks of small cards, each of which is tiny enough to be just about displayed on a single screen."[27] When the information is more than can be managed on a card, information may be condensed automatically to accommodate the display. Since you can't know how the adjusted content might be read or what information might be excluded, you need to ensure that your content is designed to be efficiently and effectively managed on a PDA. Also important in the small device environment is management of linking. More linking and more site-level depth helps keep the page length short.

Building Credibility. In all situations involving information, people want to be able to trust the accuracy of what they read. Although print media doesn't always guarantee the accuracy of information, the fluidity of electronic information make determining and developing credibility challenging. While publishing information in print form often includes review processes that help separate accurate information from junk, widespread access to the Internet means that just about anyone can author and disseminate information.

Designers and users of information need to critically consider how to establish credibility of electronic information. B. J. Fogg, a researcher at Stanford University's Persuasive Technology Lab, has developed guidelines for building information credibility in electronic environments. The guidelines in Figure 13.19 can also be used to evaluate the credibility of sites you visit.

Standards and Tools
标准与工具

Information designers use standards and other tools to create content and maintain consistency across multiple-page Web sites. Standards include definitions of site elements and processes for implementing design decisions. Though good standards may take time to develop initially, they can improve efficiency and reduce the costs of future development and maintenance because the products of many design tasks can be reused. Some standards, such as the scripting languages that allow electronic information to appear in browsers, are industry standards that have been developed and adopted over time. Documentation, such as style guides and code libraries, are used during development and for maintenance after development.

Markup Languages, Scripts, and Programming
置标语言、文字及程序

Documents on the World Wide Web are "marked up" with HTML. HTML is not programming. It is a system of tags that, when inserted into plain-text documents, tell Web browsers how to display documents. Writing documents using HTML enables your documents to be displayed on any computer that has a Web browser and an Internet connection, whether a Mac, PC, or UNIX-based workstation. HTML tags also control the appearance of pages on a screen.

FIGURE 13.19 Guidelines for Building Credibility[28]

Guidelines	Comments
1. Simplify the process of verifying the accuracy of information on your site.	Provide third-party support (citations, references, source material) for information you present, especially if you link to this evidence. Even if people don't follow these links, you've shown confidence in your content.
2. Show the actual organization sponsoring your site.	Show that your Web site represents a legitimate organization. The easiest way to do this is by listing a physical address. You can also post a photo of your offices or list membership in the Chamber of Commerce or other credible organizations.
3. Highlight the expertise of people in your organization and of the content and services you provide.	Provide information about in-house expertise. Do you have experts on your team? Are your contributors or service providers authorities? Be sure to give their credentials. Are you affiliated with a respected organization? Make that clear. Conversely, don't link to outside sites that are not credible; your site becomes less credible simply by association.
4. Show that honest and trustworthy people stand behind your site.	Show the actual people behind your site and in your organization. Find ways to convey their trustworthiness through images or text. For example, some sites post employee bios that tell about community involvement, family, or hobbies.
5. Make contacting you easy.	Make your contact information clear: phone number, physical address, and e-mail address.
6. Design your site so it looks professional (or is appropriate for your purpose).	Pay attention to factors such as layout, typography, images, and consistency. Some people quickly evaluate a site by visual design. The visual design should match the site's purpose.
7. Make your site easy to use — and useful.	Make sites easy to use and useful. Some site operators neglect users by self-aggrandizement or using excessive animation.
8. Update your site's content often; review it regularly.	Indicate the date the site was updated. People believe sites are more credible if they have been recently updated or reviewed.
9. Limit promotional content such as ads or special offers.	If possible, avoid having ads (especially pop-up ads) on your site. If you must accept advertising, clearly distinguish the sponsored content from your own.
10. Avoid errors of all types, no matter how small.	Avoid all errors. Typographical errors and broken links severely damage a site's credibility.

HTML has been revised several times and is being supplemented (and in some cases replaced) by newer markup languages. Other types of scripting tools and programming languages now work with HTML to deliver rich graphic and interactive electronic content. In addition, the development of new types of hardware and connectivity has required markup and programming languages to function with the new tools. Figure 13.20 lists several types of markup languages, scripting tools, and programming languages that you will encounter. You may not need to be a computer programmer to design electronic communication, but you should know the tools and their use.

Pages that display electronic content are plain-text documents that can be created in any text editor. However, programs are available that streamline the design process, help manage site structure and files, and allow designers with little HTML knowledge or experience to create Web pages. Some popular development programs for Web pages include Macromedia's Dreamweaver, Microsoft's Frontpage, and Adobe's GoLive.

Style Sheets and Templates 格式模板

Cascading style sheets manage the appearance of Web pages across a site. Style sheets contain information about elements such as fonts, heading levels, colors, and backgrounds. One cascading style sheet can be used to coordinate the appearance of hundreds of Web pages. If, for instance, you want the font on all your pages to be the same type style, size, and color, using a cascading style sheet ensures consistency. In addition, if you want to change the appearance of an element managed by a style sheet across the whole site, you can change one style sheet, rather than hundreds of individual Web pages.

Templates can also be used to manage the layout of Web pages. Greeked templates, which are examples filled in with "fake" content, can be used early in the development process to test the usability of a design before content is added. Greeked content can also contain styles used for the actual content.

Code libraries contain reusable scripts and codes that can be "plugged into" new pages and sites. Reusing programming for forms and other functional aspects of Web sites saves development time and ensures consistency in function.

Style Guides 格式指南

Style guides include information about the way that particular information is designed and should be maintained. Style guides can include a variety of information, from color and text choices to guidelines for writing and incorporating graphics. Though creating a style guide takes a little time, the effort is usually worthwhile, particularly in maintenance time and expense.

FIGURE 13.20 Summary of Widely Used Tools

Tags, Scripts, Styles, and Programming	Description	Web/Internet	Wireless	Client Side	Server Side
HTML	**HyperText Markup Language** is a system of tags that make up the basic markup language for the Web.	✔	✔	✔	
HTML 4.0	**HTML 4.0** is the newest version of HTML currently in use. This standard offers more types of tags but is a stricter form of HTML, which means that designers must be more careful about using tags. Browsers are moving towards accommodating this standard as a replacement for HTML.	✔	✔	✔	
DHTML	**Dynamic HTML** combines HML with other programming and scripting languages to provide interactivity and animation.	✔		✔	
XML	**eXtensible Markup Language** is a "metalanguage" for development. It does not include specific tags like HTML; instead, it contains rules for creating tags that can be used to format many types of documents. For example, XML helps information designers create content once and then format it for a variety of media.				
XHTML 1.0	**eXtensible HyperText Markup Language** combines properties of HTML and XML. As with HTML 4.0, this transitional standard offers more design capabilities for designing content and may be used in place of HTML.	✔	✔	✔	
JavaScript	**JavaScript** is a scripting language that shares features of some programming languages. JavaScript enables some functionality on Web pages, such as roll-over images and drop-down menus.	✔		✔	
CGI	**Common Gateway Interface** applies to several types of programming languages — for example, Perl is particularly popular for Web development projects — that process interactive Web content between clients and servers. For instance, CGI is required to receive and display information from Web-based forms.	✔			✔
PHP	**Hypertext Preprocessor** is a scripting language that works with HTML. It resides on the server and allows the creation of dynamic content. PHP works well with databases and can interact with various types of resources across the Internet, not just the Web.	✔			✔
WML	**Wireless Markup Language,** which derives from XML, is used to display information on wireless phones and some other types of handheld devices.		✔		
WAP	**Wireless Application Protocol** allows users to access information on handheld devices.		✔		
CSS	**Cascading Style Sheets** are used with HTML and XHTML to control the appearance of Web pages. CSS can be stored in a separate file from content pages and linked to them.	✔			

Understanding the Iterative Design Process
理解设计过程

The consistency of all aspects of an electronic communication environment is important for usability. Establishing and maintaining consistency requires coordination during the design process. In addition, maintenance procedures must be documented to ensure that consistency is continued as the site is updated. Consistency is a basic usability principle because it reduces the time users need to learn your site and the number of problems they have using your site.

Planning the Iterative Process 计划设计过程

Creating a project plan is essential, whether you are developing a site alone or as part of a team. Before you start developing a site, you need to know its purpose and scope, the overall look and feel, the resources you'll need, limitations you must contend with, and the schedule, all of which you will define and explain in the project plan.

During development, the project plan helps the development team stay on track by providing guidelines that everyone can consult. If you are developing a Web site for your company, another company, or other organization, a project plan often becomes part of your proposal. Of course, you will need to make adjustments during the project, for instance, as a result of user responses in testing. Maintain the plan throughout the project and include any changes that you make. Your project plans should address some or all of the issues identified in Figure 13.21, depending on the purpose and scope of the site.

Analyzing Existing Sites 分析已有网站

Begin the development process by analyzing existing electronic communication. The analytical process allows you to identify sites that provide information, products, or services similar to yours and provides an opportunity to test the usability of others' sites before developing your own. Analyzing other sites can cut your planning time by allowing you to identify what works and what doesn't. The goal is not to copy other sites but to learn from them. Find sites that interest you and see how well they work. As you analyze sites, identify specific design features that caused problems and those that worked well. The worksheet in Figure 13.22 can also be used to assess your own site during and after development. To complete a fair assessment, you need to actually use a site rather than just look at it.

- What's available for user response or feedback?
- How many clicks from the home page do you need to read actual content? In general, three clicks is reasonable, five is acceptable, and beyond five difficult to manage and very annoying.
- How much time is needed to download? Is the maximum download time within acceptable limits, that is, 10 seconds?

In addition to developing your own analysis guided by the questions in Figure 13.22, you may want to conduct some preliminary usability testing of these sites. This testing may be minimal, involving only three or four users, to give you a preliminary sense of how people interact with various sites. Of course, as your project develops, you will need to regularly conduct usability testing sessions on various portions of your site. This testing lets you make changes as you go along, so each iteration of the site eliminates problems identified by test participants.

Creating Prototypes of Your Web Site 创建你的网站原型

Creating prototypes, which occurs early in the design process, involves developing mock-ups of ideas for your Web site and brainstorming those ideas with team members, clients, and possibly potential users. This allows you to get feedback about your ideas before a significant amount of time, resources, and effort go into development.

Initially, you should develop low-tech storyboards as prototypes of the site. For example, try using simple index cards as "pages" of your site. Draft a scenario explaining the site and its goals. Write page names on index cards (and/or a description of site content). Meet with your team as well as clients and representative users if possible. Using a large board, tape or pin the cards to it, creating a simple display of the proposed site content and architecture. This storyboarding task helps you answer several questions:

- Is the content sufficient and useful?
- Are the names of site areas and pages helpful?
- Does the organization make sense?
- Are the pages of information in the appropriate categories and areas of the site?

Ask team members, clients, and users to comment on and make suggestions about proposed names, content, and architecture. Changes are easy to complete on the spot by writing new index cards and moving others around the board.

Why is using a low-tech storyboard often more productive when done collaboratively rather than when done individually?

From developing low-tech prototypes, you can go on to develop more complete outlines. Keep the initial designs simple. Sketch the page design and possible site structure by creating a small number of linked pages. You don't need actual content and graphics at this point; you'll be testing primarily for overall functionality and usability of the page design. Develop two or three prototypes from your best ideas and then get feedback from team members, clients, and users before proceeding.

Coordinating the Process 协调过程

Coordination requires both a team effort and a central authority. Early in the design process, the results of testing prototypes help developers decide which features and design elements work best. The team should have a shared vision of the ultimate look and feel of the site. Particularly on a large project, a project manager or steering committee should coordinate all aspects of a project so the site is coherent and consistent.

FIGURE 13.21 Questions and Tasks for Web Site Development

AREA	QUESTIONS AND TASKS
DEVELOPMENT	
Purpose(s)	■ What is the purpose of the site? **TASK:** Write a brief statement articulating as clearly as possible the primary and secondary purposes of the Web site.
Intended Audience(s)	■ Who is the primary audience for the Web site? Secondary audiences? ■ What information will they need to use your site? What tasks should they be able to complete? **TASK:** Develop user and task analyses and attach them to the project plan.
Project Requirements	■ What are the client's project requirements? ■ Can these project requirements be met? Which will need to be adjusted and in what ways? **TASK:** List any project requirements from the client. Categorize the requirements by area (i.e., content, design, graphics, technology, reporting, etc.).
REQUIREMENTS	
Project Resources	■ What hardware is required for development (computers, scanners, printers, servers)? ■ What software is required for development (for example, designing and creating pages, managing site structure and links, designing and creating graphics, project management, mounting site to server)? ■ What server capabilities are required/available? Where is the server on which the site will be mounted? Who can access the server, and mount and manage files? **TASK:** Identify what hardware and software are available and where they are located. Determine the necessary server information and supervision.
User Technology	■ What platform/browser combinations are you designing for? **TASK:** Create a matrix and indicate the combinations that you anticipate designing for. Your goal should be to accommodate users' technology to the maximum degree possible. However, if you choose not to accommodate older browsers or some platforms, provide a rationale.

	Netscape Nav 4.x	Netscape Nav 6.x	IE 4.x	IE 6.x	Other
Mac					
PC					
Handheld					
28.K modem					
56.K modem					
Broadband					
Wireless					
Other					

FIGURE 13.21 Questions and Tasks for Web Site Development (continued)

AREA	QUESTIONS AND TASKS
REQUIREMENTS	
Project Timeline and Milestones	▪ What is the deadline for delivery of the project? ***TASK:*** Moving backwards from the completion date, schedule all activities and milestones.
Teams/Team Member Responsibilities	▪ What are the human resource requirements for the project? ***TASK:*** List teams and responsibilities. List all specialties required for the project and the number of people needed to complete tasks: Graphic designers? Programmers? Database developers? Writers? Site designers? Multimedia experts? Match available personnel to responsibilities and teams.
PROJECT MANAGEMENT	
Communication	▪ How will the project be managed? How will team activities be coordinated? ▪ What are the proposal requirements (if any)? To whom will it be delivered? ▪ What status updates are required and for whom? ▪ What materials will be provided to client? Archived? ▪ How will change management be handled (process by which changes are documented, reported, approved, and implemented)? ***TASK:*** Provide an organizational chart to identify the team members and their responsibilities. Write the project specifications. Create a Gantt or PERT chart.
Documentation	▪ What documentation is required on the site (FAQ, help, etc.)? ▪ What documentation is required for site maintenance (e.g., style guide, instructions, templates)? ***TASK***: Identify the documentation required.
Quality Assurance	▪ What testing will be completed? When will testing be completed? ▪ What resources are required for testing? ***TASK:*** Create a testing plan.
Site Design/ Navigation	▪ What does the site architecture look like? ▪ What do the pages look like? ▪ What are some key paths users might take? ***TASK:*** Create the site architecture on paper. Create a storyboard of the key pages and paths. Develop names for projected section, page of the site. Prototype the site.
Content	▪ What content is to be provided on the site? How will content be acquired? ▪ What subject matter experts (SMEs) are needed to develop site content? ▪ What writing conventions will be followed? ***TASK:*** List content provided by client and content to be developed. Identify SMEs. Determine appropriate tone and style as well as spelling and naming conventions. Prepare a style guide. Write sample content to review and test.
Visuals	▪ What types of visuals are required? For site design? For content? ▪ How will visuals be created/acquired? ***TASK:*** Select and/or design the visuals.

FIGURE 13.22 — Worksheet for Website Assessment

Ratings: (4) Excellent, (3) Acceptable, (2) Weak, (1) Unacceptable, (N/A) Not Applicable

Site address: _____
Type/purpose of site: _____

Site Features	Rating	Site Features	Rating
Context		**Content**	
Sponsorship and affiliation evident and visible		Up to date	
Information easily available		Accurate and error-free	
Perspective/persuasion (news, opinion, etc.)		Verifiable	
Advertising		Reliable	
		Research-based	
		Sources listed	
Audience		Contact information provided	
Reader benefits obvious			
Appropriate for intended audience		**Visuals**	
Responses to customer queries/feedback		Relevant	
		Consistent	
Information Architecture		Aid navigation	
Clear navigation		Load time	
Type(s) and usability of navigation (list)			
Names of pages consistent		**Usability/Accessibility**	
Clicks between home page and information		Maximum download acceptable	
Use of lists, headings		Names of links consistent	
Inclusion of relevant links		Text and links readable	
		Functions on multiple platforms/browsers	
Page Design		Alt tags included with graphics	
Logical balance: content, graphics, navigation		Title tags included with links	
Effective use of white space		Help and use information provided	
Consistent use of color		All pages identified; site ID on all pages	
Use of headings aids navigation		Site map, index, or search functions	
Appropriate for rhetorical situation			
Site design consistent			

Ensuring Usability and Accessibility
确保可用性和可访性

People involved in professional communication must be aware of accessible design concepts as they relate to information development and management. Although tools like special hardware and software can help users who have disabilities, they will not make up for inaccessible information design. Developers need to follow these useful practices:

- Understand the opportunities and limitations of the virtual environment and its potential users.
- Know something about the assistive hardware and software available and be aware of how the design of electronic information could impact the technology your audience may be using.
- Concentrate on good design principles and integration rather than on what "cool" things you can do with programming languages, unless those functions help the majority of your audience receive the information and services you are offering.
- Use various methods for providing information so that you accommodate the greatest number of visitors.

WEBLINK

The more we learn about the ways that users interact with Web sites, the more that older, static sites need to be redesigned. The lessons learned from CancerNet, a Web site that provides current and accurate cancer information from the National Cancer Institute (NCI), the federal government's principal agency for cancer research, is very useful. It summarizes and illustrates data collection and user analysis, iterative prototype development, usability testing, and site launching. Go to www.english.wadsworth.com/burnett6e for a link.
   CLICK ON WEBLINK
      CLICK on Chapter 13/Web redesign success

Features of Accessible Electronic Communication
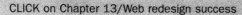
可访性电子交流特点

Developers can do a number of very simple things to help audiences better access their electronic communication environments:

- ***Provide alternative representations of information.*** Give people choices of page displays, such as with or without frames; graphic and text or text only; with or without audio; or large-font text displays. This doesn't mean just taking the page and stripping out the "cool stuff." This is about considering each rendition on its own merits.

MEETING THE CHALLENGES OF A WEB ACCESSIBILITY POLICY

面对网站可访性原则的挑战

University Web sites have a challenging array of audiences, including former, current, and potential students. The Emporia State University (ESU) Web presence originated in the mid-1990s as a way to share the wealth of knowledge at ESU with enrolled students. It developed without much oversight regarding design or accessibility into a massive compilation of sites that form a Web presence that reaches worldwide.

When the state of Kansas mandated that all agencies in the state incorporate accessibility guidelines into their Web development policy, ESU realized the complex implications of displaying information on the Internet.

Identifying the Challenges. Implementation of the Kansas Web Content Accessibility Guidelines (KWAG) was met with fierce resistance because current Web development practices would have to change. These changes presented four areas of challenges affecting the production of high-quality Web sites:

1. *Institution environment:* Balance was needed between administrative autonomy and technical experience.
   - Politics — From the inception of the university Web site, departments were given absolute control over their respective sites.
   - Technical reality — Many departments assigned office staff who had little or no skill in implementing any type of guidelines.

2. *Perceptions about the significance of the policy:* Balance was needed between the mandated changes and information about the importance of the changes.
   - Communication gap — Many stakeholders did not understand the significance of producing accessible Web pages.

3. *Resistance to change.* Institutional compliance and consistency needed to be balanced by creativity and academic freedom.
   - Ongoing resistance — Many stakeholders believed the policy detracted from creativity and academic freedom.

4. **Support for implementation.** Balance was needed between people's Web design and site management skills and their need to understand the impact of the policy change.
   - Knowledge gap — Many department Web managers lacked the basic skills to maintain a quality web site.
   - Policy problems — Many individuals at the university were unable to determine the ways in which the policy affected them.

Example of an Accessibility Persona

Making the ESU Web Accessible to Stephanie

Stephanie is an 18-year-old who is scheduled to attend ESU in the fall. She is deaf and has low vision. She uses a screen magnifier to enlarge the text on Web sites to a font size that she can read. When screen magnification is not sufficient, she also uses a screen reader to relate to a braille display.

To skim through the Kansas Web Content Accessibility Guidelines, go to **www.english.wadsworth.com/burnett6e** for a link.
   CLICK ON WEBLINK
   CLICK on Chapter 13/KWAG

WEBLINK

Stephanie has been able to enroll at ESU through the admissions Web site because the online enrollment form uses the appropriate form labels specified by KWCAG.

Stephanie is able to use much of the Web site because of accessible design in a number of important areas:
· style sheets · accessible multimedia · device-independent access · labeled frames
· appropriate form labels · table markup

Departments that don't follow the KWAG are inaccessible to Stephanie; thus, she is unable to use those university services.

Meeting the Challenges. Implementing new policy guidelines requires a common knowledge base, so ESU developed a four-part process:
- Develop personas to illustrate the legitimacy of following Web development standards such as the KWCAG.
- Develop templates that meet both state and university Web standards.
- Hold workshops that cover basic Web page management activities.
- Provide an open forum where information technology development and strategies can be discussed freely and without consequence.

Organizations regularly must decide to take the time to develop an information system the right way or to create a quick fix, which more than likely ignores multiple issues that will need to be addressed in the future.

One way to do things right from the beginning is to develop *accessibility personas*, like the one for Stephanie in the sidebar. Accessibility personas are composites representing individuals who are members of specific groups of ESU Internet users. These personas are created by grouping critical user characteristics (much like you'd do in writing usability scenarios). The likely users of one site can be represented by creating a series of personas. Such personas help personalize the legitimacy of conforming to Web standards, as the example of Stephanie shows.

Do they work? Yes. Development teams that write accessibility personas tend to create more accessible sites that are responsive to user needs.

Zachary Lavicky is the webmaster at Emporia State University. He has a seat on the State of Kansas Web Accessibility Subcommittee, where he is involved in developing and implementing Web Accessibility Standards for the state of Kansas.

- **Use alternative tagging ("ALT" tags).** When a user places the mouse on a graphic, the alternative tag enables a pop-up box with a simple text explanation of a function, link, or graphic.
- **Add transcripts and captioning to audio.** If people can't hear the audio, they won't get your message.

While these suggestions won't solve all the accessibility problems with Web-based information, they will go a long way in making that information available to a much larger audience.

Checking Web Sites for Accessibility 检查网站的可访问性

In addition to paying attention to accessible design principles, you should ensure that your Web sites are accessible by conducting usability tests through the development process. As you develop information for electronic media, ensure that your design serves people with varying needs. Design and implement a testing program that includes diverse users. Also consider using online testing services such as the World Wide Web Consortium's free HTML Validator Service.

WEBLINK

A number of useful guides to developing usable Web sites are available on the Web. Go to www.english.wadsworth.com/burnett6e for a list of links.
CLICK ON WEBLINK
CLICK on Chapter 13/Guides to usability

Individual and Collaborative Assignments
个人作业和小组作业

1. **Identify accessibility, comprehensibility, and usability**

    (a) Work in a small group to visit any three of the following Web home pages, which represent a range of national and multinational corporations as well as not-for-profit organizations.

www.admworld.com	www.nestle.com	www.ups.com
www.fedex.com	www.oracle.com	www.cocacola.com
www.dupont.com	www.birdseye.com	www.merck.com
www.bayerus.com	www.lucent.com	www.whymilk.com

    Consider these questions:

    - **Who's the sponsor?** Can users easily identify a name, logo, and tag line on the home page describing what the organization does?
    - **Who are the intended audiences?** Who are the probable users? What are their purposes for using the site?

- *How accessible is the site?* To whom is the site accessible? To users reading other languages? To users with visual disabilities? To users with limited or old computer resources? Does the home page have distracting or competing elements?
- *How easy is the site to understand?* Can users easily determine what's most important on the home page? What prior knowledge is assumed? What conventions does the home page use? What is the technical level of definitions and explanations?
- *How easy is the site to use?* How easily can users determine the site's organization from the home page? Can users find a clear place to start? How are links to other parts of the site indicated? How easy is the site to navigate?

(b) Summarize your findings in an online guide for Web site designers who are interested in identifying what users see as successful practices. Provide specific examples (correctly documented) from your visits to the Web sites.

(c) Summarize your findings in a collaborative memo written to the sponsor of one of the Web sites, highlighting the strengths and recommending improvements. Provide specific examples from your visits to the Web site.

2. **Compare impact of screen size.** Work individually to identify several Web sites that provide information in formats for both PCs and for PDAs. Compare the ways that information is displayed in each medium.

- What are the differences in screen display?
- What are the differences in the ways content is presented?
- What is gained or lost in the different screen sizes? In content? In convenience?

3. **Credibility of Web sites.** Individually select three companies as your top choices for employment and locate their Web sites. Then use the criteria in Figure 13.19, Guidelines for Building Credibility, to assess each Web site for credibility. Create an effective way to summarize your findings for each organization (for example, matrixes, paragraph descriptions, checklists). Rank order the three organizations according to your findings. Then prepare a 5–8 minute oral presentation for your class in which you summarize and support your findings.

4. **Credibility of nonprofit organizations.** Work with a small group to select the Web sites of four or five nonprofit organizations to assess their credibility. Use the criteria in Figure 13.19, Guidelines for Building Credibility, to assess each Web site for credibility. Do the task collaboratively, discussing the ways in which each criterion can be applied.

Create an effective way to summarize your findings for each organization. Rank order these nonprofit organizations according to your collective decisions. Then prepare a 5–8 minute oral presentation for your class in which you summarize and support your findings.

5. **Assess the usability of your university's Web site.** Work with a small group to assess your own university's Web site.

   (a) Use the criteria in Figure 13.22, Worksheet for Website Assessment, to consider these seven categories: context, audience, information architecture, page design, site features, visuals, and usability/accessibility. Rate each item as (4) excellent, (3) acceptable, (2) weak, (1) unacceptable, or (N/A) not applicable. Do the task collaboratively, discussing what contributes to the rating in each category. Be able to point to at least two aspects of the site that contribute to the rating in each category.

   (b) Based on your assessment, create a list of ways to improve the site.

   (c) Prepare a memo about your assessment and recommendations to submit to the university's webmaster.

6. **Create a prototype for a Web site.** Work with a small group to select a small organization that would like to create or significantly update a Web site. This organization will be your client. Interview the key people in the organization to learn what they believe their users need/expect/want on the site. Two tools from this chapter will be especially useful: Figure 13.21, Questions and Tasks for Web Site Development, and Figure 13.16, Basic Grid for NASA Web Pages. First, complete the tasks in Figure 13.21, which includes creating a prototype of the site with index cards to create a storyboard. As part of this process, sketch the grid. See if that grid can be used with only slight modifications for each page on the site, so that you have consistency and coherence in the architecture. Prepare a memo about your prototype, including the prototype, for your client.

7. **Consider privacy policies.** Visit eight to ten Web sites to locate, read, and assess their privacy policies.

   (a) Figure out a way to record and display your findings. You may need to ask additional questions. In order to have an equitable review of the sites, you need to answer the same questions on each site. Use these questions as a starting point:

   - How easy is locating the privacy policy?
   - Does the site appear to collect information about visitors? If so, what information is collected? How is it collected?
   - Does the site appear to share the collected information? With whom and why?
   - How can users "opt out" of information collection?

(b) Based on your findings, create what you consider to be an excellent privacy policy.

8. **Assess Web writing style.** Visit five Web sites in order to assess their writing style.

    (a) Use the principles of writing for the Web that are presented and discussed in this chapter to evaluate the writing on the sites. Figure out a way to record and display your findings, making sure to include examples that illustrate your points. Consider these questions as a starting point for your analysis:

    - In what ways does the writing conform to principles of effective writing for the Web?
    - In what ways does it fail to conform?

    (b) Choose a passage of content from one of the sites that does not conform to the guidelines. Revise the passage to improve the readability for the Web.

Chapter 13 Endnotes

[1] Compiled from data available from ePaynews.com. (n.d.). *Statistics for mobile commerce.* Retrieved December 21, 2003, from http://www.epaynews.com/statistics/mcommstats.html#39

[2] Winker, M. A., Flanagin, A., Chi-Lum, B., White, J., Andrews, K., Kennett, R. L., et al. (posted 3/17/2000). Principles governing AMA web sites. *Guidelines for Medical and Health Information Sites on the Internet.* Retrieved January 6, 2004, from http://www.ama-assn.org/ama/pub/category/1905.html

[3] Post, A. (2003). *The dangers of spyware* (White Paper). n.p.: Symantec Corporation. Retrieved January 6, 2004, from http://www.symantec.com/avcenter/reference/dangers.of.spyware.pdf

[4] W3C Technology and Society Domain. (n.d.). *Privacy activity statement.* Retrieved January 6, 2004, from http://www.w3.org/Privacy/Activity

[5] Haas, C. (1996). *Writing technology: Studies on the materiality of literacy.* Mahwah, NJ: Lawrence Erlbaum.

[6] McGrane Chauss, K. (1996). Reader as user: Applying interface design techniques to the web. Kairos, 1(2). Retrieved December 21, 2003, from http://english.ttu.edu/kairos/1.2/features/chauss/bridge.html; Retrieved January 3, 2004, from http://www.asis.org/Conferences/Summit2000/Information_Architecture/mcgrane.html

[7] Nielsen, J. (n.d.). *useit.com: Jakob Nielsen's website.* Retrieved January 3, 2004, from http://www.useit.com/

[8] Nielsen, J. (1994). "Response times: The three important limits." *Usability engineering.* San Francisco: Morgan Kaufmann. Retrieved January 3, 2004, from http://www.useit.com/papers/responsetime.html

[9] Nielsen, J. (1997, March 1). *The need for speed.* Retrieved January 3, 2004, from http://www.useit.com/alertbox/9703a.html; and GVU's WWW user survey.(n.d.). Georgia Institute of Technology, GVU Center, College of Computing. Retrieved January 3, 2004, from http://www.cc.gatech.edu/gvu/user_surveys/

[10] Levinson, P. (1997). *Soft edge: A natural history and future of the information revolution* (p. 146). New York: Routledge.

[11] Iowa State University Extension. (1997–2003). *Food safety project.* Retrieved December 16, 2003, from http://www.extension.iastate.edu/foodsafety/

[12] Iowa State University Extension. (n.d.). The consumer control point kitchen. *Food safety project.* Retrieved December 16, 2003, from http://www.extension.iastate.edu/foodsafety/educators/ccp.cfm?articleID=62&parent=2

[13] Iowa State University Extension. (n.d.). The consumer control point kitchen. *Food safety project.* Retrieved December 16, 2003, from http://www.extension.iastate.edu/foodsafety/educators/ccp.cfm?articleID=62&parent=2

[14] Kahn, Paul. (n.d.). *Mapping web sites.* Dynamic Diagrams Seminar on Web Site Planning Diagrams, Visualizing and Analyzing Existing Web Sites. Copyright © 2000 by Dynamic Diagrams, Inc.

[15] Bernard, M., & Hamblin, C. (2003). Cascading versus indexed menu design. *Usability News,* 5(1). Retrieved January 7, 2004, http://psychology.wichita.edu/surl/usabilitynews/51/menu.htm

[16] Adapted from Harrison, C. (2002, October). Hypertext links: Whither thou goest, and why. *First Monday,* 7(10). Retrieved December 16, 2003, from http://firstmonday.org/issues/issue7_10/harrison/index.html

[17] Fermi National Accelerator Laboratory. (n.d.). *Home page.* Retrieved December 10, 2003, from http://www.fnal.gov/; Fermi National Accelerator Laboratory. (n.d.). *Fermilab now.* Retrieved December 10, 2003, from http://www.fnal.gov/pub/now/index.html

[18] Fermi National Accelerator Laboratory. Old Home Page. Retrieved December 10, 2003, from http://www.fnal.gov/pub/help/oldhomepage.jpg

[19] Fermi National Accelerator Laboratory. (n.d.). *History of the FNAL website.* Retrieved December 10, 2003, from http://www.fnal.gov/pub/help/history.html

[20] National Aeronautics and Space Administration. (2004). *NASA news highlights.* Retrieved January 4, 2004, from http://www.nasa.gov/home/index.html

[21] National Aeronautics and Space Administration. (2004). *NASA news highlights.* Retrieved January 4, 2004, from http://www.nasa.gov/home/index.html

[22] National Aeronautics and Space Administration. (2004). *NASA news and events.* Retrieved January 4, 2004, from http://www.nasa.gov/news/highlights/index.html

[23] National Aeronautics and Space Administration. (2004). My NASA. Retrieved January 4, 2004, from http://mynasa.nasa.gov/portal/site/mynasa/index.jsp?bandwidth=high

[24] Nielsen, J. (2000). *Designing web usability* (p. 29). Indianapolis: New Riders Publishing.

[25] Ducky images: Adobe clip art from Adobe Photoshop.
Mask images: Microsoft clip art from MSOffice 2000.

[26] Adapted from Outing, S. (1999, June 18). Some advice on writing, web-style. *E&P Online.*

[27] Pearrow, M. (2002). *The wireless web usability handbook* (p. 205). Hingham, MA: Charles River Media.

[28] Adapted from Fogg, B.J. (2002, May). *Stanford guidelines for web credibility.* Retrieved November 15, 2003, from Stanford University, Stanford Persuasive Technology Lab Web site: www.webcredibility.org/guidelines

PART IV

Understanding the Communicator's Strategies
理解交流者采用的策略

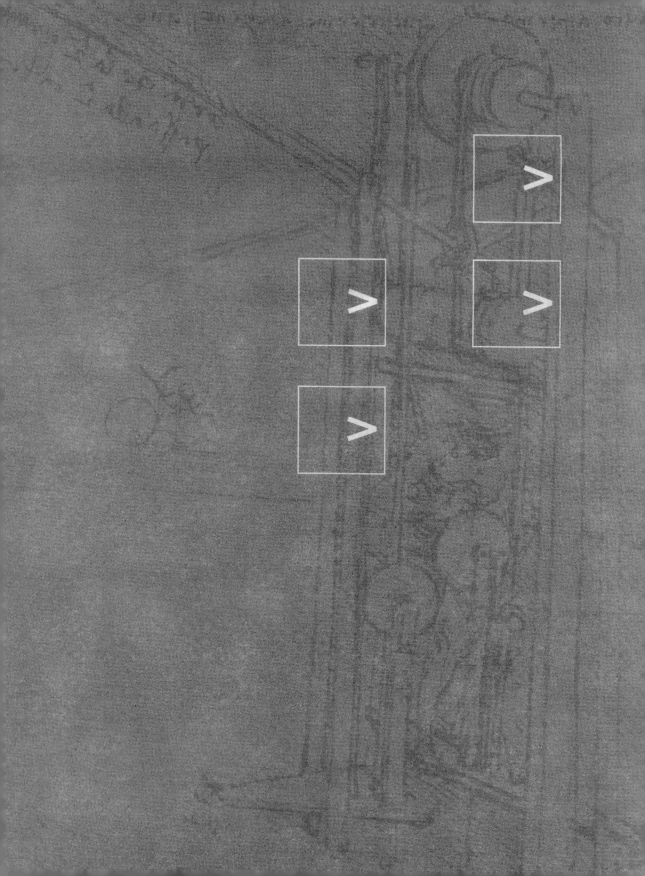

CHAPTER 14

Creating Definitions
创建定义

在准备文件或口头展示时，很有必要运用读者或客户掌握的单词和概念来定义关键术语。本章讨论了定义的需要，分析了不同定义的构成，介绍了定义在不同文件中可安放的位置。首先，本章介绍了如何在定义时避免由多义词、内容复杂性、专业术语及专业符合等造成的定义内涵歧义。然后，本章阐释了几种常用定义（如非正式定义、正式定义、操作定义、扩展定义）的构成方式。最后，本章介绍了根据文件的性质确定定义在技术文件中安放的位置（词汇表、注释、融于正文、附录或网上帮助）。

Objectives and Outcomes 学习目标

This chapter will help you accomplish these outcomes:

- Avoid problems caused by multiple meanings, complexity of meanings, technical jargon, and symbols

- Create several categories of definitions:
  - Informal definitions: synonym, antonym, stipulation, negative, analogy, and illustration
  - Formal definitions (*species* = *genus* + *differentia*)
  - Operational definitions summarizing steps involved in a function
  - Expanded definitions using etymology, history, and examples

- Make appropriate decisions about using definitions in glossaries, information notes, and appendixes

Not only do the meanings of words change, but new words come into our language as well. For example, in helping readers to understand the meaning of *hypertext,* a word that has recently entered our common academic and workplace vocabulary, you could use many forms of definition. The following brief explanation of hypertext incorporates many of the types of definition that you'll read about in this chapter.

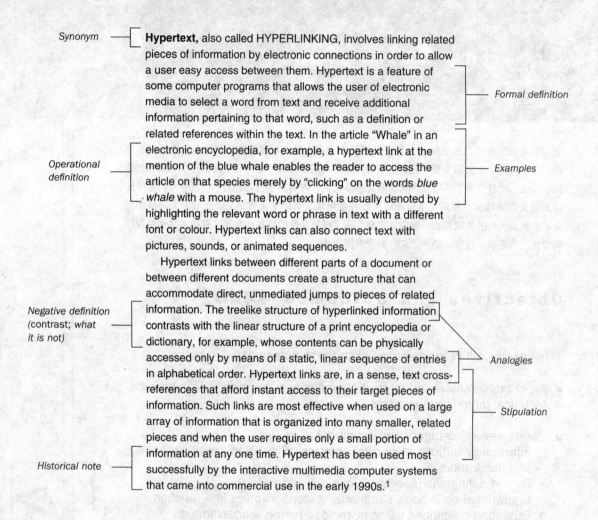

Synonym — **Hypertext,** also called HYPERLINKING, involves linking related pieces of information by electronic connections in order to allow a user easy access between them. Hypertext is a feature of some computer programs that allows the user of electronic media to select a word from text and receive additional information pertaining to that word, such as a definition or related references within the text. — *Formal definition*

Operational definition — In the article "Whale" in an electronic encyclopedia, for example, a hypertext link at the mention of the blue whale enables the reader to access the article on that species merely by "clicking" on the words *blue whale* with a mouse. The hypertext link is usually denoted by highlighting the relevant word or phrase in text with a different font or colour. Hypertext links can also connect text with pictures, sounds, or animated sequences. — *Examples*

Negative definition (contrast; what it is not) — Hypertext links between different parts of a document or between different documents create a structure that can accommodate direct, unmediated jumps to pieces of related information. The treelike structure of hyperlinked information contrasts with the linear structure of a print encyclopedia or dictionary, for example, whose contents can be physically accessed only by means of a static, linear sequence of entries in alphabetical order. Hypertext links are, in a sense, text cross-references that afford instant access to their target pieces of information. Such links are most effective when used on a large array of information that is organized into many smaller, related pieces and when the user requires only a small portion of information at any one time. — *Analogies*

— *Stipulation*

Historical note — Hypertext has been used most successfully by the interactive multimedia computer systems that came into commercial use in the early 1990s.[1]

When you prepare technical documents, oral presentations, and visuals, you need to define critical terms by using vocabulary and concepts within the audience's grasp. You can tailor a definition for different audiences by adjusting details, vocabulary, and types of examples and explanations. This chapter discusses the need for definitions, examines the construction of various types of definitions, and presents specific places to use definitions in various documents.

The Need for Definitions
定义的需要

Writers, speakers, and designers often understand the need to provide definitions of various kinds. As a result, you can find definitions included in many documents, oral presentations, and visuals that provide the audience with information they need to interpret critical terms.

At other times, much like Humpty Dumpty in *Alice in Wonderland*,[2] people use language in whatever way they want . . . and members of the audience are left to figure out the meanings for themselves. Inadequate or missing definitions cause a variety of problems. Readers may become confused by multiple meanings, complexity of meanings, technical jargon, and symbols.

Multiple Meanings 词的多义

Some words have *multiple meanings*, different definitions in other contexts, which might mislead readers. The definition of even simple terms sometimes changes entirely when the term is applied in a different field. For example, a biologist, geologist, and naval gunner would probably react differently to the everyday word *focus*:

When I use a word, it means just what I choose it to mean, neither more nor less

- In biology — the localized area of disease or the major location of a general disease or infection[3]
- In calculus — one of the points that, with the corresponding directrix, defines a conic section[4]
- In earth science — the location of an earthquake's origin[5]
- In photography — the adjustment of a camera lens to a particular image to ensure a sharp and clear picture[6]
- In physics — the small area of a surface that light or sound waves converge upon[7]
- In naval gunnery — the rotation and elevation of a gun to accurately hit a target[8]

Indeed, definitions are frequently necessary for common words if their meaning is ambiguous or unclear to the audience. Examples include such words as *base, cell, cover, limit, positive, stock,* and *traverse.*

Words with multiple meanings are especially treacherous for one of the largest audiences — nonexpert professionals. Imagine a manager with a background in agronomy reading a memo from a graphic artist that includes the phrase "insufficient crop." The context may make the meaning clear, but only after a moment or two of hesitation. To eliminate problems caused by multiple

> What other words can you think of that are used in multiple disciplines or professionals and have multiple meanings?

> What problems might occur if you introduce and define key terms near the beginning of a training manual and then throughout the manual substitute a variety of synonyms for these key terms to add some variety to your writing?

meanings, assess your audience and decide whether any of your terms has a meaning that members of that audience might think of before discerning the intended technical definition. If they might be confused, include an unobtrusive parenthetical definition.

Complexity of Meaning 意义的复杂性

Complexity can be considered in two broad ways. First, definitions can be simple or detailed, depending on the intended audience. The following two definitions of *volt* illustrate two levels of complexity. The first definition comes from a general dictionary like those in public schools and homes; the second comes from a technical dictionary.

> This first definition would satisfy most general readers.

- *volt* — standard unit of electromotive force; after Alessandro Volta, an Italian electrician[9]

> The second definition requires some technical knowledge because of the vocabulary (ampere, watt, electromagnetic units), kind of details, and amount of information.

- *volt* — the derived SI unit of electric potential defined as the difference of potential between two points on a conducting wire carrying a constant current of one ampere when the power dissipated between these points is one watt. Also the unit of potential difference and electromotive force. 1 volt = 108 electromagnetic units. Symbol V (= W/A). Named after Alessandro Volta (1745–1827).[10]

Your decision about the complexity of the definition depends on your assessment of both the intended audience and the situation. You need to decide what information is needed in order for the audience to comprehend and be able to use the term in the context of the document, oral presentation, or visual.

A second way to think about complexity involves the factors that contribute to definitions themselves. For example, *case definitions* are "sets of criteria used by public health agencies in the surveillance, or monitoring, of disease syndromes. In the United States, case definitions are established by the Centers for Disease Control and Prevention (CDC).[11] An especially controversial case definition is the one for AIDS. In 1981, the CDC started to track the cluster of opportunistic infections, which eventually came to be called AIDS. It is now recognized as "a syndrome . . . characterized by more than two dozen different illnesses and symptoms as well as by specific indications on blood test findings."[12] The initial case definition was established by the CDC in 1982 and then underwent major revision in 1985 (to include 20 conditions, three of which were types of cancer) and again in 1987 (to include three more conditions).

The complex definition of AIDS evolved as medical knowledge expanded and as social and political pressures brought attention to two problems: an inadequate case definition and new uses of the definition beyond its original epidemiological purposes. For example, by the early 1990s, the case definition being used to assess the effects of AIDS was inadequate, in part because it didn't sufficiently acknowledge "certain populations, namely women, injecting drug users, and communities of color. . . . Physicians, activists, and, in particular, HIV-positive women, began a movement to force the CDC to expand the surveillance definition of AIDS."[13] So in 1993, the case definition evolved a third time to include three additional conditions and a system of categorization that more accurately reflects the all affected populations.

This example illustrates that definitions — especially complex definitions — need to be contextualized. They work as long as they are accepted by the majority of people in a particular community as accurate, but when they cease to be usable, they can be challenged and revised.

For a link to the case definition of AIDS, go to **http://english.wadsworth.com/ burnett6e**. You'll learn about the evolution of a case definition as knowledge changes and about the legal and financial implications of case definitions.
 CLICK ON WEBLINK
  CLICK on Chapter 14/AIDS

WEBLINK

Technical Jargon 技术术语

Definitions are frequently needed when technical rather than everyday terms are used. You should assess whether readers are familiar with the terms; if so, no definitions are necessary. As the Peanuts cartoon shows, you can easily misjudge the level of technical information an audience can handle.[14]

The following paragraph contains technical vocabulary that the writer could be fairly certain the intended readers already know; the magazine is a trade publication for the plastics industry, and the intended readers are professionals knowledgeable about plastics. The specialized technical terms, italicized here, were not italicized in the original.

> *Ratios* are indexed via a digital thumbwheel. *Reinforcement* is loaded into the emptied tank (by means of a *positive vertical auger conveyor*) and activated to achieve a uniform density; *polyol* is then added from bulk storage tanks and mixed with *reinforcement*. With initial production now under way, no requirement for *heat-tracing* of mixing tanks has been observed, and this is probably due to the effective but essentially *shearless mix action* of the *orbital auger principle* employed.[15]

Under what circumstances and in what types of documents might a writer take the time and effort to define terms for audiences who have technical expertise?

Sometimes, however, technical terminology unfamiliar to the audience is necessary. For instance, a process may be introduced that requires a technical explanation employing new terms. In such cases, the writer should define the terms. The following sentence, from a short article about safety precautions necessary to protect workers who use industrial robots, defines the unfamiliar term *dwell-time*.

> Perhaps the most dangerous condition exists when people are unaware of a robot's *dwell-time*. (Dwell-time is the temporary period of inactivity between motions.)

Figure 14.1 illustrates longer definitions incorporated into an informational sales brochure for *diamond laps,* instruments used to make metal surfaces flat. The

FIGURE 14.1 Incorporated Definitions[16]

Accessibility
- The figures are placed to closely follow the textual references.

Comprehensibility
- The broad characteristics are identified in the opening paragraph.
- Informal parenthetical definitions help readers move quickly through the information.

Usability
- The features of surface texture — "roughness, waviness, lay, and flow" — are (1) forecast in a sentence, (2) defined in an accessible bulleted list, and (3) illustrated in figures.

FINISH/FLATNESS CONCEPTS

SURFACE FINISH

The surfaces produced by machining and other methods of manufacturing are generally irregular and complex. Of practical importance are the geometric irregularities generated by the machining method. These are defined by height, width and direction, and other random characteristics not of a geometric nature.

The general term employed to definethese surface irregularities is *surface texture,* the repetitive or random deviation from the nominal surface (Figure 1) that forms the pattern of the surface. It includes roughness, waviness, lay, and flaw.

- Roughness consists of fineirregularities in the surface texture produced by the machining process (Figure 2).
- Waviness is the widely spaced component of surface texture. It has wider spacing than roughness (Figure 2). It results from cutting tool runout and deflection.

FIG. 1

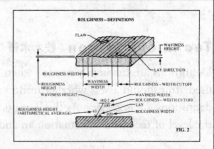
FIG. 2

- Lay is the direction of the predominate surface pattern and it is determined by the machining process used in producing the surface (Figure 2).
- Flaws are irregularities that occur at scattered places, without a predetermined pattern. They include cracks, blow holes, checks, ridges, scratches, etc. (Figure 2).

Roughness is definedas the arithmetical average (AA) deviation of the surface roughness expressed in microinches from a mean line or roughness centerline (Figure 3). AA has been adopted internationally and is often referred to as CLA or c.l.a. (centerline, average). Many instruments still in use employ an average deviation from the roughness centerline, which is the root mean square average (RAMS) deviation of surface roughness, also expressed in microinches. RMS, while used frequently, has actually been obsolete since

definitions are given credibility because they are taken from *Machining Data Handbook*, a standard machinists' reference book. The company includes the definitions to educate its customers about the comparative benefits of its product.

Symbols 符 号

Technical language can be nonverbal, as in the symbolic language of mathematics, chemistry, and physics. For example, the equation explaining conservation of matter and energy ($E = mc^2$) is completely understandable to a physicist and, in fact, to virtually all physics students, who would know that E = energy, m = mass, and c = velocity of light and could translate the symbolic statement into a

FIGURE 14.1   Incorporated Definitions[16] (continued)

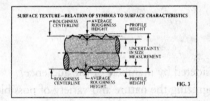

FIG. 3

about 1950. Roughness measuring instruments calibrated for RMS will read 11 percent higher, on a given surface, than those instruments calibrated for AA. The difference is usually much less than the point-to-point variations on any given machined surface.

The commercial ranges of surface roughness produced by various machining processes are shown in the table. A range of finishes can be obtained by more than one process; however, the selection of a surface finish involves more than merely designating a particular process. The ability of a process operation to pro-duce a specific surface roughness or surface finish depends on many factors. In turning, for example, the surface roughness is geometrically related to the nose radius of the tool and the feed per revolution. For surface grinding, the final surface depends on the type of grind-ing wheel, the method of wheel dressing, the wheel speed, the table speed, cross feed, down feed, and the grinding fluid. A change in any one of these factors may have a significant effect on the fnish of the fnal surface produced.

Type of Surface	Roughness Height (Microinches)
Honed, lapped, or polished	2
	4
	8
Ground with periphery of wheel	4
	8
	16
	32
	63
Ground with flat side of wheel	4
	8
	16
	32
	63
Shaped or turned	32
	63
	125
	250
	500
Side milled, end milled or profile	63
	125
	250
	500
Milled with periphery of cutter	63
	125
	250
	500

Comprehensibility
- The figures are carefully labeled with callouts.
- The figures are explained in the accompanying text.

Usability
- Types of surfaces produced by various machining processes and the corresponding roughness are presented in an accessible table, with the degree of roughness listed in ascending order in microinches.
- Even though the information is technical, it is presented so that it can be understood by professional nonexperts — in this situation, probably managers who have to approve decisions that may in part be based on the flatness that can be achieved with certain materials and equipment.

verbal statement. Yet the symbols might be confusing even to highly educated people not trained in physics or a related field.

Simply defining the symbols will not ensure that nonexperts comprehend the content of either the symbolic or verbal statement. The definitions you construct need to do more than identify the unfamiliar terms; you must consider the audience's knowledge and adjust the definition to the appropriate level. These definitions illustrate two of the possibilities:

- $E = mc^2$ means that *energy* is equivalent to *mass* times the square of the constant *velocity of light*.
- $E = mc^2$ means mass-energy is conserved. The energy produced directly from the loss of mass during a nuclear fission or fusion reaction is equal to that mass loss times the square of the constant velocity of light.

You need to understand the concepts behind the symbols in order to provide an explanation appropriate for the audience's education and experience.

Construction of Definitions
构建定义

Effective definitions answer questions considered by members of the audience, *before* they verbalize those questions. Recognizing the nature and variety of possible questions helps you construct your definitions, recognize when a definition is appropriate, and determine the effectiveness of existing definitions when editing. After the initial "What is it?" you can ask yourself some common questions:

Physical Characteristics	■ What does it look like?
	■ What are its physical features?
Comparison	■ How is it classified?
	■ What is it similar to?
	■ How does it differ from similar objects (theories, procedures, situations)?
Whole/Parts	■ What are its distinguishing characteristics?
	■ What are its components (structural parts and functional parts)?
Function	■ What does it do?
	■ How does it work (function, operate)?
Operation	■ Who uses it?
	■ What are examples of its use?
	■ What is its value?

A variety of techniques will aid you in answering these questions when constructing definitions, depending on the category: a formal, informal, operational, or expanded definition.

Formal Definitions 正式定义

Because dictionaries use *formal definitions* in many entries, people often believe that is the only way to define a term — identifying the broad category to which a term belongs as well as its distinctive characteristics. As a writer, you may be expected to construct clear and accurate formal definitions for new products and processes when no definition exists and for existing products and processes when current definitions are inadequate. The format of formal definitions is always the same.

Species	equals	Genus	plus	Differentia
term being defined		Class or category to which the term (species) belongs		distinguishing characteristics that differentiate this species from other species in the same genus

A simple example illustrates the structure and demonstrates the application of guidelines that you should follow when constructing effective formal definitions.

Species	equals	Genus	plus	Differentia
A robin	is	a bird	with	a red breast and yellow beak.

You should make the genus as narrow as possible. A robin is a bird, but can the category be more specific? Yes. A robin is a type of thrush, so the formal definition can be revised.

Species	equals	Genus	plus	Differentia
A robin	is	a thrush	with	a red breast and yellow beak.

You should make the differentia as inclusive as possible to eliminate the possibility of mistakenly identifying one species with another. Do robins have additional characteristics that differentiate them from other thrushes? Again, yes. A robin has a distinctive black back and wing tips. A more complete formal definition for robin can be constructed:

Species	equals	Genus	plus	Differentia
A robin	is	a thrush	with	a red breast, yellow beak, and black back and wing tips.

Formal definitions answer questions such as these: How is it classified? How does it differ from similar objects? What distinguishes this from related objects? What are the identifying characteristics? The need to construct your own formal definitions arises when dictionary definitions are inadequate or nonexistent. The following example of a formal definition was constructed for a specific report. Notice that in this example, the genus is purposely kept narrow and the differentia are inclusive.

Species	equals	Genus	plus	Differentia
Hypertext	is	electronically linked pieces of information	with	connections that allow users easy access between them.

Informal Definitions 非正式定义

Informal definitions tend to be the type we insert in communication without realizing that we're defining a term. We integrate informal definitions casually and comfortably and frequently out of necessity into our normal writing and speech. The six types of informal definitions presented in Figure 14.2 are particularly useful for technical communicators: synonym, antonym, negative, stipulation, analogy, and illustration.

Three of these types — stipulation, analogy, and illustration — deserve additional discussion because they are so useful in technical documents and presentations. They are especially good at providing the audience with information to differentiate a specific term from similar ones. For example, the following definition begins by providing a synonym, presenting an additional definition, and then offering an example to help the audience understand the concept of *domain name*. But perhaps the most helpful part of the definition is the set of the stipulations of specific extensions for particular situations. The stipulations are what the audience is likely to remember.

Synonym ——— **domain name.** The address or URL of a particular Web site, it
Additional definition ——— is the text name corresponding to the numeric IP address of a computer on the Internet. For example: www.netlingo.com is
Example ——— the domain name for the numeric IP address "66.201.69.207." There is an organization called InterNIC that registers domain names for a fee, to keep people from registering the same name. As of February, 2002, here is the approximate number of registered names for each top-level domain:

* .com - 22.5 million
* .net - 3.9 million
* .org - 2.5 million
* .info - 700,000
* .biz - 500,000
* .name - 150,000
* .coop - 5,000
* .museum - 2,000

Stipulations ——— To register a domain name, you can contact a company (such as Network Solutions, Inc.) or you can ask your ISP or hosting company to register names for you. In addition to the suffixes listed above, there is also .edu, .gov, .mil, and the list of country codes, as well as the following:

* .arts for arts and cultural entities
* .firm for businesses
* .pro for professional
* .rec for recreation and entertainment
* .store for merchants
* .web for Web services[17]

FIGURE 14.2 Types of Informal Definitions

Term	Definition	Examples	Comment
Synonym	A word that means essentially the same thing as the original term is a synonym.	microbe = germ helix = spiral Corrugated paperboard is the technical term for what is popularly known as cardboard. The bellows in a thermostatic element is made of a paper-thin, hardened (heat-treated) copper to make it strong, elastic, and corrosion resistant.	Synonyms usually answer such questions as "What is it similar to? What do I know that it resembles?"
Antonym	A word that is opposite in meaning to the original term is an antonym.	deviating - direct indigenous - foreign	Antonyms answer the obvious question, "What is the opposite?"
Negative	Explaining what something is not provides readers with useful information.	Machine rivets, usually made from metals such as aluminum or titanium, are unlike the rivets used in iron work in that they do not need to be heated before insertion.	Negatives respond to such questions as "What similar things should I not equate with this object? What similar things might mislead me?"
Stipulation	Stipulative definitions specify the meaning of a term for a particular application or situation.	When the term x [not necessarily mathematical, just any term] is used in this paper, it means . . .	Stipulations respond to such questions as "What are the limitations of use?"
Analogy	An analogy directly compares the unfamiliar to the familiar to identify major characteristics of the unfamiliar term.	A kumquat is a citrus fruit about the size and shape of a pecan. The skin is much thinner than that of a tangerine, and entirely edible. When fully ripe, the kumquat is a motley orange-green, much like an unprocessed orange.	An analogy responds to the same questions as a synonym: "What is this similar to? What related object has characteristics I'm already familiar with?"
Illustration	An actual drawing or diagram can illustrate a term.	[diagrams, drawings]	Visuals respond to the question, "What does it look like?"

Analogies, another kind of informal definition, are particularly powerful when explaining unfamiliar concepts or objects, especially for audiences that lack expert knowledge of the topic. They link the familiar and the unfamiliar. The following example begins with a visual display of how the word *modem* was coined and then provides a formal definition. The analogy that follows, though, is probably what will help an audience unfamiliar with a modem remember its primary function.

modem

short for: MOdulator, DEModulator

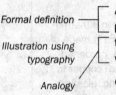

Formal definition — A hardware device you connect to your computer and to a phone line. It enables the computer to talk to other computers through the phone system. Basically, modems do for computers what a telephone does for humans.

Illustration using typography

Analogy — Generally, there are three types of modem: external, PC card, and internal.

Most computers now have internal modems so you can plug the telephone cord directly into the back of the computer.[18]

An actual drawing or diagram can illustrate a term. In many cases, a visual definition is far more efficient, accurate, and easy to understand than a verbal definition. In Figure 14.3, annotated drawings accompany a definition so readers can readily understand the explanation of the terms *capillary attraction* and *capillary repulsion.*

Sometimes visual definitions are not merely desirable but essential. Visuals respond to the question, "What does it look like?" For example, both acetone and propionaldehyde molecules contain three carbon atoms, six hydrogen atoms, and one oxygen atom. Although each molecule has the same number and kind of atoms, they are arranged differently, resulting in two compounds with different characteristics. The chemical formulas in Figure 14.4 state the differences verbally, but the addition of the diagrams brings those differences into focus.

FIGURE 14.3   Illustration to Increase Comprehension[19]

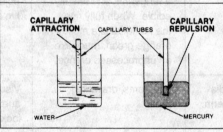

capillary attraction, the force that causes a liquid to rise in a narrow tube or when in contact with a porous substance. A plant draws up water from the ground and a paper towel absorbs water by means of capillary attraction.

capillary repulsion, the force that causes a liquid to be depressed when in contact with the sides of a narrow tube, as is mercury in a glass tube.

FIGURE 14.4 Visuals Essential to Show Critical Differences

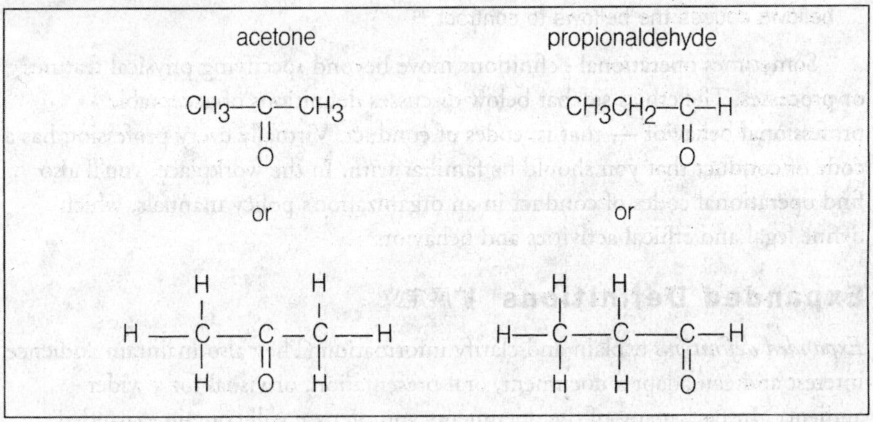

acetone

CH_3-C-CH_3
$\quad\ \ \|$
$\quad\ \ O$

or

H   H
| |
H—C—C—C—H
| ‖ |
H   O   H

propionaldehyde

CH_3CH_2-C-H
$\qquad\quad\ \|$
$\qquad\quad\ O$

or

H   H
| |
H—C—C—C—H
| | ‖
H   H   O

Operational Definitions 操作定义

The term *operational definition* means different things to different technical professions. For example, for experimental researchers, operational definitions specify the activities (the operations) that researchers use to measure a variable. In contrast, for engineers, operational definitions specify the functions or workings of an object or process. In fact, although these two uses of operational definition are different, they both depend on a definition to identify the key steps that make up a process, either to clarify the process or to measure it.

Situations that lend themselves to operational definitions require answers to questions such as these: How does it work? How can I measure or test it? How can I determine if its function is successful? What are the steps in its operation?

An operational definition summarizes or outlines the primary steps involved in the function, usually in chronological order. An effective operational definition can form the basis for a detailed process explanation (see Chapter 16). Whereas an operational definition usually outlines the major steps in a procedure, a process explanation provides specific details of each step, often describing the relationships between steps as well as offering theoretical background. The following example shows how useful an operational definition can be when defining a term:

> A thermostatic element with a remote bulb is a temperature-sensitive instrument that converts a temperature change into a mechanical force. The instrument consists of three copper parts (bulb, capillary tube, and bellows) soldered together, with a liquid sealed inside. The bulb contains liquid that turns to a gas when heated. Since the gas requires more volume per unit weight than the liquid, the pressure in the bulb increases, forcing gas through the capillary tube and into the bellows. This increase in the volume of gas causes the bellows to expand. Just the opposite happens when the bulb is cooled. This loss of heat in

Why is a formal definition a useful way to begin? Why is identifying the physical structure useful? Where does the actual operational definition start?

> What are the primary steps in this process? How could you illustrate this process?

the bulb causes some of the gas in the bulb to condense into its liquid state. Since the liquid has a much smaller volume per unit weight, the pressure drops, which pulls gas back from the bellows. A decrease in the volume of gas in the bellows causes the bellows to contract.[20]

Sometimes operational definitions move beyond specifying physical features or processes. The ethics sidebar below discusses definitions of acceptable professional behavior — that is, codes of conduct. Virtually every profession has a code of conduct that you should be familiar with. In the workplace, you'll also find operational codes of conduct in an organization's policy manuals, which define legal and ethical activities and behaviors.

Expanded Definitions 扩展定义

Expanded definitions explain and clarify information. They also maintain audience interest and can adapt a document, oral presentation, or visual for a wider audience. In fact, many of the documents you prepare will contain expanded definitions. What are the most common forms of expanded definitions? Etymology, history, and examples. To determine which form is most appropriate to use in a particular situation, you need to analyze both the audience and the task.

- Presenting the *etymology* (the linguistic origin) of a term is appropriate for general audiences.
- The *history* of a term is also appropriate for general audiences; audiences with technical expertise may need recent historical information as well.
- Relevant *examples* have value for all audiences.

ETHICS SIDEBAR 职业道德规范知识吧

> What would you include in an operational definition of professional conduct for a new organization?

Professional Codes of Conduct 职业行为规范

Many professional organizations provide their members with ethical guidelines, sometimes referred to as codes of conduct — that is, definitions of what constitutes acceptable professional behavior. Codes of conduct have many purposes, including providing members of professional organizations with possible responses to ethical dilemmas. They also help build the credibility of the organization (and its profession) to the outside community.

A useful code of conduct for technical professionals is the Society for Technical Communication (STC) code of conduct, available at this Web address:

www.stcconsultants.org/ethics.html

This code considers legality, honesty, confidentiality, quality, fairness, and professionalism.

The STC code, like almost all professional codes of conduct, is designed to influence the way technical communicators act both toward others within their profession and toward those outside the profession. For example, the STC code of conduct requires that its members avoid conflicts of interest in fulfilling professional responsibilities and activities. If a conflict of interest does arise, STC members are expected to disclose it to people who are interested or concerned and obtain their approval before moving ahead with a project.

An online listing of codes of conduct, sponsored by the Illinois Institute of Technology Center for the Study of Ethics in the Professions, is available at this Web address:

www.iit.edu/departments/csep/

In additional to an enormous number of actual codes of ethics from a large array of professional organizations, you'll also find discussions about ways to use codes of ethics, the process of authoring codes of ethics, and links to other sources about codes of ethics.

- Are you aware of a code of conduct in your field of study? Should you be?
- How much of a code of conduct is common sense?
- Codes of conduct do not always clearly indicate how or even if an organization will enforce the code. How should codes of conduct be enforced? Can they be? Should codes of conduct be viewed as rigid rules or as advice?

Etymology. Etymologies anticipate questions such as these: How did this object get its name? How old is this word? Where did this word come from? What are its historical precedents? Presenting the linguistic origin of a term sometimes gives insight into its current meaning(s). Etymological information is found in dictionaries or specialized reference books. In a dictionary entry, this information is most frequently presented in abbreviated form inside square brackets. Every dictionary contains a page near the front of the volume that will help you understand its abbreviations.

Etymologies are a useful part of a definition if knowledge of the original meaning will increase your audience's understanding of the modern meaning and usage. Such explanations are particularly appropriate if you are writing for general audiences, although etymologies also add interest to definitions for more technical audiences. The following example demonstrates how etymologies can be used effectively as a technique for definition.

> The word rivet comes from the Vulgar Latin word *ripare*, which means to make firm, or from the Middle French words *rivet* or *river*, which means to clinch.[21]

History. Presenting historical background about the development and use of the term or subject puts its current meaning into perspective. History can cover several thousand years (if the subject is chemistry, which began at least as early as the magicians in the Egyptian pharaohs' courts) or decades (if the subject is lexan, which was invented in the 1960s). The use of historical background anticipates questions such as these: What are the subject's origins? How long have such objects (concepts) existed? How has the history affected modern development? How were the original objects (concepts) different from modern ones? The example in Figure 14.5 begins with the history of anthrax in 70 BC and takes readers quickly up to the present day.

WEBLINK

Anthrax has been in the news, but not many people know more than what they hear or read in dramatic headlines. Figure 14.5 presents the first of six screens that define anthrax by presenting a brief history of the disease. For a link to the other five screens, go' to http://english.wadsworth.com/burnett6e.
   CLICK ON WEBLINK
      CLICK on Chapter 14/anthrax

FIGURE 14.5   Example of Definition Using History[22]

Part IV   Understanding the Communicator's Strategies

Examples. Using specific examples to illustrate the application of a term effectively expands a definition. Defining a concept with an example can be particularly effective, as in the following example, "Rayleigh-Taylor Instability and ICF," taken from a sidebar in the article "Diagnostics for Inertial Confinement Fusion Research," from *Energy and Technology Review,* a publication of Lawrence Livermore National Laboratory.

> We are all familiar with the Rayleigh-Taylor instability. Consider, for example, what happens if a layer of water is carefully laid on top of a lower-density liquid, such as alcohol, in a container. The heavier water will find its way through the lighter alcohol to the bottom of the container if the container is disturbed. The mechanism that initiates this fluid interchange is the Rayleigh-Taylor (RT) instability: fingers of the heavier fluid start poking into the lighter fluid, and bubbles of the lighter fluid rise through the heavier fluid until eventually the interchange is complete.[23]

Placement of Definitions
定义的位置

Writers of technical material have five basic choices for placing and incorporating definitions, although the choices are not mutually exclusive:

- glossary
- information notes and sidebars
- incorporated information
- appendixes
- online help

Where are definitions placed so they are most convenient for you as a reader? Where are you most likely to use them? Where are they least obtrusive?

Glossary 词汇表

A *glossary* is a mini-dictionary usually located at the beginning or end of a technical document. Sometimes glossary definitions are located on the page where a term initially appears, either as a footnote or as a marginal annotation. A glossary at the beginning is particularly useful when readers are unfamiliar with the information and must know the terminology in order to comprehend the document. The disadvantage of an initial glossary is that, without having read the document, readers may lack a frame of reference and may not be able to judge which terms to focus on. A glossary at the end of a document provides definitions and explanations readers can refer to as they need the information. Probably the most useful place for definitions is close to the initial use of the term. When a terminal glossary is used, the terms should be marked in some way (boldface, italics, asterisks) as they occur in the body to let readers know that they can find the definition in the glossary.

Individual entries can employ many of the forms of definition: formal, informal, operational, or expanded. Figure 14.6 shows an excerpt from excerpts from two glossaries. Like most workplace documents that use definitions,

---

FIGURE 14.6   Excerpts from Two Glossaries[24]

National Geographic.com

Adaptive radiation
the evolution of a single ancestor species into several new species within a relatively short period of time and in a certain geographic area. The plants and animals of the Galápagos Islands are a result of adaptive radiation, where one plant or one animal species diversified into many species that fill a variety of ecological roles. For example, more than a dozen species of finches evolved from a single founding species that colonized the islands from the mainland of South America.

Various kinds of examples increase readers' understanding.

Atoll
a ring-shaped coral reef or string of coral islands, usually enclosing a shallow lagoon

Biodiversity
the variety of life on Earth and the interconnections among living things

Biogeography
the study of living systems and their distribution. Biogeography is important to the study of the Earth's biodiversity because it helps with understanding where animals and plants live, where they don't, and why.

Biotic
refers to the living components of the environment (such as plants, animals, and fungi) that affect ecological functions

Boreal
pertaining to the north

Entries sometimes begin with an informal definition.

Brackish
slightly salty or briny. Brackish water is saltier than fresh water but less salty than seawater.

*ST*atistical *E*ducation through *P*roblem *S*olving (STEP)

Box and Whisker Plot (or Boxplot)
A box and whisker plot is a way of summarising a set of data measured on an interval scale. It is often used in exploratory data analysis. It is a type of graph that is used to show the shape of the distribution, its central value, and variability. The picture produced consists of the most extreme values in the data set (maximum and minimum values), the lower and upper <u>quartiles</u>, and the <u>median</u>.

A box plot (as it is often called) is especially helpful for Indicating whether a distribution is skewed and whether there are any unusual observations (<u>outliers</u>) in the data set.

Entries often begin with a formal definition that is sometime explained.

Box and whisker plots are also very useful when large numbers of observations are involved and when two or more data sets are being compared.

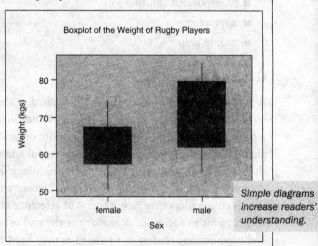

Simple diagrams increase readers' understanding.

See also <u>5-Number Summary</u>.

Cross references that help readers locate additional information are signaled, here by underlining and color.

these glossaries do not restrict themselves to one kind of definition; instead, they incorporate a variety of types of definitions to address the readers' anticipated needs.

Information Notes and Sidebars 注 释

When readers need extended information, it may interrupt the flow of the text if included in the main discussion. Presenting this information as information notes or sidebars gives readers the option of reading the additional information if they need it.

Information notes may simply define a term or concept; they also enable writers to provide examples, cite related studies, explain tangential concepts, present possible explanations, and so on. They can be placed on the bottom of a page or collected at the end of a document along with source or reference notes. Technical reports for decision making usually contain information notes that offer brief definitions or explanations, since their audience usually has little time. Technical documents for research or academic purposes may include more detailed information notes for readers who might want to investigate an idea in greater depth.

Sidebars usually provide more elaborated information than footnotes or endnotes. The sidebar and accompanying illustration in Figure 14.7 are taken from an article about balloon angioplasty in the *Harvard Health Letter*. This newsletter, published by the Harvard Medical School, says its overall goal is to "interpret medical information for the general reader in a timely and accurate fashion." The sidebar defines the categories of blockages that occur in arteries. The accompanying illustration helps readers visualize both the blockages and the tools surgeons use to unclog arteries.

Appendixes 附 录

Lengthy documents intended for readers with widely varying backgrounds often have difficulty appealing to the entire range of readers. For example, nonexperts can be confused if a document jumps into the subject without sufficient explanation. Technical experts can be bored or even offended if the documents include too much elementary material. One way to resolve this dilemma is to include *appendixes* that provide both operational and expanded definitions of critical concepts. Readers already familiar with the material can glance at the reference to the appendix in the text and continue reading, virtually uninterrupted. Readers who need to review the background material will appreciate the detailed, illustrated definitions and discussions.

Online Help 网上帮助

Virtually all software companies provide users with critical information electronically via online help systems rather than in print manuals. *Online help* systems are designed to provide users with information immediately, in several

FIGURE 14.7 Illustrated Sidebar from a Health Newsletter[25]

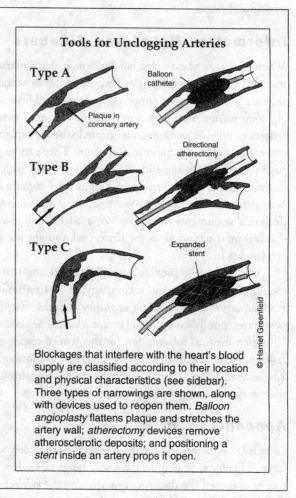

WHAT TYPE OF BLOCKAGE?

Physicians use *coronary angiography* to determine the location, size, shape, and to some degree the composition of atherosclerotic lesions that narrow the coronary arteries. This information helps predict who is a good candidate for balloon angioplasty, who is likely to have a better result with a more spe-cialized procedure, and who should go straight to coronary artery bypass graft surgery.

A popular classification system devised by the American College of Cardiology and the American Heart Association divides blockages into three categories. (*See illustration.*)

Type A: These are simple lesions in easily accessible locations that are concentric, less than 10 mm long, and contain little or no calcium and no clots. They are ideal for treatment with balloon angioplasty.

Type B: These somewhat complex, irregular narrowings are 10–20 mm long, with moderate-to-heavy calcifcation and some *thrombus* (clot), and are situated in a bend or vascular junction. Balloon angioplasty is slightly less likely to restore blood flow and slightly more likely to have complications.

Type C: This category includes heavily calcifed lesions, total blockages more than three months old, and narrowings located in a sharp turn or in a deteriorated bypass graft. The success rate for balloon dilation is signifcantly lower so bypass surgery, stenting, or atherectomy may be a better choice.

Balloon angioplasty is most successful for patients who are male, less than 70 years old, with normal left ventricular function (pumping ability), who have no more than two blocked arteries and no history of diabetes, heart attack, or bypass surgery.

Blockages that interfere with the heart's blood supply are classified according to their location and physical characteristics (see sidebar). Three types of narrowings are shown, along with devices used to reopen them. *Balloon angioplasty* flattens plaque and stretches the artery wall; *atherectomy* devices remove atherosclerotic deposits; and positioning a *stent* inside an artery props it open.

different formats. For example, the word processing program used to prepare the manuscript for this textbook has a "balloon help" option; when activated, it provides the user with a callout that includes brief definitions and explanations of many features and functions on the computer desktop.

In addition to the balloons, this same software has a number of other online help features, which is typical of most software:

- an alphabetic index of all help topics available to users of this software
- a list of frequently used topics that often saves time

- an on-screen box that provides hints and wizards (shortcuts to common practices)
- a searchable database to answer questions

Virtually all of these online help options include various kinds of definitions to assist users who are confused or stuck.

Individual and Collaborative Assignments
个人作业和小组作业

1. **Identify types of definitions.** Read the following examples and identify each type of definition. Some of the examples have more than one type of definition embedded. Discuss the appropriateness of each definition for the audiences.

    (a) From a teacher's manual: The word for chemistry comes from the Middle East; long ago the sacred name for Egypt was *Chemia,* which means black and probably referred to the fertile black soil of the Nile valley. In those ancient times almost any kind of change was mysterious, such as the change of wood to ash when it burns, or the transformation of sand into glass. Men who understood how to make some things change were considered to be magicians (at least we might call them that today). From their mysterious abilities to cause changes, the word for the study of change was derived.[26]

    (b) From a dictionary: Chemistry — The study of the composition of substances and of the changes of composition which they undergo. The main branches of the subject are inorganic chemistry, organic chemistry, and physical chemistry.[27]

    (c) From a Web site defining network terms: Hypertext — A system of writing and displaying text that enables the text to be linked in multiple ways, to be available at several levels of detail, and to contain links to related documents. The term was coined by Ted Nelson to refer to a nonlinear system of information browsing and retrieval that contains associative links to other related documents.[28]

    (d) From a technical report: The reduction in speed of the steam turbine engine is necessary to achieve efficiency. The efficient speed for operating the turbine is higher than the speed of the shaft. The transmission of your automobile functions similarly by converting a high engine speed to a lower wheel speed.

    (e) From a scientific journal in an article about lipid barriers in biological systems: The current model views the mammalian stratum corneum as a two-component system ("bricks and mortar") consisting of protein-rich cells (bricks) embedded in a lipid matrix (mortar), with these intercellular lipids being primarily responsible for the integumental water barrier.[29]

(f) From a Web site defining network terms: Search engine — A Web site (actually a program) that acts as a card catalog for the Internet. Search engines attempt to index and locate desired information by searching for the <u>keywords</u> a <u>user</u> specifies. The ability to find this information depends on computer indices of Web resources (maintained in a <u>database</u>) that can be <u>queried</u> for these keywords. These indices are either built from specific resource lists (as is the case with a <u>search directory</u>) or created by Web programs with strange-sounding names that seem to be inspired by insects: <u>bots</u>, <u>spiders</u>, <u>crawlers</u>, and <u>worms</u>.

From a <u>surfer's</u> point-of-view, search engines can be quite tiresome and not very efficient if you don't know how to use them correctly. On top of that, different engines are good for different kinds of searches, so it's a good idea to read the engine's advanced search section before you do a search. In many cases, using <u>Boolean logic</u> will help narrow down the results for you and better optimize your search results.

SEARCH TIP: The best way to get the most out of a search engine is to understand its features. Always check the site's help page or advanced search page when you arrive, to find out what features are available. Then use them — they really help. Be specific and enter all of the words you are looking for. Pick your search site smartly: If you are looking for a bio of a football figure, use a directory, but if you want to see every instance where his name appears, use an engine.[30]

2. **Determine three levels of definitions for the same term.** Work with a classmate who is in the same discipline or field (if possible) and identify a concept or term that you would like to research. Check dictionaries, texts, encyclopedias, handbooks, professional journals in the reference and periodical section of your library, and various Web sites. Make copies of the definitions you select, and document your sources, using the appropriate formats from the Usage Handbook. Identify the major distinctions among the various definitions, and evaluate the effectiveness of each definition for the intended audience. Prepare a brief oral report for your classmates.

3. **Incorporate definitions into a document.** Imagine that your audience is managers of small businesses who have been resistant to converting their businesses to use computers. They need some elementary information about computers. You are revising a newsletter article dealing with computer basics that will contain a complete glossary at the end of the article, but you believe that brief definitions should be incorporated into the article itself so the readers don't have to regularly check the glossary while they're reading. Rewrite this basic paragraph, incorporating the following definitions (or parts thereof) as you believe is appropriate for this resistant audience.

Every computer system has two types of components, hardware and software. Most visible is the hardware, typically a central processing unit (CPU) and peripheral equipment. Less visible, but usually even more critical, is the software. Too often computer buyers and sellers focus on stylish, competent-looking hardware, rather than on the software that determines what a system can or can't do for a particular business. Another often overlooked expense is the backup storage equipment that generally is needed in addition to basic system components.

- *Backup storage.* Copies of data files, used as a safeguard against damage or loss.
- *Computer system.* A computer plus software plus one or more pieces of peripheral equipment.
- *CPU (central processing unit).* The part of a computer that performs calculations and processes data according to the instructions specified by the software. *CPU* is sometimes used interchangeably with *computer.* See also *microcomputer.*
- *Hardware.* The computer itself or any item of peripheral equipment.
- *Peripheral equipment.* Input-output and data storage devices: printers, keyboards, CRTs, remote terminals, and tape and disk drives.
- *Software.* The programs, or instructions, that tell the computer how to respond to specific user commands.[31]

4. **Identify audience for a document that uses definitions.**

   (a) Carefully read the following paper, "The Fugue." [32]

   (b) Marginally annotate to identify all the types of definition the writer uses.

   (c) Identify probable audiences for this paper.

The Fugue

A fugue is a polyphonic form of music that is most easily recognized by several reappearances of a short melodic theme. Fugues are usually written in from two- to five-part harmonies. Each part blends with the other parts to form harmony, but it is also a melodic line as well. This characteristic of a fugue makes it unique. Writing a short melody with simple harmony is easy; however, if the supporting parts do not form a melody very similar to the melodic theme first stated in the fugue, then the composition cannot be called a fugue.

A fugue is similar to a canon or a round, but a canon usually has only two parts that are always exactly alike. One part begins the canon and the second part enters later, duplicating the first. An example of a canon is shown in Figure 1.

Figure 1 *Canon*

(By the way, can you name that tune?)

The fugue, however, always has the second part entering in a different key. This new key is called the dominant key and is fivetones higher than the original key, the tonic key. (See Figure 2.)

Figure 2 *Tonic-Dominant Relationship*

There are, then, two important characteristics of a fugue:
1. The melodies are imitative.
2. The imitation occurs in related keys.

The fugue is commonly divided into three distinct sections: exposition, development, and stretto.

The exposition consists of the statement of the melodic theme and its answer in the dominant key. These statements and answers may occur several times, depending upon the number of parts written into the composition. Most frequently, fugues are written in four parts and require two statements and two answers.

The development is the most exciting and improvisational part of the fugue. Indeed, the fugue is so-named because of the action within the development. Fugue is derived from the Latin *fugere,* meaning to fee or run away. The development runs away from the straightforward statements and answers of the exposition and adds color and variety to the composition. The development uses the following techniques to achieve interest:

1. Countersubject—playing a new theme with the original theme
2. Augmentation—playing the theme more slowly
3. Diminution—playing the theme more quickly
4. Inversion—playing the theme upside down

The stretto section of the fugue is a restatement of the original theme by all the parts. They often overlap unexpectedly and reach a climax to provide a dramatic end to the fugue.

The fugue was a popular form of composition during the Baroque era. Most of the major composers have written fugues or parts of fugues in larger compositions. However, Bach remains the most famous and prolifc writer of fugues.

---

5. **Identify an audience, context, and purpose.**

   (a) Carefully study the diagram, titled "It Does a Body Bad,"[33] that defines immediate and long-term effects of stress.

   (b) Identify audiences for whom this presentation would be appropriate and effective; what would be possible context(s) and purpose(s)?

IT DOES A BODY BAD

■ **These are some** immediate and long-term effects of stress. If long-term symptoms persist for more than a few weeks and interfere with your ability to work or perform normal daily activities, see a physician:

Brain
Instant: Hypothalamus and pituitary glands, which stimulate other organs and release stress hormones (primarily adrenaline, cortisol and norepinephreine), kick in.
Long-term: Mental and emotional problems, including insomnia, depression, anxiety, personality changes, irritability, sleeping problems, exhaustion.

Face/Head
Instant: Face "flushes" as blood flow increases.
Long-term: Muscles in the head, neck, jaw can tighten, causing chronic headache, neck ache, jaw pain, tics.

Lungs/Breathing
Instant: Lungs speed up to take in more air and deliver more oxygen to muscles, producing a breathless feeling.
Long-term: Stress can worsen chronic lung problems, such as asthma or emphysema.

Muscles
Instant: Muscles become more efficient and stronger, sometimes producing seemingly superhuman strength, speed, reaction.
Long-term: Muscle aches, soreness, pain, tension, upper and lower back, shoulder, neck problems.

Kidneys
Instant: A rush of anti-diuretic hormone (adh), decreased blood supply and tightened muscles decrease urine output and temporarily shut down the kidneys. Defecation and urination are prevented.
Long-term: Diarrhea or uncontrolled urination may occur as muscles relax, blood supply increases and hormones level out.

Senses
Instant: Pupils dilate. Smell is heightened.

Salivary glands
Instant: Salivary glands stop secreting saliva, making the mouth feel dry.
Long-term: Mouth ulcers, sores.

Heart
Instant: Heart pumps more blood to muscles, heart rate increases, producing a pounding, fluttering feeling in the chest. Blood pressure increases.
Long-term: Heart disease, heart attack, and high blood pressure.

Liver
Instant: Releases more sugar into the blood to provide muscles with instant energy. May also release more cholesterol into the blood.

Stomach/Digestive system
Instant: Stomach secretes more acid, producing a feeling of "butterflies" or gurgling. Digestion shuts down temporarily.
Long-term: Ulcers, colitis, irritable bowel syndrome, gastritis, heartburn.

Skin
Instant: Skin turns pale as blood is drawn toward internal organs. Palms and feet sweat to cool the body.
Long-term: Outbreaks of rashes or other skin problems, including eczema, psoriasis, hives.

Blood
Instant: Blood clotting mechanisms improve with stress.

SOURCES: *The Complete Manual of Fitness and Well Being* (Reader's Digest; 1984); Dr. Howard Schertzinger Jr. of Queen City Sports Medicine Rehabilitation; The American Institute of Stress, Yonkers, N.Y.

GANNETT NEWS SERVICE

Then identify inappropriate or ineffective contexts, purposes, and audiences.

(c) Describe (and, if appropriate, do thumbnail sketches of) other ways to define the psychological effects of stress.

6. **Write a paper incorporating definitions.**

    (a) Work with a classmate who is in the same discipline or field (if possible) and identify a concept or term that you would like to define.

    (b) Write a multiparagraph paper incorporating various forms of definitions for that single term. Your paper should resemble the samples in Assignments #3 and #4. Make sure to include visuals if appropriate for illustrating or clarifying the term. Document any sources used in preparing the paper.

7. **Analyze definitions.** Visit the following Web site: **www.search.eb.com**.

    (a) Choose a term from your discipline and search for it in the online *Encyclopedia Britannica* and *Merriam-Webster's Collegiate Dictionary* (**www.m-w.com**).

    (b) Identify additional Web sites that provide useful definitions of your term.

    (c) Create a rubric that lists the criteria for analyzing the effectiveness of each definition, and then use your rubric to assess each definition by identifying the different purposes and audiences.

8. **Define Web structures.** Create a table in which you define and illustrate various ways Web sites can be structured — for example, sequentially, hierarchically, and so on. Imagine your table will be in a book about Web design for managers who need to understand options for their company's Web site and make decisions about the most effective structures for various purposes and audiences.

9. **Revise glossary entries.** As you carefully read the following entries, you'll see that they are not parallel in sentence structure or specificity. Revise the glossary definitions so they're consistent, comprehensible, and usable for interested nonexperts.

Turbine Glossary[34]

Anemometer: Measures the wind speed and transmits wind speed data to the controller.

Blades: Most turbines have either two or three blades. Wind blowing over the blades causes the blades to "lift" and rotate.

Brake: A disc brake that can be applied mechanically, electrically, or hydraulically to stop the rotor in emergencies.

Controller: The controller starts up the machine at wind speeds of about 8 to 16 miles per hour (mph) and shuts off the machine at about 65 mph. Turbines cannot operate at wind speeds above about 65 mph because their generators could overheat.

Gear box: Gears connect the low-speed shaft to the high-speed shaft and increase the rotational speeds from about 30 to 60 rotations per minute (rpm) to about 1200 to 1500 rpm, the rotational speed required by most generators to produce electricity. The gear box is a costly (and heavy) part of the wind turbine and engineers are exploring "direct-drive" generators that operate at lower rotational speeds and don't need gear boxes.

Generator: Usually an off-the-shelf induction generator that produces 60-cycle AC electricity.

High-speed shaft: Drives the generator.

Low-speed shaft: The rotor turns the low-speed shaft at about 30 to 60 rotations per minute.

Nacelle: The rotor attaches to the nacelle, which sits atop the tower and includes the gear box, low- and high-speed shafts, generator, controller, and brake. A cover protects the components inside the nacelle. Some nacelles are large enough for a technician to stand inside while working.

Pitch: Blades are turned, or pitched, out of the wind to keep the rotor from turning in winds that are too high or too low to produce electricity.

Rotor: The blades and the hub together are called the rotor.

Tower: Towers are made from tubular steel (shown here) or steel lattice. Because wind speed increases with height, taller towers enable turbines to capture more energy and generate more electricity.

Wind direction: This is an "upwind" turbine, so called because it operates facing into the wind. Other turbines are designed to run "downwind," facing away from the wind.

Wind vane: Measures wind direction and communicates with the yaw drive to orient the turbine properly with respect to the wind.

Yaw drive: Upwind turbines face into the wind; the yaw drive is used to keep the rotor facing into the wind as the wind direction changes. Downwind turbines don't require a yaw drive, the wind blows the rotor downwind.

Yaw motor: Powers the yaw drive.

Chapter 14 Endnotes

[1] Hypertext. (2000). In *encyclopedia Britannica* (15th ed.). Chicago: Encyclopedia Britannica.

[2] Carroll, L. (1871). Chapter 6: Humpty Dumpty. Illustrator John Tenniel. *Through the Looking Glass*. Retrieved November 12, 2003, from http://www.sabian.org/Alice/lgchap06.htm

[3] Focus. (1940). In *American pocket medical dictionary*. Philadelphia: Saunders.

[4] Thomas, G. B., Jr. (1972). *Calculus and analytic geometry* (5th ed., p. 479). Reading, MA: Addison-Wesley.

5 Earthquake. (2000). In *Encyclopedia Britannica* (15th ed.). Chicago: Encyclopedia Britannica.

6 Polaroid Corporation. (1974). *The square shooter* (p. 3). Cambridge, MA: Author.

7 Semat, A. (1966). *Fundamentals of physics* (p. 96). New York: Holt, Rinehart, & Winston.

8 Bureau of Naval Personnel. (1965). *Principles of naval ordnance and gunnery* (p. 4) (NAVPERS 10783-A). Washington, DC: U.S. Navy.

9 Volt. In *Webster's new school and office dictionary.*

10 Volt. In *Penguin dictionary of science.*

11 McGovern, T., & Smith, R. A. (1998). Case definition of AIDS. In *Encyclopedia of AIDS: A Social, Political, Cultural, and Scientific Record of the HIV Epidemic.* Retrieved November 12, 2003, from http://www.the body.com/encyclo/aids.html

12 McGovern, T., & Smith, R. A. (1998). Case definition of AIDS. In *Encyclopedia of AIDS: A Social, Political, Cultural, and Scientific Record of the HIV Epidemic.* Retrieved November 12, 2003, from http://www.thebody.com/encyclo/aids.html

13 McGovern, T., & Smith, R. A. (1998). Case definition of AIDS. In *Encyclopedia of AIDS: A Social, Political, Cultural, and Scientific Record of the HIV Epidemic.* Retrieved November 12, 2003, from http://www.thebody.com/encyclo/aids.html

14 © 1999, *Peanuts* reprinted by permission of United Features Syndicate.

15 Snealler, J. (1982). Mass production of RRIM parts start up on automotive lines. *Modern Plastics, 59* (January): 48.

16 Source: *Machinability Data Center* (p. 3). Cincinnati, OH: Metcut Research Associates. Reprinted with permission.

17 NetLingo.com. (n.d.). *Domain name.* Retrieved November 12, 2003, from http://www.netlingo.com/inframes.cfm

18 NetLingo.com. (n.d.). *Modem.* Retrieved November 12, 2003, from http://www.netlingo.com/inframes.cfm

19 Capillary attraction and capillary repulsion. In *Scott Foresman advanced dictionary.* Reprinted with permission of Scott Foresman.

20 Drake, C. (n.d.). Operational definition of a thermostatic element. *Technical and Scientific Writing, 42,* 225.

21 Rivet. (1980). In *Webster's new world dictionary.*

22 The Office of the Public Health Service Historian. (n.d.). *a brief history of anthrax.* Retrieved November 12, 2003, from http://lhncbc.nlm.nih.gov/apdb/phsHistory/resources/anthrax/anthrax.html

23 Rayleigh-Taylor instability and ICF. (1992). In Diagnostics for inertial confinement fission in research. *Energy and Technology Review,* (July). Livermore, CA: Lawrence Livermore National Laboratory.

24 *Wild*/World Glossary. *National Geographic.* Retrieved April 1, 2004, from http://www.nationalgeographic.com/wildworld/glossary.html

Easton, V. J., & McColl, J. H. (1997). *Statistics Glossary,* vl.1. Retrieved April 1, 2004, from http://www.stats.gla.ac.uk/steps/glossary/sampling.html

Copyright Statement and Licence Agreement http://www.stats.gla.ac.uk/steps/licence.html

25 Source: Bittl, J. A., & Thomas, P. (1996, January). Opening the arteries: Beyond the balloon. *Harvard Health Letter, 21,* 4–6. Copyright © 1996, President and Fellows of Harvard College. Reprinted by permission.

26. Mandell, A. (1974). *The language of science* (p. 23). Washington, DC: National Science Teachers Association.
27. Chemistry. In *Chamber's technical dictionary*.
28. Reproduced by permission. Copyright © 1995 by Netlingo, Inc. The Online Computer Dictionary, www.netlingo.com
29. Hadley, N. F. (1989). Lipid water barriers in biological systems. *Progress in Lipid Research, 28,* 23.
30. NetLingo.com. (n.d.). *Search engine.* Retrieved November 12, 2003, from http://www.netlingo.com/inframes.cfm
31. Adapted from Computerspeak glossary. (1980 May). *Inc.,* pp. 102–103. Copyright © 1980 by Inc. Publishing Corporation, 38 Commercial Wharf, Boston, MA 02110. Reprinted with permission of *Inc.* magazine.
32. Source: Stanhope, C. The fugue. *Technical Communication EN 4676,* Northern Essex Community College.
33. MacDonald, S. (1995, November 27). Treating stress. *Des Moines Register,* p. 3T. Reprinted with permission of the Des Moines Register. Copyright © 1995.
34. U.S. Department of Energy/Energy Efficiency and Renewable Energy. (2004). Inside the wind turbine. *Wind Energy Basics.* Retrieved January 2, 2004, from http://www.eere.energy.gov/windandhydro/wind_how.html

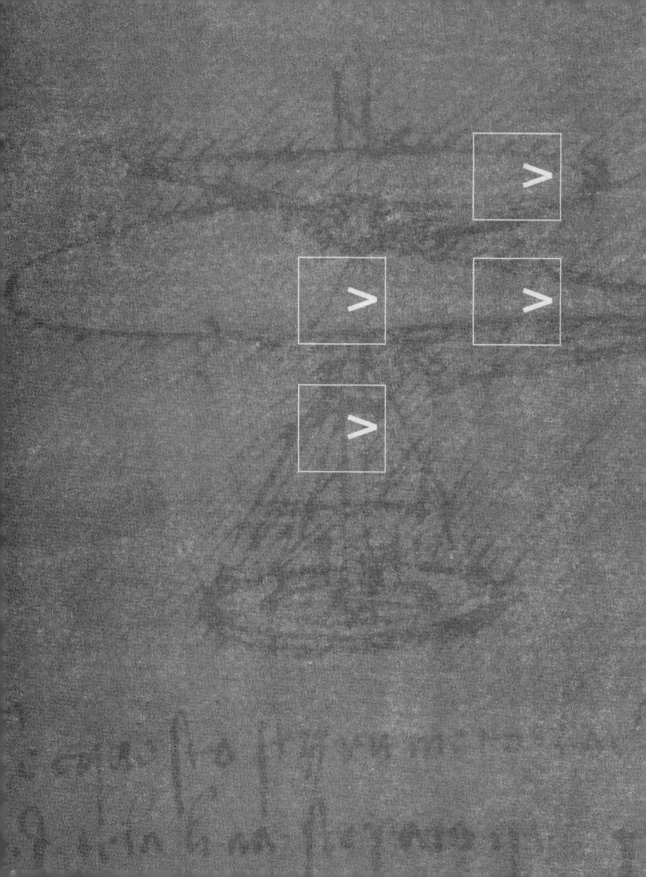

CHAPTER 15

Creating Technical Descriptions
创建技术描述

技术描述是信息文本创建的重要组成部分。技术描述指的是恰当呈现关于某个物体、物质、机械装置、有机体、系统及位置等的详细信息。本章首先介绍了技术描述的定义,然后阐释了技术描述在观察记录、培训手册、技术手册、研究提案、研究报告、市场营销材料、公众宣传和教育中的应用。最后,本章指出准备技术描述时须注意明确交流对象的需求、确定描述的组成部分、使用准确的语言、设计合理的视觉呈现方式(如绘图、照片、地图、图表等)以及选择合适的排版格式。

Objectives and Outcomes 学习目标

This chapter will help you accomplish these outcomes:

- Understand that technical descriptions can be used to organize specific details about objects, substances, mechanisms, organisms, systems, and locations for an identified audience

- Summarize physical characteristics, answering questions you expect your readers to have about appearance, acceptability, and impact

- Use technical descriptions in observation notes, manuals and training materials, proposals and reports, marketing and promotional materials, and public information and education

- Prepare technical descriptions:

Since the beginning of the seventeenth century, scientists have been describing four of Jupiter's moons — Io, Europa, Ganymede, and Callisto — although over nearly 400 years, the level of detail has changed considerably. The inquiry started in 1610, when Galileo Galilei announced "the occasion of discovering and observing four planets, never seen from the very beginning of the world up to our own times, their positions, and the observations made during the last two months about their movements and their change of magnitude. . . ."[1]

In his journal, Galileo carefully recorded his observations of these four satellites, establishing size as "greater than [another that was] exceedingly small," luminescence as "very conspicuous and bright," and location as "deviated a little from the straight line toward the north."

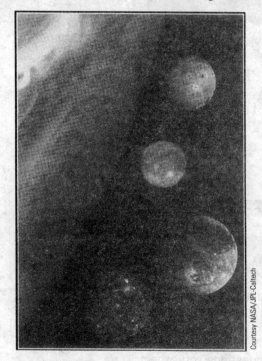

"This 'family portrait,' a composite of the Jovian system, includes the edge of Jupiter with its Great Red Spot, and Jupiter's four largest moons, known as the Galilean satellites. From top to bottom, the moons shown are Io, Europa, Ganymede and Callisto."[2]

January 11. [My observations] established that there are not only three but four erratic sidereal bodies performing their revolutions round Jupiter. . . .

January 12. The satellite farthest to the east was greater than the satellite farther to the west; but both were very conspicuous and bright; the distance of each one from Jupiter was two minutes. A third satellite, certainly not in view before, began to appear at the third hour; it nearly touched Jupiter on the east side, and was exceedingly small. They were all arranged in a straight line, along the ecliptic.

January 13. For the first time four satellites were in view. . . . There were three to the west and one to the east; they made a straight line nearly, but the middle satellite of those to the west deviated a little from the straight line toward the north. The satellite farthest to the east was at a distance of 2' from Jupiter; there were intervals of 1' only between Jupiter and the nearest satellite, and between the satellites themselves, west of Jupiter. All the satellites appeared of the same size, and though small they were very brilliant and far outshone the fixed stars of the same magnitude.

These same four moons have been the object of intense scrutiny by the National Aeronautics and Space Administration (NASA). The mission of *Voyager 1* and *Voyager 2,* beginning in 1977, was to collect data about Jupiter's "miniature solar system," including the four Galilean satellites. In vivid contrast to Galileo's brief comments, the *Voyager Bulletin* (a mission status report that regularly reported the discoveries) described the moons in considerable detail:

Of all the satellites, Io generated the most excitement. As *Voyager 1* closed in on Io, the puzzle was why its surface, so cratered and pocked when viewed from a distance, began to look smoother and younger as the spacecraft neared. . . . But the mystery was solved with the discovery of active volcanoes spewing sulfur 160 km (100 mi) high and showering it down on the crust, obliterating the old surface. Infrared data indicated hot spots at the locations of the plumes identified in the photographs, confirming the find. Io is undoubtedly the most active known surface in the solar system, surpassing even the Earth.[3]

After *Voyager1* came *Galileo*, whose mission, from 1989–2003, was to study Jupiter in even greater detail. NASA's Space Science News Web site regularly reported on the descriptions coming from the *Galileo* project, noting that "since the first volcanic plume was discovered by Voyager in 1979, Io has remained under intense scrutiny." Based on data from *Galileo*, earlier generalizations were replaced with more detailed descriptions.

For a world dominated by fiery volcanoes, it's curious that Io is also very, very cold. The ground just around the volcanic vents is literally sizzling, but most of Io's surface is 150 degrees or more below 0°C. The moon's negligible atmosphere traps little of the meager heat from the distant Sun. As soon as volcanic gases spew into the air, they immediately begin to freeze and condense. The plumes of Io's sizzling volcanoes are very likely made up of sulfur dioxide snow.[4]

Like the observations of Galileo Galilei and the *Voyager* spacecraft, the *Galileo* mission provided valuable data about Jupiter and its moons, including Io, until the spacecraft was destroyed in 2003 (Figure 15.1). The excerpts from Galileo

FIGURE 15.1 End of Galileo Mission[5]

NASA put Galileo on a collision course with Jupiter for two reasons. First, Galileo's propellant was nearly depleted. "Without propellant, the spacecraft would not be able to point its antenna toward Earth or adjust its trajectory, so controlling the spacecraft would no longer be possible." Second, NASA wanted to eliminate any chance of an impact between Galileo and Jupiter's moon Europa, which Galileo discovered may have a subsurface ocean. "The possibility of life existing on Europa is so compelling and has raised so many unanswered questions that it is prompting plans for future spacecraft to return to the icy moon."[6]

Galilei's journal, from the *Voyager Bulletin,* and from the NASA Space Science News Web site illustrate several characteristics of description that are discussed in this chapter. Most important, the descriptions include specific details, presented in an organized manner to meet the needs of an identified audience.

For a link to more information about the inventor Galileo Galilei (1564–1642), including his remarkable inventions, go to **http://english.wadsworth.com/burnett6e**.
  CLICK ON WEBLINK
    CLICK on Chapter 15/Galileo Galilei

For a link to more information about NASA's 14-year *Galileo* mission to Jupiter, which ended in September 2003, go to **http://english.wadsworth.com/burnett6e**.
  CLICK ON WEBLINK
    CLICK on Chapter 15/Galileo Mission

Defining Technical Description
定义技术描述

Descriptions summarize physical characteristics, answering questions you expect your readers to have about the appearance or composition of an object, substance, mechanism, organism, system, or location. Regardless of a description's length or subject, it is characterized by verifiable information that responds to assumed questions.

1. What is it? How is it defined? By whom?
2. What is its purpose? What is its importance or impact?
3. What are the characteristics of the whole? What is "normal" or "typical"? What are within acceptable tolerances or specifications?
   - What does it look like (size, shape, color)?
   - What are its characteristics (material or substance, weight, texture, flammability, density, durability, expected life, method of production or reproduction, and so on)?
4. What are its parts? What is "normal" or "typical"? What are within acceptable tolerances or specifications?
   - What is the appearance of each part (size, shape, color)?
   - What are the distinctive characteristics of each part?

What additional characteristics might be important for descriptions in your professional field?

5. How do the parts fit together? How do they work together? What defines effective function?

Which of these questions are answered depends on the depth of detail required by the description. Complex descriptions clearly answer more questions.

Sometimes technical description constitutes an entire document, oral presentation, or visual. However, in most situations a technical description is limited to a single segment of a longer document or presentation. For example, descriptions could range from a few lines included in a one- or two-page memo to several paragraphs in a longer report. So, a description of equipment could be just one part of a report about monitoring airport noise that is interfering with animals in an adjoining wildlife refuge. Or the description of equipment could take up one section in a proposal to purchase a new X-ray machine.

Do technical descriptions matter? Do they have any impact beyond providing accurate information about physical features? The ethics sidebar below shows that if descriptions are inadequately presented and explained, readers may underestimate their importance or even neglect them entirely. Sometimes the results can be deadly.

ETHICS SIDEBAR 职业道德规范知识吧

"The decision was flawed": Ethical Responsibility and the Challenger Explosion "决定不是完美的"：职业责任与"挑战者号"爆炸

One of the most tragic accidents in NASA history was the space shuttle *Challenger* explosion in 1986. The explosion occurred when fuel leaked out of the fuel tanks and mixed with engine exhaust. The leaks were traced to defective seals, called O-rings, on the fuel tanks. During launch, the O-rings were charred by the hot engines enough that they allowed fuel to leak out.

Researcher Paul Dombroski believes the explosion occurred in part because of an ethical failure of the technicians and administrators involved to act on the information they had, not from a lack of information about the O-rings.[7] Technical descriptions of the fuel tanks, written after each previous shuttle flight, revealed that the O-rings were being charred during launch. Although technicians and administrators knew the O-rings were burned, the burning was described in the reports as "allowable erosion" and "acceptable risk." While some engineers questioned these descriptions (and the integrity of the O-rings) the night before

If you were in a similar situation, with millions or even billions of dollars and lives on the line, could you have the ethical strength to speak up? How would you do it? See Chapter 16 for a discussion about whistleblowers.

Courtesy of NASA

> *In February 2003, the space shuttle Columbia was destroyed in a disaster that claimed the lives of its seven-person crew. Follow the WEBLINK below to help you form an opinion about the ways in which various kinds of communication problems contributed to the Columbia disaster.*

the launch, they were unable to provide strong enough arguments to persuade administrators to cancel the launch. The technical descriptions were not in question; everyone agreed that O-rings were charring. However, the contextual pressures to launch influenced the way that technical information was interpreted. The O-rings were deemed safe enough, and seven lives were lost.

Dombrowski uses this example to illustrate that technical professionals cannot necessarily rely on conventional procedures to deal with ethical dilemmas. Technical professionals must recognize when the information in a document is not enough, even when it is entirely accurate. They should be willing to take personal responsibility to make sure they have done all that is possible to convey the full picture and explain the implications of descriptions that would otherwise go unnoticed.

WEBLINK

Following the space shuttle *Columbia* disaster, a Columbia Accident Investigation Board (CAIB) was formed. In August 2003, the CAIB released a report that said, "unless the technical, organizational, and cultural recommendations made in this report are implemented, little will have been accomplished to lessen the chance that another accident will follow." For a link to more information about the *Columbia*, including the final CAIB report, transcripts and videos of the press conferences, and background information about the missions and crew, go to **http://english.wadsworth.com/burnett6e**.
   CLICK ON WEBLINK
      CLICK on Chapter 15/Columbia

Using Technical Description
使用技术描述

> *How could you write a description that would be sure to get the attention of managers who needed to know the information for decision making?*

How do you know when to use a technical description? You can decide whether to include a description and what kind of details to incorporate by examining the context, purpose, and task of your document.

- Will a description help accomplish *your purpose* of providing information, persuading readers or listeners, or helping them complete a task?
- Will a description help members of the audience accomplish *their purpose* of gathering information, making a decision, or completing an action or activity?
- Will a description help prevent problems?

The following discussion identifies and illustrates some common applications for technical descriptions: observation notes, reference and training materials, reports and proposals, marketing and promotional materials, and public information and education.

Observation Notes 观察记录

Many situations require accurate first-hand descriptions, particularly in medicine, field study, and scientific research. Technical experts observe, select, and record relevant data, often employing abbreviations and jargon specific to the field. The initial purpose of observation notes is to maintain an accurate record. Later, the notes may be extended or transcribed so others can read them, or they may be used as the basis for a more formal document.

The *Manual of Pediatric Therapeutics,* a reference volume for pediatric practitioners, outlines the longstanding and widely used criteria for immediate evaluation of newborns. This evaluation, based on observation by medical professionals, provides a detailed physical description of the newborn. The excerpt in Figure 15.2 provides information for the delivery room observation and evaluation.

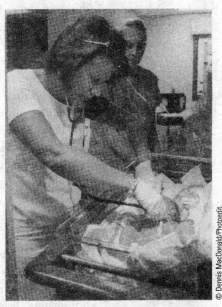

Training Materials 培训手册

Both student interns and new employees often need descriptive overviews of the tools and systems with which they'll work, so technical descriptions can be an appropriate part of initial training. For example, the short catalog description, as

In the delivery room, a newborn infant is screened with an Apgar test. Here, the heartbeat is being checked.

FIGURE 15.2   **Apgar Score: Description Based on Observation**[8]

Accessible
- The outline makes the hierarchy clear.
- The five critical signs are emphasized with italics.

Comprehensible
- The purpose of the Apgar score is clearly stated.
- Technical vocabulary restricts the information to experts.
- The embedded reference to the table helps readers link the text and table.

Usable
- The explanation precedes the application of the system.
- Time-sensitive instructions are presented.
- Presenting critical criteria and rating in a table make information easy to use.

I. EVALUATION OF THE NEWBORN
  A. **Delivery room.** Immediate assessment of the newborn infant by the Apgar scoring system should help to identify infants with severe metabolic imbalances. At 1 and 5 minutes after delivery (the times at which feet and head are both first visible), the infant is to be evaluated for five signs — *heart rate, respiratory effort, muscle tone, reflexes* and *irritability* and *color* — and given a rating of 0, 1, or 2 (as defined in Table 5-1). In the extremely compromised infant, prompt and efficient resuscitation is far more important than his exact Apgar score.

TABLE 5-1
Apgar Score *(Score infant at 1 and 5 minutes of age)*

Sign	0	1	2
Heart rate	absent	slow, less than 100	100 or over
Respiratory effort	absent	weak cry, hypoventilation	crying lustily
Muscle tone	flaccid	some flexion, extremities	well-flexed
Reflex irritability	no response	some motion	cry
Color	blue, pale	blue hands and feet	entirely pink

shown in Figure 15.3, provides only sketchy details about a circular inspection mirror — sufficient for ordering the tool but not for learning about it.

An intern or new employee would not know why this tool is used, how it's used, or what special features it has that make it important. The description of a circular inspection mirror in Figure 15.4, which presents a more detailed description than the catalog does, could be used as background reading during initial orientation to introduce this basic piece of inspection equipment. Notice that both the text and the figure are essential for a complete description; either by itself provides only partial information. Notice also that while the information is precise and carefully organized, the language is easy to understand and the tone is friendly, so the audience is more likely to read the information sheet and understand why this particular small tool is important.

Technical Manuals 技术手册

Most manuals include a technical description of the mechanism or system that the manual deals with. The description usually appears in one of the manual's early sections, often providing a general overview followed by more detailed information. It introduces the user, operator, technician, or repairperson to the physical characteristics of the mechanism or system. Technical descriptions in manuals are usually accompanied by a variety of visuals: the entire mechanism or system, exploded views, blowups, and phantom and cutaway views of individual parts and subparts.

FIGURE 15.3 — Catalog Description of a Circular Mirror[9]

Accessible
- Features and details are differentiated by headings.
- Information is presented in easy-to-read lists.

Comprehensible
- Vocabulary is basic.
- A photo depicts the overall appearance.

Usable
- Dimensions are clearly identified.

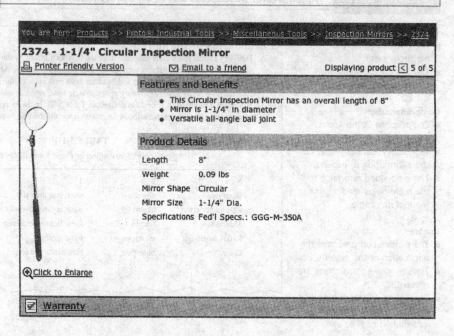

FIGURE 15.4   Circular Inspection Mirror[10] Information Sheet

CIRCULAR INSPECTION MIRROR

Everyone working in our group uses a circular inspection mirror. It looks similar to a hand mirror used by a dentist to inspect teeth, with one exception: this mirror swivels separately from the handle.

Function. The circular inspection mirror is one of the most important tools you'll use to visually inspect general electrical and mechanical equipment for production flaws. The mirror helps you observe areas that — because of the angled displacement within the unit — are normally hidden from view.

Components. The inspection mirror shown in Figure 1 consists of three main parts: mirror, universal swivel joint, and handle.

An especially important feature is the lack of distortion in the 1⅛"-mirror, which reflects identical size figures. The mirror's durable stainless steel casing adds ⅛" to the overall diameter, making the total diameter of the mirror 1¼".

  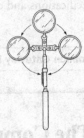

Figure 1. Circular Inspection Mirror

The mechanics incorporated in the swivel design allow a complete 360° spherical positioning of the mirror with no movement of the handle.

Attached by spot welding to the inside of the casing back is a small stem extending ⅜" and concluding in a round bearing. This bearing is positioned inside a two-bearing universal joint.

The simple universal joint uses two encloser plates held together by a nut and screw. Impressed in the plates are four concave pockets that prevent the bearings from leaving the joint but allow maximum rotation to the attached handle or mirror. By tightening and loosening the screw, you can adjust the mirror to the desired tension.

Also located inside the universal casing and opposite the bearing attached to the mirror is the second bearing, which connects to a hard tempered-steel handle that is approximately 6" long.

Safety. The rough surface of the metal handle is covered for 3" with orange plastic insulation that protects you from electrical shock and possible electrocution.

Convenience. An additional feature of the circular inspection mirror is a pocket clip, located toward the middle of the handle, which allows the tool to be carried like a pen in your shirt pocket.

Accessible
- Run-in headings identify the four topics the audience should understand and remember.
- The serif font is sufficiently large to read easily.
- The paragraphs are very short, which is appropriate for this kind of quick reference document.

Comprehensible
- Second-person "you" lets readers know this information is related to them.
- Vocabulary is technically accurate but easy to understand.

Usable
- The figure is embedded in the text in the appropriate place and referred to directly.
- Critical information — lack of distortion, adjustability, safety — is clear.

Figure 15.5 provides users with information about CGI. Because this information is available electronically, users can select the path that best matches their own needs and experience. For example, users are told, "If you have no idea what CGI is, you should read this introduction." And if they click that hyperlink, they get Figure 15.6. Users are also told that is they have a basic idea of what CGI is, they can select a primer. And if they click that hyperlink, they get Figure 15.7.

Proposals and Reports 研究提案与研究报告

If a description helps the audience understand and approve a proposal, it should be included. This type of description usually gives an overview and then provides details appropriate for the primary reader(s). For example, a proposal from a manager of research and development (R&D) to the company comptroller about an equipment purchase would logically include a description of the equipment. However, the description would not be detailed because the equipment's technical specifications and capabilities are not relevant for that audience. If secondary

FIGURE 15.5 Common Gateway Interface[11]

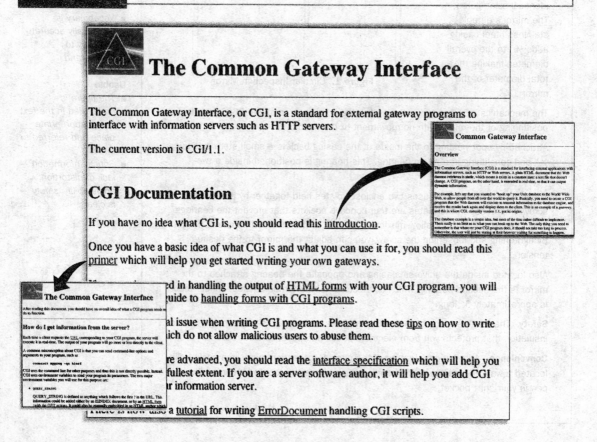

FIGURE 15.6 Common Gateway Interface for Novices Who Need an Introduction[12]

Common Gateway Interface

Overview

The Common Gateway Interface (CGI) is a standard for interfacing external applications with information servers, such as HTTP or Web servers. A plain HTML document that the Web daemon **retrieves** is **static**, which means it exists in a constant state: a text file that doesn't change. A CGI program, on the other hand, is **executed** in real-time, so that it can output **dynamic** information.

For example, let's say that you wanted to "hook up" your Unix database to the World Wide Web, to allow people from all over the world to query it. Basically, you need to create a CGI program that the Web daemon will execute to transmit information to the database engine, and receive the results back again and display them to the client. This is an example of a *gateway*, and this is where CGI, currently version 1.1, got its origins.

The database example is a simple idea, but most of the time rather difficult to implement. There really is no limit as to what you can hook up to the Web. The only thing you need to remember is that whatever your CGI program does, it should not take too long to process. Otherwise, the user will just be staring at their browser waiting for something to happen.

FIGURE 15.7 Common Gateway Interface for Beginners Who Need a Primer[13]

The Common Gateway Interface

After reading this document, you should have an overall idea of what a CGI program needs to do to function.

How do I get information from the server?

Each time a client requests the URL corresponding to your CGI program, the server will execute it in real-time. The output of your program will go more or less directly to the client.

A common misconception about CGI is that you can send command-line options and arguments to your program, such as

    command% myprog -qa blorf

CGI uses the command line for other purposes and thus this is not directly possible. Instead, CGI uses environment variables to send your program its parameters. The two major environment variables you will use for this purpose are:

- QUERY_STRING

    QUERY_STRING is defined as anything which follows the first ? in the URL. This information could be added either by an ISINDEX document, or by an HTML form (with the GET action). It could also be manually embedded in an HTML anchor which

readers for the same proposal are familiar with R&D operations, an appendix could discuss technical details. In contrast, a proposal to a state's environmental control commission from a local community to preserve a wetlands area would include a detailed description of the geographic area as a main part of the proposal. The members of the commission would need the details to make an informed decision about the validity of the preservation plan.

Several types of reports incorporate descriptions. For example, a report about changes in the work flow in an assembly area because of new automatic insertion equipment could logically include a description of this equipment. A supervisor writing to the division manager would emphasize features of the equipment that have affected the work flow. Generally, any report justifying or recommending acquisition or modification of equipment or facilities should include a description.

Marketing and Promotional Pieces 市场营销材料

Technical descriptions in marketing materials are usually both informative and persuasive. Positive (and, of course, subjective) terms are often incorporated into the initial description. The information presents an overview, identifying major components and characteristics. Additional information is often condensed on specification sheets (specs). Promotional and marketing materials frequently include visuals that first display the entire object or mechanism and then highlight its special features.

Figure 15.8 shows a technical description that balances text and visuals. It's an excerpt from a four-page, four-color, 11" × 17" glossy marketing brochure for a Ruud Achiever 90 Plus Modulating Gas Furnace with Contour Comfort Control. The brochure defines and describes a modulating gas furnace in several ways because it will be unfamiliar to many homeowners who are considering buying a furnace. Figure 15.8 is one of the critical parts of the brochure, describing the furnace with a cutaway view of the furnace itself and succinct explanations of each of the major components.

Public Information and Education 公众宣传和教育

Much of the technical and scientific information presented to the public in newspapers, general-interest magazines, and Web sites includes a substantial amount of description, simply because people need to know *what* something is before they make decisions about its value. Sometimes the presentation of this information follows the same general organization as presentations in more technical documents (that is, as text supported by visuals). At other times, though, the presentation to general readers uses a small amount of text to support dramatic visuals.

An example of a useful Web site providing valuable public information — much of it technical description — is one sponsored by the Danish Wind Industry Association. Because wind energy is an international technology and

FIGURE 15.8 Technical Description of a Modulating Gas Furnace[14]

FEATURES

① Comfort For Life
The primary heat exchanger at the heart of this furnace is made of solid stainless steel. We are so confident of its quality that we give it a limited lifetime warranty.

② Direct Spark Ignition & Remote Flame Sensor
Direct spark ignition is an extremely efficient way to light the burner and eliminates the need for a standing pilot. And for added safety during operation, the remote flame sensor constantly monitors the burner flame to ensure it is burning as it should.

④ Modulating Gas Valve & ③ Burner
To keep you comfortable while it keeps your energy bills low, the gas valve delivers fuel to the burner at a variable rate, as required, to maintain the desired temperature. You get the heat you need, when you need it. Designed to provide the most efficient air/gas mixture, the shutter-free design of the burner eliminates the need for adjustments. The burner always delivers its flames directly into the primary heat exchanger for the greatest efficiency.

⑤ Two-Speed Induced Draft Blower
Working in conjunction with the modulating burner, Ruud's induced draft blower quietly pulls hot combustion gases through the heat exchangers and vents them safely outdoors. And it does this at one of two speeds, depending on the operating level of the burner. Most of the time it runs at the slower speed, meaning lower electricity usage and operation that is more quiet.

⑥ Modulating ECM Blower Motor
The advanced ECM blower motor varies in speed depending on your demand for heat. And in continuous fan mode, this motor is so efficient that it uses less electricity than a 75 watt light bulb. This motor always operates at just above a whisper, far more quietly than a conventional blower motor, to help keep your home warm and peaceful.

⑥ Integrated Furnace Control
The "brain" of this furnace is the patented integrated control board. This unique design has two processors that check the actions of each other to ensure optimum performance. The control directs the actions of the blower motor, the inducer motor and other furnace components to give you the heating capacity you need.

⑦ Secondary Heat Exchanger
One secret behind the superb efficiency of this furnace is the secondary heat exchanger. It captures heat that escapes your primary heat exchanger and uses it to warm your home. It is also backed by a limited lifetime warranty.

⑧ Easy-Access Washable Filter
With the air filter kept clean, your furnace will perform better and operate more efficiently. And with this furnace, you won't have to deal with the hassle and expense of replacement filters because it's equipped with a permanent, washable filter that's easy to access and clean.

Accessible
- Strong figure-ground contrast makes the diagram easy to see.
- The font is sufficiently large to be legible in home lighting.
- Each bulleted and numbered item is in a contrasting color for easy legibility.

Comprehensible
- The description presumes readers' purposes: (1) consider the purchase of a new furnace, (2) understand the distinctive features.
- Definitions of critical features are embedded in the text.
- Analogies help nonexperts.

Usable
- Numbers in the bullets refer to critical features on the diagram in ascending order of importance to furnace function.
- Each bulleted and numbered item has a key phrase heading to make content easy to locate.
- The cutaway view enables readers to see the interior of the furnace.

because Denmark is part of the European Union, the home page (Figure 15.9) gives users the choice of accessing the information in Danish (naturally), German, English, Spanish, and French. If you choose Danish, you see a page with several choices, each briefly described: a guided tour, a manual for calculations, experiments, class activities for schools, and a Quicktime video. Figure 15.10 shows part of the initial Danish page and the English page, with descriptions of the options the site offers.

WEBLINK

The Danish Wind Industry site (Figures 15.9 and 15.10) can be useful to you in two ways. First, you can learn a great deal about wind energy. Additionally, you can study a tutorial designed for a broad audience and assess whether you like the approach. For a link, go to **http://english.wadsworth.com/burnett6e**.
   CLICK ON WEBLINK
      CLICK on Chapter 15/wind energy

FIGURE 15.9 Danish Wind Industry Association Home Page Offering Access in Five Languages[15]

FIGURE 15.10 — Danish Wind Industry Association Contents Page in Danish[16] and in English[17]

WINDPOWER.ORG

< > Søg Print zoom

- ▶Dansk
  - ─ Hjem
    - ▶Rundtur
    - ▶Vindkrafthåndbog
    - ─ Spørgsmål
    - ─ Quiz om vindkraft
    - ▶Nyhedsarkiv
    - ▶Publikationer
    - ▶Kontakt
    - ─ © Copyright
    - ─ Fabrikanter
    - ─ Komponenter
    - ─ Links
    - ▶Web video
    - ─ Download websted
    - ─ Webbutik
    - ▶Vind med Møller
  - ─ Deutsch
  - ─ English
  - ─ Español
  - ─ Français

ENERGIFORLIG SKABER OPTIMISME
Det energipolitiske forlig indgået 29. marts 2004 er en anerkendelse af, at vindmølleindustrien er en vigtig velfærdsdynamo, som skaber beskæftigelse til mere end 20.000 danskere.
"Kontinuiteten på det strategisk vigtige danske vindkraftmarked er en forudsætning for, at vi fortsat kan beholde førertrøjen i den skærpede konkurrence på det globale marked," siger Vindmølle-industriens direktør Bjarne Lundager Jensen.
Læs pressemeddelelsen

ÅRSBERETNING 2003
Hent Vindmølleindustriens årsberetning 2003 som pdf.

VINDFORMATION
Download december 2003 og tidligere numre af kvartalsbladet.

STATEN KAN TJENE PÅ CO_2-KØB
»Køb af CO_2-kvoter baseret på vindkraftprojekter kan give nettogevinster til statskassen«, fortæller Vindmølleindustriens direktør Bjarne Lundager Jensen.
Se pressemeddelelsen og download rapporten

UD AF DET BLÅ er en 28 minutters Quick Time video med introduktion til vindkraft.

RUNDTUR I VINDKRAFTENS VERDEN er den mest besøgte del af dette websted. Den har mere end 100 sider om vind, placering af vindmøller, teknologi, elnet, miljø, økonomi og historie.

VIND MED MØLLER er et websted til skolebrug med opgaver og lærervejledning. Målgruppen er 5. klasse og opefter, men mange andre synes, dette er en sjov og hurtig måde at lære om vindkraft.

WINDPOWER.ORG

< > Search Print zoom

- ▶English
  - ─ Home
    - ▶Guided tour
    - ─ Wind energy manual
    - ─ FAQs
    - ─ Wind energy quiz
    - ▶News
    - ▶Publications
    - ▶Contact
    - ─ Copyright
    - ─ Manufacturers
    - ─ Components
    - ─ Links
    - ▶Web video
    - ─ Download web site
    - ─ Web shop
    - ▶Wind With Miller
  - ─ Dansk
  - ─ Deutsch
  - ─ Español
  - ─ Français

ENERGY AGREEMENT ENSURES CONTINUITY IN DENMARK
"The broad energy agreement reached 29. march 2004 shows, that there is a broad consensus in the Danish Parliament behind continued wind power development", says Bjarne Lundager Jensen, managing director of the Danish Wind Industry Association.
"Danish politicians recognize that the wind industry is an important engine for growth and welfare contributing billions of Euros to the Danish balance of payments as well as creating employment for more than 20.000 Danes."
Read press release

NEW SCIENCE PROJECT
Download a pdf with building instructions and experiments with a paper wind turbine - complete with a gearbox.

WIND VIDEO Out of the Blue is a 28 minute Quick Time video introducing wind energy.

THE GUIDED TOUR is the most visited section of this web site. It has more than 100 pages on wind, turbine siting, technology, electrical grid, environmental and economic aspects of wind energy and history.

WIND WITH MILLER is a web site for schools with class assignments and a teacher's guide. The target audience is 5th grade and up, but many others think this is a fun and fast way to learn about wind energy.

© Copyright 2004 Danish Wind Industry Association
Updated 29 March 2004
http://www.windpower.org/en/core.htm
Version 4.1

Preparing a Technical Description

准备技术描述

To prepare a technical description, you need to identify the audience and task, determine the components, choose precise diction, design effective visuals, and select an appropriate format.

Audience's Task 交流对象的需求

Technical description should address the intended audience. The only way for you to make sure the description meets the needs of members of your audience is to analyze their purpose in reading the document and identify the questions they expect to have answered. You may find talking with representatives of the actual users very productive. At this stage, you should ask several questions:

> *What additional questions might be useful to anticipate?*

- Why do users want or need the information? What is their task? In what ways will the information be important?
- Do they need information in order to understand a more detailed discussion that follows? Do they need to make a decision?
- Are users interested in a general overview or a detailed description?
- What details do the users need: Dimensions? Materials? Assembly? Function? Capabilities? Benefits?

Giving insufficient information leaves the audience with unanswered questions, but be equally wary of including unnecessary information; you may obscure facts you want to convey.

As you prepare a technical description, select information that responds to the audience's probable questions. The more removed the audience is from actually using the information in the description, the more general it can be. For example, the excerpt from the *Voyager Bulletin* at the beginning of this chapter is easy to read despite the inclusion of specific data; the readers of this status update report are generally interested nonexperts, not astrophysicists or aerospace engineers. Precisely identifying the audience also helps you decide on such crucial aspects of the description as components, diction, visuals, and format.

Components 组成部分

Before you can describe something, you must separate it into parts or components because the description emphasizes the physical characteristics of each part. But people's concepts of "part" differ greatly. For instance, should a description of the moon Io be separated according to elements, geologic structures, or electromagnetic fields? Or consider the case of mechanical engineers asked to specify the number of parts in a simple house key. Their answers range from 1 to 27, with the mode (the number occurring most frequently) being 5. Their answers differ because they do not define *part* in the same way.

You can easily see that how you partition something depends on your purpose as the writer and on the background and task of the audience. Components can usually be separated into structural parts and functional parts.

- *Structural parts* comprise the physical aspects of the device, without regard to purpose. For example, a simple house key is made of a single piece of metal.
- *Functional parts* perform clearly defined tasks in the operation of the device. Although the key has a single structural part, it has multiple functional parts.

Applying your knowledge about the audience can help you decide whether one method of separating an object into its parts is more appropriate than another. Thinking about the audience and the purpose for writing the description also helps you decide whether you need to describe all the parts or only some of them.

> What other items have distinct structural and functional parts? What are the structural and functional parts of a fiberglass sailboat hull? A screwdriver? A car tailpipe?

> How many parts does your house/apartment key have? What about your car key?

Diction 语言使用

The diction of a technical description should be precise, so that the information is verifiable. You can achieve this precision in three ways: choose the most specific terms appropriate for your audience, choose technically accurate terms, and consider the value of metaphor to convey descriptions.

Audience-appropriate Terms. Whether you select general or specific terms depends on the needs of your audience. Generally, nonexperts need accurate information, but they do not require extraordinary detail. Readers with more technical background need more technical details. For example, a general description of a lawnmower might appear in an advertising flyer from a chain store sent to all residents in an area. A more detailed description could be in a product brochure that sales reps could use to explain the mower's specifications to interested customers. Figure 15.11 presents two lawnmower descriptions that illustrate how characteristics can be described using general or specific diction, depending on audience needs.

Accurate Terms. A second way for a writer to ensure precision is to use the most accurate terms available. For example, many writers should differentiate more accurately between two- and three-dimensional objects. How often have you heard someone mistakenly refer to a ball as *round* instead of *spherical* or a box as a *square* rather than a *cube*? These geometric shapes — sphere/circle, cube/square, cone/pyramid/triangle — are commonly misused.

> What other terms have you heard people misuse?

Not only is careless diction inaccurate, it also causes confusion for the audience. For example, if a three-dimensional object is described as triangular, how will the audience know if the solid form is really a cone or a pyramid? Figure 15.12 on page 565 reviews the terminology of geometric shapes. You can use these terms for figures, solids, and surfaces if your audience is familiar with them. If your audience is unlikely to know these terms, you may need to define the term or use a diagram.

FIGURE 15.11 Gaining Precision in Technical Descriptions

What other details might be important to engineers? To repair technicans? To consumers?

General Abstract Terms		Specific Concrete Terms
dependable mower	(specify brand)	Briggs and Stratton
powerful	(specify amount)	4 cycle, 3 1/2 HP
self-propelled	(specify type)	rear-wheel belt-to-chain drive
wide blade	(specify size)	21" blade
adjustable height	(specify variation)	7 positions, 1-3"
powerful, dependable, self-propelled mower with wide blade adjustable to cut different heights		Briggs and Stratton mower with 4-cycle, 3 1/2 HP engine; self-propelled by rear-wheel belt-to-chain drive; 21" blade; 7 cutting heights from 1-3"

Figurative Language. A third way to ensure precision is to consider whether figurative language such as metaphors, similes, and analogies would give readers a clear description. The example in Figure 15.13 on page 566 is taken from *Air & Space*, a publication read by aerospace engineers. The example presents a technical description of a microelectromechanical system (MEMS) that embeds both verbal and visual metaphors. The visual metaphor uses a playing card to illustrate the size of the MEMS in relation to the stealth aircraft that uses it. The language includes not only metaphors (e.g., "smart cars," "radar signatures"), but also similes (e.g., "like a spoiler," "flap-like surfaces," "as delicate as butterfly wings") and analogies (e.g., "sequins too small for a Barbie doll's cocktail dress").

Visuals 视觉手段

Precise visuals are as important in effective technical descriptions as is precise diction. Visuals enable the audience to form a mental image of the subject being described. Of course, all visuals should be labeled and titled and referred to in the text. Dimensions are usually more appropriately presented in visuals so the text is not cluttered or difficult to read.

In organizing a typical technical description of a mechanism, you could have an introductory section with a drawing or a photograph that shows the overall

FIGURE 15.12 Geometric Shapes[18]

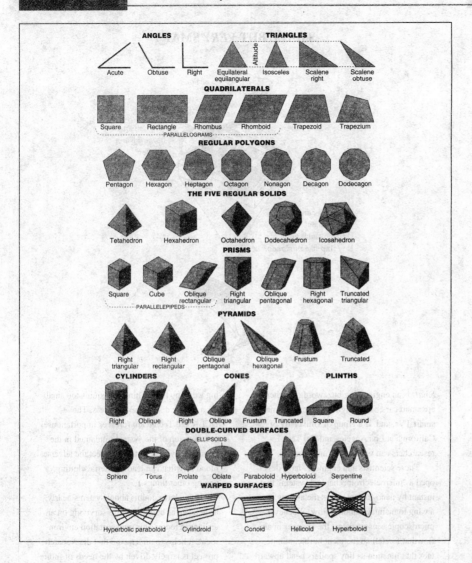

features. In organizing the rest of the description, you could use detailed views, such as phantom or cutaway views, to show the location of parts, as well as enlarged drawings, which could be placed adjacent to the text that describes them. Figure 15.14 on page 567 suggests that different types of visuals can be used to illustrate the exterior, the interior, and individual components as they relate to the whole. (Chapter 12 discusses visuals in more detail.)

FIGURE 15.13 Visual and Verbal Metaphor in Technical Text[19]

How effective is the visual metaphor of a playing card to illustrate the relative size of MEMS?

What specific examples of figurative language such as metaphors, similes, and analogies can you identify in this article?

How does the figurative language help readers understand the features of MEMS?

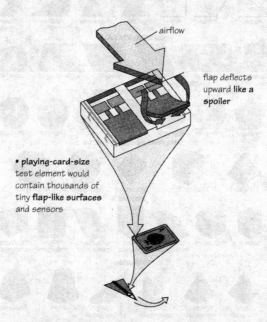

SMALL BUT *VERY* SMART

airflow

flap deflects upward **like a spoiler**

• **playing-card-size** test element would contain thousands of tiny **flap-like surfaces** and sensors

Smart is an engineering buzzword . . . ; there are smart cars, smart highways, smart bombs, smart TVs, and, if a group of University of California at Los Angeles and Cal Tech researchers can work it out, smart wings.

These scientists and engineers have developed a "microelectromechanical system" that, instant by nano-instant, alters the airflow over a wing to maintain laminar flow. Whenever microscopic sensors detect the changes in airflow that foretell an incipient burble, minute tabs that function as tiny spoilers bend upward into the airflow to create counter-burbles that cancel out the boundary layer separation.

Microelectromechanical systems—let's henceforth revert to the official acronym MEMS—include devices (flaplets, in this case) so small that thousands of them can be built into microchips that also house the controlling sensors as well as the actuators that activate the surfaces themselves. (We're talk-

ing *way* tiny here: Think of sequins too small for a Barbie doll's cocktail dress. The UCLA/Cal Tech team foresees important uses for a version of the system implanted in the human body to detect and correct the adverse blood flow that can lead to arterial clotting, among other things.)

If you have doubts about systems nearly as delicate as butterfly wings surviving on an airliner in today's air transportation environment, it helps to understand that the research project is largely driven by the needs of future military aircraft. For stealthy airplanes, MEMS arrays that maintain laminar flow could also be used as substitutes for conventional movable control surfaces, which can create radar signatures when they're deflected. Deflect a bunch of MEMS on one wing or the other, say, and considerable lift asymmetry can be created, literally invisibly, rolling the airplane just the way an aileron would.

FIGURE 15.14   Visuals for Technical Descriptions

Purpose of Visual	Selected Visual to Use in Technical Descriptions
Visuals to give an overview	- photographs - realistic drawings - topographic or contour maps
Visuals to describe interior components, to give an image of the way the parts fit together	- phantom views (drawings that depict an exterior surface as transparent so the inside structure can be viewed) - schematics and wiring diagrams - cross-section maps
Visuals to describe individual parts in relation to the whole, to give an image of each individual component	- exploded views (drawings that separate all the components and display them in the proper sequence and relationship for assembly) - cutaway views (drawings that slice a section out to show a full or partial cross-section) - blueprints - photographs or drawings of individual parts
Visuals to show patterns	- photographs - videos - realistic drawings - pairs or groups of photographs or drawings

What kinds of visuals have you seen used in technical descriptions?

Some concepts and mechanisms are extraordinarily difficult to explain without the use of visuals. One example is the subject of the recent book *Self-Organization in Biological Systems,* which explores "diverse pattern formation processes in the physical and biological world."[20] What kinds of patterns? Zebra stripes. Stamen clusters. Designs on butterfly wings. The visual images provide explicit descriptions, as shown in the photos below and on the next page.

The primary author of *Self-Organization in Biological Systems,* Scott Camazine, describes self-organization as "the various mechanisms by which pattern, structure and order emerge spontaneously in complex systems . . . the pattern of sand ripples in a dune, the coordinated movements of flocks of birds or schools of fish, the intricate earthen nests of termites, the patterns on seashells, the whorls of our fingerprints, the colorful patterns of fish and even the spatial pattern of stars in a spiral galaxy."[21]

WEBLINK

Self-organization first catches our attention because of the amazing visual patterns. Then it captures our attention because of the mathematical "rules" that can be followed to simulate these patterns. For a link to an article in *Natural History* about this way of describing patterns and for extraordinary still and animated images that illustrate the principles, go to **http://www.english. wadsworth.com/burnett6e**.
   CLICK ON WEBLINK
     CLICK on Chapter 15/self-organization

Organization 信息组织

When preparing a technical description, you have to make decisions about the sequence of information. Writers conventionally organize technical descriptions in spatial order to give the audience a clear view of appearance and structure. Occasionally, writers use chronological order, describing the components in order of assembly, or use priority order, describing the components in order of importance. Figure 15.15 outlines a conventional sequence of information you can use to plan a detailed technical description.

FIGURE 15.15 **Planning a Technical Description**

What visuals would be appropriate for various sections of a technical description?

Title

1.0 Define the object (or substance, mechanism, organism, system, or location) in the introduction.
    1.1   Define the object. Identify whose perspective the definition is from.
    1.2   Identify the purpose of the object. Indicate the importance or impact of this purpose.
    1.3   Describe the characteristics of the whole. Indicate acceptable tolerances or specifications.
    1.4   Present a visual that provides an overall view of the object.
    1.5   Identify the parts of the object.

2.0 Present a part-by-part description arranged in order of the parts' assembly, location, or importance.
    2.1   Describe part one.
        2.1.1   Define the part.
        2.1.2   Identify the purpose of the part.
        2.1.3   Describe the general appearance of the part (including a visual if useful).
        2.1.4   Describe the characteristics of the part. Indicate acceptable tolerances or specifications.
            2.1.4.1   Identify the general shape and dimensions.
            2.1.4.2   Identify the material type and characteristics (color, flammability, optical properties, solubility, density, conductivity, magnetism, and so on).
            2.1.4.3   Identify the surface treatment, texture.
            2.1.4.4   Identify the weight.
            2.1.4.5   Identify the method of manufacture.
            2.1.4.6   Identify the subparts of part one.
        2.1.5   Describe its attachment to other parts.
    2.2   Describe part two.
        . . . and so on

3.0 Conclude the description.
    3.1   Explain how the parts fit together.
    3.2   Explain how the parts function together. Explain what criteria are used to establish effectiveness.

Technical descriptions should have a title if they are printed as a separate document or a section heading if they are incorporated into one section of another document. The introductory section usually begins with a definition suitable for the intended audience. The definition can include or be followed by a statement of the purpose or function of the document, as in this example:

> As the new owner of a wood-burning stove, you should be familiar with its structure and components. This information will help you safely maintain your stove as a supplemental source of home heat.

The introductory material presents an abbreviated version of the description. It includes characteristics of the whole: overall shape and major dimensions, primary color and texture, and any distinctive aspects. A photograph or realistic drawing often supplements this overall description. The final part of the introductory section partitions the whole into its major parts, in the order they will be described. This partition can be illustrated with an exploded or cutaway view.

To appeal to a particular audience, you may incorporate into the introductory material elements that increase audience interest and background knowledge but do not add substantively to the technical content. Keep in mind that experts are usually annoyed by the inclusion of what they consider extraneous information. However, if you are writing for or speaking to a general or nonexpert audience, consider some of these elements that may add interest or appeal to the introductory section:

- *Background information:* What is the history? What are current developments?
- *Parts–whole relationships:* Where does the object fit in relation to similar ones?
- *Qualitative distinctions:* What separates it from similar objects?

The body of a technical description involves a part-by-part description arranged in order of location, assembly, or importance. Each section of the body follows the same format. Initially, the part, and sometimes its purpose, is defined. Then a description of the general appearance of the part, including shape, major dimensions, and material, follows, often accompanied by a visual presenting detailed dimensions. The outline in Figure 15.10 identifies additional characteristics that are relevant for some audiences. Specifics are added according to the needs of the audience.

An architect designing a passive solar house would want information about surface treatments, optical and insulating properties, and weights of specially treated glass. An interior designer would be more concerned with color and texture. Both would be interested in subparts and methods of attachment to other parts.

The conclusion explains how the parts fit and function together. Just as you can stimulate reader interest in the introduction, you can also create a more lively conclusion by including some of these elements:

- *Applications:* How is it used?
- *Anecdotes or brief narratives:* Who uses it?
- *Advantages/disadvantages:* What are the benefits and/or problems?

Often a technical description does not have a concluding section, but simply ends when the last part has been fully described.

Individual and Collaborative Assignments
个人作业和小组作业

1. **Identify parts for analysis.** (a) Identify ways to describe the following subjects. Each can be separated into a number of different parts or subsystems. (b) Add one subject from your own profession to each category and identify its parts or subsystems, too.

   An organism such as a wolf can be separated in a number of ways. Some ways include by cellular composition; by categories of fluids, such as blood; by categories of systems, such as muscles; by categories of physical functions, such as reproduction and respiration; and by categories of ecological functions, such as controlling the elk population.

Subjects	Examples	Parts or systems
Objects	- golf ball - wood screw	
Mechanisms	- carbon monoxide detector - kidney	
Substances	- granola - ocean water	
Systems	- immune system - workflow in office	
Organisms	- decathlon athlete - experimental variety of corn	
Locations	- site of a new building - protected wetland	

2. **Distinguish between structural and functional parts.** Identify the structural and functional parts for one column of the following items. Both word lists and diagrams will help you identify the distinctions.

AAA battery	comb	light bulb	pocket lighter
ballpoint pen	field daisy	magnet	pocket knife
baseball	flashlight	oxygen tank	scissors
candle	hand saw	pinecone	zipper

3. **Choose appropriate diction for specificity.** Some descriptions might be inappropriate because they're negative or vague.

   (a) Under what circumstances might the following descriptions be inappropriate? Suggest possible alternatives that would provide more detailed and accurate descriptions.

   - big equipment shed
   - cheap replacement part
   - cold weather complicated step
   - easy-to-assemble desk
   - fast microprocessor
   - fast photocopier
   - fat patient
   - hard surface
   - recent decision
   - sharp angle

   (b) What other general description terms can you think of that might be inappropriate? In what circumstances?

4. **Consider audience needs.** Imagine that you work for a company that manufactures modular houses and sells directly to individual customers. Several publications are being prepared, and you have been assigned responsibility for creating descriptions of the modular houses. How would you identify the parts of the modular houses for the following audiences?

   - government agency with information about fuel-efficient construction methods
   - production line manager
   - architect
   - lumber wholesaler
   - municipal wiring and/or plumbing inspector
   - prospective homeowner

5. **Choose visuals for certain descriptions.** Several kinds of visuals are described in this chapter. Which would be appropriate to incorporate into a description of each of the following items? What would make one kind of

visual more appropriate than another kind for each item — considering, for example, context, purpose, and audience?

- apple, from bud to harvest
- computer mouse
- condominium complex
- crankshaft
- espresso coffee maker
- gas well
- human leg
- landfill
- mints: catnip, spearmint, peppermint, applemint
- paint sprayer
- reclining chair or geriatric chair
- septic tank and leach field
- silicon chip
- snowblower
- sprocket gears (as on a bicycle)

6. **Analyze technical descriptions.**

   (a) Bring two examples of technical descriptions to class. If possible, locate one description in a U.S. publication and the other description from a publication outside the United States.

   (b) Work with classmates in a small group to conduct a preliminary analysis of two of the technical descriptions your group brought in, considering at least these points:

   - *Context.* What assumptions seem to have been made about the context in which the descriptions will be used?
   - *Audience.* For what audience is each intended? Has the writer accurately analyzed the audience(s)?
   - *Visuals.* Are the visuals appropriate and helpful? Are additional visuals needed? Do the visuals differ in descriptions from different cultures?
   - *Format.* Does the format make the descriptions easy to read? Does the form differ in descriptions from different cultures?

   (c) Based on your preliminary analysis, create an evaluation rubric that shows how you've incorporated the criteria discussed above as well as other criteria that you and your classmates have determined are helpful in analyzing and assessing technical descriptions.

   (d) Test and refine the rubric by using it to conduct a complete analysis and evaluation of at least two other descriptions you and your classmates brought in.

   (e) Give a brief oral presentation to the class about the criteria you selected and the assessment of one of your group's descriptions.

7. **Select two visuals.** Writers and designers frequently decide to use more than one visual in combination to convey information to readers. The figure below[22] shows a cross section of an eye and then shows an enlargement of a segment of that cross section. The cross section shows the basic structure; the enlargement shows how these structures work. The caption explains to readers how they can interpret the drawings.

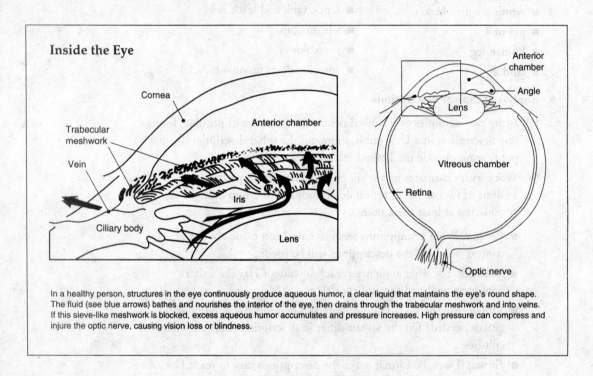

Inside the Eye

In a healthy person, structures in the eye continuously produce aqueous humor, a clear liquid that maintains the eye's round shape. The fluid (see blue arrows) bathes and nourishes the interior of the eye, then drains through the trabecular meshwork and into veins. If this sieve-like meshwork is blocked, excess aqueous humor accumulates and pressure increases. High pressure can compress and injure the optic nerve, causing vision loss or blindness.

Select a concept or mechanism that is important in your discipline. Locate two figures from the Web that work together to describe the concept or mechanism (although you may not have found them together). Write a clear, succinct description that can serve as a caption for the two visuals. (Make sure to provide appropriate citations.)

8. **Write a technical description.**

   (a) Select an object, mechanism, substance, organism, or location from the following lists, or choose another subject that relates to your field:

Objects	*Mechanisms*	*Substances*
electrical cable	cider press	photographic developer
drill bit	pool filter	acetylene
shotgun shells	spinning reel	baking powder
contact lenses	spinning wheel	baby food
mallet	camera lens	blood sample
gable roof	combination lock	measles vaccine
computer chip	solar panel	yogurt
polarizing filter	smoke alarm	plant fertilizer
photographic film	semicircular canals	effluent
golf club	transit	cough medicine

Systems	*Organisms*	*Locations*
respiratory system	termites	a harbor mooring
photovoltaic system	dolphins	cross section of well site
braking system	tapeworms	R&D section of a plant
electronic auto inspection system	algae	forest marked for logging
planetary system	chickens	layout for vegetable garden
HVAC system	yeast	geologic fault
irrigation system	mosquitoes	archaeological excavation
photocopying machine	foxgloves	traffic cloverleaf pattern
scrubber for contaminants	pumas	underground storage tank
	protozoa	runway grid for airport

   (b) Modifying the format outlined in Figure 15.15, write a description that appropriately considers context, audience, and purpose of your description.

   (c) After writing your description, work in a small group to compare and contrast it with those written by other students. Examine the organization, selection of details, adjustment for audience, and use of visuals. Explain your reasons for the choices you made in designing and developing your description.

Chapter 15 Endnotes

1. Galileo, G. (1960). The sidereal messenger. In F. R. Moulton & J. J. Schifferes (Eds.), *The autobiography of science* (2nd ed., pp. 65–76). Garden City, NY: Doubleday.

2. NASA. (n.d.). PIA00600: Family portrait of Jupiter's great reds and the Galilean satellites. *Planetary photojournal.* Retrieved November 15, 2003, from http://photojournal.jpl.nasa.gov/catalog/PIA00600

3. NASA-Jet Propulsion Laboratory. (1979, February). Mission status report. *Voyager Bulletin, 36*(23), 3.

4. Science@NASA. (n.d.) Io's alien vocanoes. Retrieved November 16, 2003, from http://science.nasa.gov/newhome/headlines/ast04oct99_1.htm

5. NASA. (n.d.). *Galileo: Journey to Jupiter.* Retrieved November 15, 2003, from http://galileo.jpl.nasa.gov/

6. NASA. (2003, September 17). *Galileo end of mission status.* Retrieved November 15, 2003, from http://www.jpl.nasa.gov/galileo/news/release/press030921.html

7. Dombroski, P. (1995). Can ethics be technologized? Lessons from Challenger, philosophy, and rhetoric. *Technical Communication Quarterly, 38*(3), 146–150.

8. Parkman, R. (1997). Management of the newborn. In J. W. Graef & T. E. Cone, Jr. (Eds.), *Manual of pediatric therapeutics* (pp. 99–100). Boston: Little, Brown and Company. Reprinted with permission of Little, Brown and Company.

9. Stanley PROTO. (n.d.). *Inspection mirror.* Retrieved November 15, 2003, from http://www.stanleyproto.com/default.asp?CATETORY=INSPECTION+MIRRORS&TYPE=PRODUCT&PARTNUMBER=2374&Sdesc=1%2D1%2F4%26quot%3B+Circular+Inspection+Mirror

10. Cocozziello, D. Circular inspection mirror. *Technical and Scientific Writing,* 42.225. University of Massachusetts at Lowell.

11. *The common gateway interface.* (n.d.). National Center for Supercomputing Applications at the University of Illinois at Urbana-Champaign. Retrieved November 15, 2003, from http://hoohoo.ncsa.uiuc.edu/cgi/

12. *Overview.* (n.d.). Retrieved November 15, 2003, from the University of Illinois at Urbana-Champaign, National Center for Supercomputing Applications Web site: http://hoohoo.ncsa.uiuc.edu/cgi/intro/html

13. *How do I get information from the server?* (n.d.). Retrieved November 15, 2003, from the University of Illinois at Urbana-Champaign, National Center for Supercomputing Applications Web site: http://hoohoo.ncsa.uiuc.edu/cgi/primer.html

14. Ruud Air Conditioning Division. (2002). *Achiever 90 plus modulating gas furnace with contour comfort control* (No M22-6003). [Brochure]. Fort Smith, AR: Ruud.

15. Danish Wind Industry Association. (2003). Home page. Retrieved November 15, 2003, from http://www.windpower.org/index.htm

16. Danish Wind Industry Association. (2003). Contents in Danish. Retrieved November 15, 2003, from http://www.windpower.org/da/core.htm

17. Danish Wind Industry Association. (2003). Contents in English. Retrieved November 15, 2003, from http://www.windpower.org/en/core.htm

[18] French, T. E., & Vierck, C. J. (1970). *Graphic science and design* (p. 79). New York: McGraw-Hill. Reprinted with permission of McGraw-Hill Book Company.

[19] *Air & Space*. (1995, June/July). p. 35.

[20] *About the book*. (n.d.). (n.a.). Retrieved November 15, 2003, from http://www.scottcamazine.com/personal/selforganization/about.htm

[21] Camazine, S. (n.d.). *Self-organization in biological systems*. Retrieved November 15, 2003, from http://www.scottcamazine.com/personal/research/index.htm

[22] Illustration by Harriet Greenfield, in Dryer, E. B. (1994, October). Preserving eyesight with foresight. *Harvard Health Letter*, 19(12), 4–6. Copyright © 1994, President and Fellows of Harvard College. Reprinted by permission.

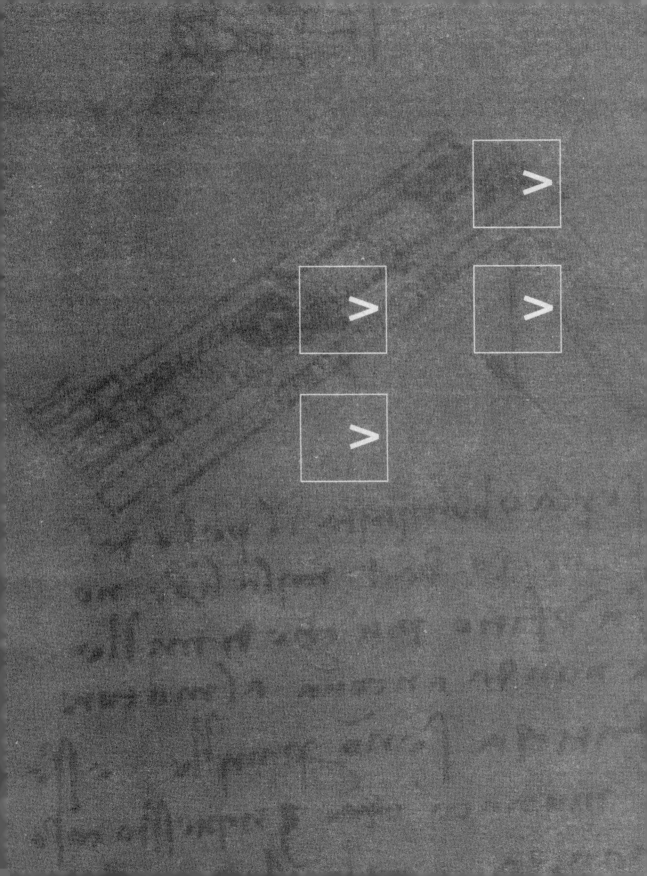

CHAPTER 16

Creating Process Explanations
创建过程解释

过程解释说明某个行动的步骤，在信息交流中起着重要作用。本章首先介绍了过程解释的定义，然后阐释过程解释在大文件（如使用手册、培训材料、市场营销材料、公众宣传信息）中的应用。最后，本章用实例说明如何准备过程解释。

Objectives and Outcomes 学习目标

This chapter will help you accomplish these outcomes:

- Understand that process explanations present an overview of sequential actions in chronological order

- Use process explanations as part of larger documents, including manuals, orientation and training materials, marketing and promotional materials, and public information

- Use a conventional sequence of technical description, process explanation, and benefits or advantages that an audience can use

- Prepare effective process explanations by following these steps:

Process explanations play an important role in technical communication by providing information about the sequence of steps in any action, from blood donation to operation of a jet engine. Generally, *process explanations* (also called process descriptions) provide an overview or background, regardless of the audience's specific tasks. They are often embedded in a longer discussion that has already presented a definition and general description, as in this example taken from a U.S. Department of Energy (DOE) Web site about the Wind Energy Program:

> So how do wind turbines make electricity? Simply stated, a wind turbine works the opposite of a fan. Instead of using electricity to make wind, like a fan, wind turbines use wind to make electricity. The wind turns the blades, which spin a shaft, which connects to a generator and makes electricity. Utility-scale turbines range in size from 50 to 750 kilowatts. Single small turbines, below 50 kilowatts, are used for homes, telecommunications dishes, or water pumping.[1]

What works in process explanations? Analogies the audience can understand, statement of purpose, explanation of actions, and relation of equipment to application. All of these strategies in the short DOE process help explain how wind turbines make electricity.

Sometimes process explanations don't need to be any longer or more complicated than the example above, but workplace professionals usually need more detailed, technical information. For example, managers often read process explanations in marketing brochures to help them make purchasing decisions. Supervisors often read process explanations, like those in many manuals, to gain an understanding of a process they're responsible for but don't actually do themselves. Technicians and operators are usually encouraged to read a process explanation before following the directions to actually conduct a process. General audiences find that process explanations satisfy their curiosity about many things — how wine is made, how hurricanes are tracked, how oil wells are drilled.

WEBLINK

For a link to a terrific Web site, howstuffworks.com, go to **http://english.wadsworth.com/burnett6e.** The site is frequently updated and has very interesting process explanations.
CLICK ON WEBLINK
CLICK on Chapter 16/howstuffworks

Defining Processes
定义过程

Process explanations explain sequential actions to members of an audience who need enough details to understand an action or process, but not enough to necessarily enable them to complete it. The following example of one step in a mechanical inspection process illustrates the difference between a process explanation and directions (which you'll read more about in Chapter 21). The process explanation identifies the general nature of the task; it is valuable precisely because it provides an overview rather than focusing on the details. In contrast, this step of the directions that enables a mechanical inspector to complete the task is very specific:

Process Explanation

A mechanical inspector initially ensures that the labels on the packages are correct.

Directions

Ensure that the computer-printed label contains all of the following information:

- customer contract number
- contract annex and line item
- part number
- nomenclature
- NSN (national stock number)
- quantity
- date packaged
- serial number (if applicable)

Accurate, accessible processes are a large part of what makes an organization function safely and legally. When the processes are inaccurate or inaccessible, problems arise. Most organizations work diligently to keep processes accurate and up to date; in fact, many organizations have built-in reviews to assure that all processes are current. However, some organizations have flawed processes — sometimes by accident, sometimes on purpose — that put people at risk. When an organization ignores such problems, some people believe they have an ethical, professional responsibility to make the problem public. These whistleblowers, now protected by law, make the workplace safer for everyone, but usually at great cost to themselves. The ethics sidebar on the next page addresses the risks and benefits of whistleblowing.

Visual inspection is a critical part of quality control/quality assurance (QC/QA). Not only do supervisors and managers need process explanations that provide an overview of the requirements and parameters of the inspection process, but the inspectors themselves need instructions that provide the specific steps required to implement rigorous inspection.

ETHICS SIDEBAR
职业道德规范知识吧

Whistleblowers: Ethical Choices and Consequences
告发者：职业道德的选择与后果

> *Would you be able to face the potential scorn and repercussions of being a whistleblower? Would you be compromising your personal ethics to keep information secret you felt the public should know? How do you make such a difficult ethical decision?*
>
> *How would you write a process explanation for a process with potentially harmful aspects?*

Dealing with the consequences of an ethical conflict can be difficult, especially when the conflict arises because of a difference between an employee's personal values and an organization's goals. Some technical professionals, faced with workplace situations they find unethical, decide their only viable option is to reveal corporate secrets to the public. These professionals, referred to as whistleblowers, jeopardize their career and personal safety because they believe the public's right to know supersedes corporate obligations.

For ethical, legal, or financial reasons, whistleblowers publicly expose a company's internal secrets. Movies like *The China Syndrome, Silkwood, The Insider,* and *Erin Brockovich* dramatically indicate the extreme repercussions some whistleblowers have faced. In these movies and in the actual situations on which these movies were based, the whistleblowers lost their jobs, found their careers finished, and faced personal assaults. While these movies dramatized extreme examples, many whistleblowers deal with less dramatic but still very important issues. Beyond the probable loss of a job, many whistleblowers have a difficult time getting hired at other companies within the same field and often must change careers.

So, faced with these negative consequences, why would a technical professional choose to be a whistleblower? Legal regulations provide one answer: a technical professional has a legal obligation to inform the public of potential harm. Researcher Carolyn Rude refers to this legal obligation as the "duty of due care":

> Technical communicators could be negligent, legally and ethically, if they knew that a product being documented could be hazardous, knew of the responsibility to provide clear instructions and adequate warnings but did not make an effort to do so, or to investigate hazards in the use of the product. (p. 179)[2]

Legal requirements are not the only factor behind the decision to become a whistleblower. Technical professionals may also respond from a sense of responsibility to the community. Reporter Todd Crowell of the online news service *Asia Now* believes whistleblowers "can be the catalysts for needed change" within a company.[3] Crowell believes that a whistleblower could have prevented Japan's worst nuclear power plant accident. Workers at the plant used an unauthorized operations manual that sacrificed safety for expedience; using this manual, employees accidentally set off a uranium chain reaction in 1999 that killed one worker and exposed hundreds of citizens to dangerous levels of radiation. Crowell believes the accident could have been avoided if someone had been willing to expose the improper procedures being used.

Making the decision to reveal company secrets is not easy, and it does not come without consequences. However, the consequences of not revealing information can be equally troubling.

To read more about whistleblowers and the issues involved, go to **http://english.wadsworth.com/burnett6e** for relevant links.
  CLICK ON WEBLINK
    CLICK on Chapter 16/whistleblowers

Using Process Explanations
使用过程解释

Process explanations often appear in the same kinds of documents as technical descriptions. You can decide whether to include a process explanation and, if so, what kind of details to incorporate by examining the purpose and task of your document. Will the process explanation help accomplish your purpose? Will it help the reader understand the process? The following discussion identifies and illustrates some of the common applications of process explanations: manuals, reports, orientation and training materials, marketing and promotional materials, and public information and education.

Reports 报 告

Reports — whether print documents or online help systems — frequently provide the audience with background information for understanding critical technical processes. The following sequence of information is typical, especially in a report's introductory section:

- *Technical description* — what a mechanism is
- *Process explanation* — how it works
- *Benefits or advantages* — why it's useful

This sequence is a particularly important part of documentation accompanying equipment that may be unfamiliar to either the user or manager.

The example in Figure 16.1 is from a type of short, regularly published report: a U.S. Geological Survey Fact Sheet. This particular fact sheet describes the testing process used by the Cone Penetration Testing (CPT) truck, which is used in geologic-hazard, hydrologic, and environmental studies. As a rapid and cost-effective approach, CPT is particularly useful in urban environments.[4] This USGS fact sheet balances text about the overview, process, and benefits with a simple and effective figure, a photograph, a sounding chart, and a diagram illustrating the relationship among the equipment, process, and output.

Task Manuals 使用手册

One of the most frequent uses of process explanations is in task manuals. While the primary purpose of such manuals is to provide clear, step-by-step instructions to complete a task and to include cautions to avoid problems, users often

FIGURE 16.1 Process Explanation Combining Textual and Visual Information[5]

Accessible
- Information is chunked in relatively short paragraphs.

Comprehensible
- Critical technical vocabulary is defined or explained.

Usable
- A specific title identifies the focus.
- Headings identify the categories of information.
- Benefits are clearly identified, making decisions about use much easier.

Subsurface Exploration with the Cone Penetration Testing (CPT) Truck

The U.S. Geological Survey Cone Penetration Testing (CPT) truck is a fast and inexpensive way to conduct shallow subsurface exploration. Detailed data are available immediately, permitting on-the-fly mapping of stratigraphy and other subsurface features. CPT is a useful tool in geologic-hazard, hydrologic, and environmental studies. This rapid and cost-effective approach is particularly advantageous in urban environments because no drill spoils are produced.

Overview. Cone penetration testing (CPT) permits rapid exploration of shallow (less than 30 meters) subsurface conditions while minimizing retrieval of subsurface materials, an inconvenient and occasionally expensive byproduct of conventional drilling. CPT uses sensors that are pushed into the ground to infer the properties of both soils and pore fluids. Known as direct-push technology, this method can map the vertical and lateral extent of stratigraphic layers as well as the distribution of subsurface contaminants. Standard engineering correlations allow the geotechnical properties of stratigraphic layers to be inferred.

Process. A CPT sounding is made by pushing a small probe into the ground. Typically, a 3.6-centimeter-diameter probe (cone) is pushed into the ground to depths ranging from 15 to 30 meters. The cone is advanced downward at a constant velocity of 2 centimeters per second, using hydraulic rams that apply the full 23-ton weight of the CPT truck to push the probe rods to depth, as shown in Figure 1. In typical CPT soundings, the resistance to penetration is measured. Continuous measurements are made of the resistance to penetration of the tip and the frictional sliding resistance of the sleeve of the cone. The penetration resistance, which is digitized at 5-centimeter depth intervals, permits detailed inferences about stratigraphy and lithology. Soil type is inferred from a chart that compares these two measurements with the known physical properties of various soils.

Benefits. CPT is a much more rapid and cost effective approach than conventional drilling for shallow subsurface exploration. Typically, four to five 15- to 30-meter-deep soundings per day can be accomplished, in contrast to one or two per day with conventional drilling and sampling. Soundings also have the great advantage of not producing any drill cuttings, spoils, or fluids. This aspect is particularly advantageous where subsurface contaminants are present or suspected. Data are automatically logged onto a rugged field computer and are ready for immediate viewing and analysis in the field. CPT is a reliable and efficient method for stratigraphic profiling and obtaining soil-engineering parameters for geotechnical design, as well as being widely accepted and encouraged by regulators as an effective environmental-investigation technology.

FIGURE 16.1   Process Explanation Combining Textual and Visual Information[5] (continued)

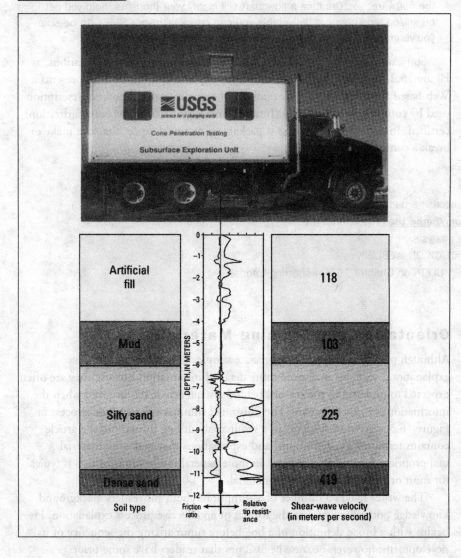

Accessible
- Color is used effectively in the accompanying figure to identify the probe and to differentiate the soil types of comparable shear-wave velocities.

Comprehensible
- The accompanying figure effectively incorporates a photograph, sounding chart, and diagram to show how the equipment, process, and output are related.

complete complex tasks more accurately and more cooperatively if they understand the overall process. A process explanation preceding step-by-step instructions is worth the time to prepare and the space to present.

Flowcharts are an effective way to present such overviews, as Wendy Phillips, a technical communicator at SYNERGEX.com, explains:

> I consider flowcharting processes very important to the documentation of any product. If you write programmer reference guides, you need to flowchart both

how the software works and how it fits together with other software tools. For end-user documentation, you need to flowchart the process of how the user uses the software. . . . Creating a flowchart will clarify your thoughts, help you get organized, and create a deliverable you can check with your SMEs (to be sure you've grasped the big picture about how the product works).[5]

Software is not the only product that benefits from process explanations, as Figure 16.2 illustrates. Rather than a textual explanation, Figure 16.2 presents a Web-based flowchart — a single example of a quality control process description used by companies that are ISO (International Organization for Standardization) certified. In this case, the process is packaging, a critical aspect that can make or break a company.

WEBLINK

To access a basic tutorial about flowcharting, go to **http://english.wadsworth.com/burnett6e**. The tutorial reviews types, tips, symbols, and suggestions for analysis.
CLICK ON WEBLINK
   CLICK on Chapter 16/flowcharting tutorial

Orientation and Training Materials 培训材料

Although managers frequently appreciate simple, straightforward process explanations, students may need more detailed information because they are often expected to understand the reasons behind a sequence of actions even when the information is just a summary. The illustrated summary of a natural process in Figure 16.3 is given to students in a seminar about bog formation; the article contains terminology, definitions, and explanations that make the material inappropriate for readers interested in more general information, which is typical for most orientation and training materials.

The writer makes a number of assumptions about his readers' background knowledge but still adheres to the format of an effective process explanation. He begins with a broad definition of a bog before summarizing the sequence of its development; however, because he assumes that readers have some prior knowledge, he does not define all technical terms. The writer uses chronology to explain the development but also orients readers with precise spatial references.

Marketing and Promotional Materials 市场营销材料

Some actions are far easier to delineate than bog development. For instance, Figure 16.4 presents an example written primarily for professionals; it explains the operation of a thermal inkjet cartridge for computer printers. This example provides a good illustration of the way in which process explanations are often

FIGURE 16.2 Visual Overview of a Process[6]

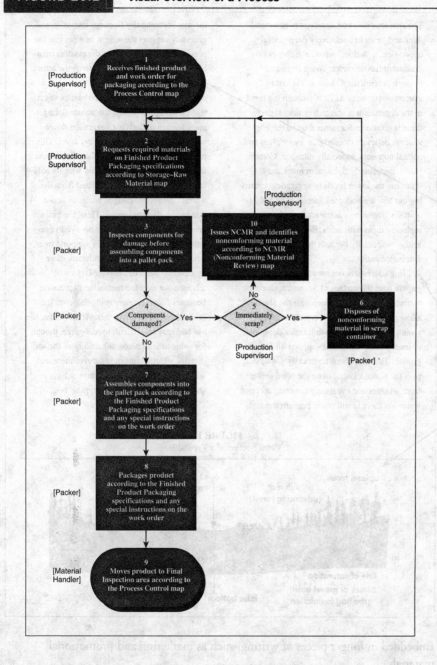

Accessible
- Conventional flowchart shapes and bright colors differentiate the steps.
- The figure-ground contrast makes the text easy to read.

Comprehensible
- The flowchart templates — for example, a rectangle is a process step; a diamond is a decision box — are recognizable by most professionals.
- Arrows remove any ambiguity about the flow of the process.
- Identifying the people associated with each step makes individual responsibilities clear.
- The flowchart defines the overall scope of this part of the quality control process.

Usable
- The four shadowed boxes are linked to other parts of the process, so clicking on those boxes moves users to a related flowchart.
- The use of a flowchart and active links assumes the audience has specialized prior knowledge.

FIGURE 16.3   Illustrated Summary of a Natural Process[7]

Accessible
- The two-column layout creates short lines that make the information accessible.
- The elements in the pen-and-ink drawing are legible.

Comprehensible
- Explanations help readers understand the origin of common terms such as "quaking bog" and phenomena such as the high level of acidity of bog water.
- The chronology of the process is clearly signaled to readers by phrases such as "succession begins" and "growth proceeds."

Usable
- The drawing illustrates each of the main elements identified in the text.

As you read the article about bog development, identify the technical terms that are not defined. Explain whether the lack of definitions hinders your understanding.

The characteristic bog develops over several thousand years in a relatively deep glacial depression, a "kettle," which is either poorly drained or has no outlet. Water is gained through precipitation alone and is lost by evapotranspiration. As flow through the pond in the depression is sluggish or nonexistent, there is no source for minerals, and the bog water is deficient in nearly all major plant and animal nutrients, especially nitrogen. Certain plants, particularly Sphagnum moss, may dominate the lower levels of vegetation, crowding out less well-adapted species. The Sphagnum also withdraws nutrients from the water, replacing them with acids. Bog water is, thus, acidic—especially beneath the Sphagnum-dominated zones.

Bog succession begins as horizontal growth over the surface of the water, since the bottom is generally too deep near the shore to allow plants to root as in a typical marsh or swamp. This lateral growth forms a dense mat of intertwining stems that supports all further growth. This mat characteristically grows out over the water, closing in on the pond center from all sides and eventually covering all open water. As there is still water beneath the mat, the mat is essentially floating; though it will generally support the weight of a person, the person gets the feeling that the earth is trembling. From this phenomena stems the term "quaking bog."

Growth proceeds upon the mat as vegetation builds up vertically, the accumulating mass forcing underlying vegetation downwards and below the static water level. This plant matter decays slowly, if at all, because the acidity of the water coupled with its coldness (it is, after all, well insulated from the warmer air above) inhibits bacterial action that causes decomposition. Thus, the basin becomes filled with partially decayed vegetation, and the mat eventually supports trees, which grow first over the landward, more "grounded" parts of the bog. Trees will advance out over the mat as the depression becomes filled, ultimately closing over the original open bog altogether. At this stage, the old bog may be difficult to recognize, though for some time to come, the acidity of the soil dictates which plants may survive there and which may not. The accompanying figure shows the cross section of a typical bog.

FIGURE 1
Cross Section of a Typical Bog

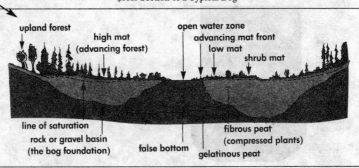

embedded in longer pieces of writing, such as marketing and promotional materials.

The process explanation makes more sense in the context of complete information. In this case, the first five paragraphs provide an overview that

FIGURE 16.4 Process Explanation of How a Thermal Inkjet Cartridge Works[8]

THERMAL INKJET REVIEW, OR HOW DO DOTS GET FROM THE PEN TO THE PAGE?

In its simplest form, an inkjet device consists of a tiny resistor aligned directly below an exit orifice. Ink is allowed to flow into the resistor area, and when the resistor is heated, the ink on the resistor essentially boils and forces a tiny droplet of ink out of the aligned orifice. This is called firing the nozzle.

A cross-sectional view of a single inkjet nozzle is shown in Fig. 1. On the foor of the firing chamber is a resistor. This resistor is patterned onto a silicon substrate using conventional thin-film farication procedures. Leads are connected to the resistor through the thin-film substrate. These leads ultimately travel out to the flexible circuit on the body of the print cartridge, through which a voltage can be applied across the resistor. The resistor is the heart of the thermal inkjet device, and the size of the resistor is the primary factor governing the volume of the ejected droplets.

FIG. 1.
An exploded cross-sectional view of a singleinkjet nozzle

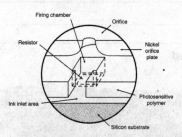

The walls of the firing chamber are made up of a photosensitive polymer. This polymer serves to define the walls of the firing chamber and determines the spacing between the resistor surface and the orifice. The thickness of this photosensitive barrier and the dimensions of the firing chamber are critical to the production of a well-formed droplet.

The photosensitive polymer also defines the dimensions of the inlet area to the firing chamber. Ink enters into the firing chamber through this inlet area. Like the barrier thickness, the inlet dimensions greatly affect the characteristics of the ejected droplet.

Finally, a gold-plated nickel orifice plate sits on top of the barrier. An orifice is formed in this plate directly above the firing chamber. This orifice hole is formed using an electro-forming process. The diameter of the orifice has a direct bearing on the volume and velocity of the ejected droplets.

To fire a drop, a voltage pulse is applied across the resistor. This pulse is typically very short, on the order of 2 to 5 microseconds in duration. The voltage pulse causes the resistor to heat up, temporarily bringing the resistor surface to temperatures up to 400°C. Heat from the resistor causes ink at the resistor surface to su-perheat and form a vapor bubble. Formation of this vapor bubble is a fast and powerful event, and expansion of the bubble forces some of the ink in the firing chamber out of the orifice at velocities of typically 10 meters per second.

By the time a droplet is ejected, the resistor has cooled down and the vapor bubble has collapsed. Through capillary forces, more ink flows into the firing chamber through the inlet area, thus readying the system for the firing of another droplet. The frequency at which the printhead can repeatedly fire droplets is determined by several factors including the inlet dimensions, the barrier thickness, and the fluid properties of the ink.

The device described above is essentially a droplet generator. The device designer has a fair amount of control over the characteristics of the ejected droplets. For example, the volume of the ejected droplet can be controlled by changing the size of the resistor—bigger resistors give droplets of larger volumes. In addition, the diameter of the orifice can be used to control droplet volumes. Droplet velocity is also controlled primarily by the diameter of the orifice.

The frequency at which droplets are ejected can be controlled by altering the size and shape of the barrier and by changing the rheological properties of the ink. . . .

Droplet characteristics, as they relate to print quality on the media surface, can be optimized through careful control of orifice profiles and resistor/orifice alignment. . . . Ink properties such as surface tension, viscosity, and thermal stability all play important roles in the production of useful droplets.

Accessible
- The enlarged cross-sectional view lets readers see insider the nozzle.
- Serif font is conventional for documents that exceed one or two pages.

Comprehensible
- The initial paragraphs provide an overview that defines this type of printer, illustrates its critical parts, and explains their purpose and importance.
- The explanation of the process of firing a drop of ink is embedded in the overall document.
- Clear transitions help readers understand the chronology of the process.
- The concluding paragraphs discuss the effect that the process has on the product.

Usable
- Relatively short paragraphs increase ease of moving through the text.
- The figure is placed in the text following the text reference.

defines, describes, and illustrates the printer, identifying the critical components that readers need to know in order to understand how the process of firing a drop of ink works. The overall definition and description are followed by two paragraphs that identify the sequence involved in firing a drop of ink. The concluding three paragraphs deal with ways in which the process can be controlled to produce high-quality printing.

Public Information and Education 公众宣传与教育

Readers of general-interest publications such as daily newspapers or Web sites are often interested in technical information, but they may not have the experience or expertise to understand complex explanations. Instead, they need simple and appealing explanations. Depending on the subject and the audience, these explanations can be largely visual or largely textual.

Figure 16.5 is a primarily visual presentation that explains how acid rain is formed. Although the term *acid rain* is familiar to most people, the complex natural process by which it is formed is not. Figure 16.5 simplifies the process with a drawing that includes the major elements of the cycle of acid rain formation and provides an explanation appropriate for its intended audience.

FIGURE 16.5   A Primarily Visual Process Explanation[9]

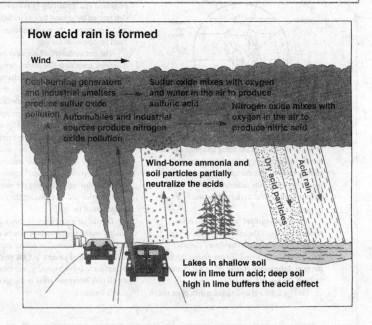

Accessible
- Readers will relate to the easily identified elements such as cars and exhaust, factories and smoke stacks.

Comprehensible
- Each major step in the process is identified, but few details are provided.
- Clear causal relationships are identified.
- The visual elements reinforce the information in the text.
- Active voice is appropriate here.

Usable
- Users typically enter the figure at the upper left corner and follow the arrows to move through the process.

Explain whether simplified process explanations such as the one about acid rain in Figure 16.5 should be avoided. Do they mislead readers by omitting key information?

To read more about the entire printing process, go to **http://english.wadsworth.com/burnett6e** for relevant links.
   CLICK ON WEBLINK
      CLICK on Chapter 16/printing process

Preparing Processes
准备过程

In preparing a process explanation, you need to consider the audience and purpose, identify the steps in the process, select or design visuals, and organize information.

Audience and Purpose 交流对象与目的

Identifying members of your audience and their purpose for reading your document or listening to your oral presentation will help you to prepare a process explanation. Most professionals are initially interested in an overall explanation of an action rather than the precise details necessary to complete that action. You need to ask not only who is going to use the process explanation and why, but you also need to know the circumstances under which they're likely to need such an explanation.

Identification of Steps 确定步骤

An essential part of preparing process explanations involves listing the steps of the action. If the time needed for each step or the time between steps is important, it too should be recorded. The sequence of steps forms the basis for the process explanation and also aids in designing visuals. For example, a common procedure in a hospital pediatrics unit is setting up a croup tent, which aids infants and children in breathing by surrounding them with moist, oxygen-enriched air. Both parents and young patients demonstrate anxiety about the tent, but parents seem to calm down (and thus the children relax) after they learn about what the croup tent does, how it is set up, and how it operates. The brief outline in the following example identifies the basic steps you could use to prepare a process explanation.

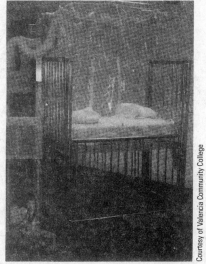

Courtesy of Valencia Community College

1. Defining a croup tent
2. Setting up a croup tent
    a. Metal frame attached to crib
    b. Canopy placed over the frame
    c. Water bottle filled and attached to frame
    d. Ice placed in chamber
    e. Valve inserted and hoses attached

3. Operating a croup tent
   a. Oxygen flow turned on to prescribed level
   b. Oxygen forced through water
   c. Oxygen enters tubing and passes through ice
   d. Moist, cooled oxygen enters tent

Visuals 视觉手段

You can choose from several types of visuals to illustrate the overall sequence of a process. Most common are flowcharts that give a visual overview in the same way that the introductory section of the text defines the action and identifies the major steps. Other visuals that provide an overview of the entire sequence are timelines and schedules.

A drawing can effectively show each element in a process, as in the cross section of a bog accompanying Figure 16.3. More common, though, are step-by-step changes that can be illustrated in a variety of ways: time-lapse photographs, drawings with overlays of changes, and drawings showing the final product. One other way is to use sequential drawings, as in Figure 16.6, which shows eight steps in the deployment of a satellite, from launch through to the final operational position. In this example, the steps in the action view are accompanied by very brief captions that are supplemental rather than essential; the drawing can stand alone.

FIGURE 16.6 Sequential Drawing Showing a Process: Satellite Deployment[10]

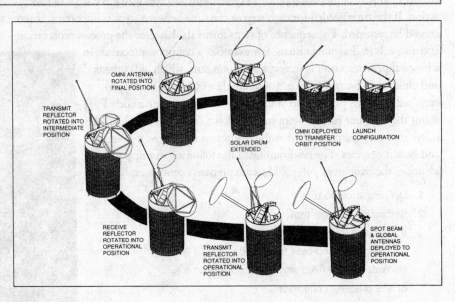

Accessible
- The curved band shows the path of deployment.

Comprehensible
- The very brief captions for each stage of deployment are in parallel structure.
- The drawings are much easier to understand quickly than comparable textual explanations.

Usable
- Locating any particular stage of deployment quickly would be easy.

Process explanations can be presented in a number of ways, depending on the audience. **Go to http://english.wadsworth.com/burnett6e** for links to three different ways to display identical information — in this case the process of peer-review, publication, and discussion in the online scientific journal *Atmospheric Chemistry and Physics (ACP)* and its discussion forum *Atmospheric Chemistry and Physics Discussions (ACPD)*.

   CLICK ON WEBLINK
      CLICK on Chapter 16/ACP and ACPD

WEBLINK

Diction 文字使用

The audience and purpose of your process explanation affect your diction, or the language you use. One of your most important decisions is whether to select active or passive voice. If you want to emphasize the operator, the doer of the action, or the activating agent, use active voice. However, if you want to emphasize the recipient of the action or if the person doing the action is insignificant or unimportant, use passive voice. Figure 16.7 summarizes these key

FIGURE 16.7   Active or Passive Voice in Process Explanations

Active Voice	Passive Voice
Use active voice when the action involves a person and you want to emphasize the operator or doer of the action. EXAMPLE: *Dr. Hunt attended* a seminar to learn about new techniques for treating kidney disease.	**Use passive voice** when the action involves a person and you want to emphasize the recipient of the action *or* when the person doing the action is insignificant or unimportant. EXAMPLE: *The marathon runner was treated* for dehydration by the doctor on duty in the emergency room.
Use active voice when the action does not involve a person and you want to emphasize the activating agent. EXAMPLE: *Torrential rains weakened* the dam.	**Use passive voice** when the action does not involve a person and you want to emphasize the recipient of the action. EXAMPLE: *The machine was activated* by the automatic timer.

factors in making a decision and provides examples. (See the Usage Handbook on the Web site for more details about active and passive voice.)

Organization and Format 组织与格式

Because process explanations are chronological, writers often use headings to distinguish their major steps. Section headings and subheadings help readers by signaling the movement from one part of the process to the next. Processes follow a format, summarized in Figure 16.8, that can be varied according to audience

---

FIGURE 16.8 — **Planning a Process Explanation**

Title
1.0 Identify the process in an introduction.
   1.1 Define the process.
   1.2 Identify purpose or goal.
   1.3 *Optional:* Identify the intended audience and the purpose.
   1.4 *Optional:* Explain background needed by the intended audience.
   1.5 *Optional:* Identify the relevant parts, materials, equipment, ingredients, and so on.
   1.6 *Optional:* Design a flowchart or other visual to provide an overview.
   1.7 Enumerate the major steps.

2.0 Present a step-by-step explanation of the process in chronological order, including cause-and-effect explanations as necessary.
   2.1 Explain step one of the process.
      2.1.1 Define step one.
      2.1.2 Present the purpose or goal of step one.
      2.1.3 *Optional:* Identify the necessary parts, materials, equipment, or ingredients for step one.
      2.1.4 *Optional:* Illustrate step one.
      2.1.5 Present chronological details of step one, including any substeps.
      2.1.6 *Optional:* Present chronological details of the substeps if they're relevant to the audience.
      2.1.7 *Optional:* Explain the theory or principle of this step's operation or function if it's relevant to the audience.
      2.1.8 Explain how this step relates to the next step.
   2.2 Explain step two . . .

3.0 *Optional:* Present a conclusion if it will increase the reader's understanding of the sequence, its theory, or applications.
   3.1 Summarize the major steps only if the action is long and/or complex.
   3.2 Discuss the theory or principle of operation if it has not already been incorporated in the primary discussion.
   3.3 Explain applications if they're not self-evident.

needs. The less expert the audience, the less complex the information should be. However, less-informed nonexperts often need very careful explanations, which may take up more space than the highly technical explanations appropriate for experts. You will notice that a number of the steps are optional; they can be included or not, depending on the audience's needs.

Examining a Sample Process Explanation: Develping Low-Cost Roofing Materials

过程解释案例分析：
开发低耗屋顶材料

When Nilsa Cristina Zacarias was the Coordinator of the Research Division of the Appropriate Technology Center (CTA: Centro de Tecnologia Apropiada) in Asuncion, Paraguay, she wrote a process explanation as part of a final report for a German agency. This agency had funded a pilot project to develop building materials that low-income people in rural areas of a developing country could make and install themselves.

The logging industry in Paraguay's forests produces a great deal of sawdust, which is considered waste. One of Zacarias's colleagues, a researcher in CTA's laboratory, was supported by the International Development Research Center in Canada to develop an ecologically sound, low-cost material that could be used to make roofing material. Zacarias field-tested this process to determine if it could be used in an actual community. Figure 16.9 shows one of her early drafts of this process explanation, with comments about things that she wants to change in her revision.[11]

Zacarias knew that her readers weren't going to complete the process themselves, but she wanted them to understand it. Because her process explanation was part of a much longer report, she wanted to keep this section brief and easy to read, while emphasizing the economic and ecological goals expected by the funding agency. She decided that using a modified outline structure would make the process easy for readers to skim quickly (Figure 16.10), and that passive voice would be appropriate since her emphasis was on the process rather than the people completing the process. She also knew that including a figure would help readers visualize the way sawdust plates were attached to a roof. Although her explanation of building sawdust plates has few details, it follows the basic structure of more elaborated process explanations.

Construction in rural areas of developing countries depends on low-cost, readily available materials. One solution creates building materials from local resources. For example, sawdust, a byproduct of logging, is mixed with cement. The mixture is poured into wooden molds and dried for use as plates in roof construction.

FIGURE 16.9 Preliminary Draft of Process Explanation

BUILDING WITH SAWDUST PLATES

Add an introductory paragraph.

Three major steps are necessary to build with sawdust plates: 1. treating the sawdust, 2. fabricating the plates, and 3. placing the plates.

List steps to help them stand out.

Make wording of headings and steps parallel.

1. **Treatment**~~ing~~ the sawdust

   Sawdust is submerged into boiling water treated with 2% ferric sulfate for 10 minutes. Then the sawdust passed through a strainer and rinsed with cold water. Finally it is placed on a clean surface to dry.

2. **Fabrication**~~ing~~ the plates   (cement:sawdust)

   First the sawdust and the cement are mixed with 1:7 proportion. Water is added until the mixture gets a determined level of plasticity. Second, this mixture is poured into wood molds and floated for getting a flat surface with a wood or steel float. This procedure is fast, but it has to be conducted with a smooth pressure. After fabrication, the plates could be lifted and put into storage for the drying process.

   How long?

3. **Placement**~~ing~~ the plates

   How the plates are placed over the roof and fastened with bolts to the wooden structure. The plates are painted with a white, waterproof paint to protect the surface against the rain and sun.

Separate each major step to make the process easier to read.

FIGURE 16.10 Revision of Process Explanation Using an Outline

BUILDING WITH SAWDUST PLATES

Accessible
- Listing steps makes them easier to read.

Fabricated sawdust plates are an inexpensive alternative building material for low-cost roof construction. These plates are fabricated by mixing sawdust (waste from the logging industry) with cement and water. After the plates are fabricated, they can be used to insulate abnormally high roof temperatures from the interior rooms.

Three major steps are necessary to build with sawdust plates:
1. treating the sawdust.
2. fabricating the plates, and
3. placing the plates.

Comprehensible
- Introductory paragraph situates the process for readers.
- Text is more coherent when steps and section headings are parallel.
- Clarifying substance for each proportion reduced ambiguity.

Comprehensible
- Rationale helps readers understand the process.

1. **Treating the sawdust**
   - (To avoid having the sawdust rot) it is submerged into boiling water treated with 2% ferric sulfate for 10 minutes.
   - Then the sawdust is passed through a strainer and rinsed with cold water.
   - Finally it is placed on a clean surface to dry.

2. **Fabricating the plates**
   - First the sawdust and the cement are mixed with 1:7 proportion (cement:sawdust). Water is added until the mixture gets a determined level of plasticity.
   - Second, this mixture is poured into wood molds and floated for getting a flat surface with a wood or steel float. This procedure is fast, but it has to be conducted with a smooth pressure.
   - (After 12 days of fabrication) the plates can be lifted and put into storage for the drying process.

- Specifying time helps readers better understand the fabrication process.

- Identifying the substeps in the process makes the simplicity of the process immediately apparent.

3. **Placing the plates**
   - The illustration shows how the plates are placed over the roof and fastened with bolts to the wooden structure.
   - The plates are painted with a white, waterproof paint to protect the surface against the rain and sun.

- Adding an illustration helps readers understand how the plates are attached to the existing roof.

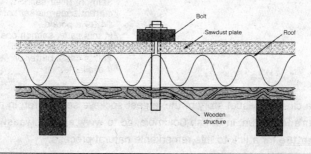

Usable
- Outline structure makes information easy to locate.

PROCESSES INVOLVING SOCKEYE SALMON
捕获、保存、烹调三文鱼的过程

The processes involved in catching, preserving, and cooking salmon have a long tradition in Native culture in Alaska. Sockeye salmon, which belongs to the family Salmonidae and is one of the seven species of Pacific salmonids in the genus *Oncorhynchus*, is a critical part of subsistence and commercial fishing in Alaska.[12]

Subsistence, an essential source of employment and sustenance for people in rural Alaska, enables people to feed and clothe their families. Even though wild food supplies one-third of the calories required by rural Alaskans (who make up 20 percent of the population of the state), subsistence accounts for only two percent of the combined fish and game harvest in Alaska.[13]

Traditionally, sockeye salmon has been central to the life of the Tlingit Indians in Alaska, which accounts for their long history in the development of fishing equipment and techniques[14] as well as preservation and preparation processes.

The processes continue, not only as part of the Tlingit heritage but as part of contemporary life. However, as people move to towns and cities, some of the traditional processes are modified. The following poem, "How to Make Good Baked Salmon from the River," by Tlingit elder, Nora Marks Dauenhauer, captures and honors the details of the traditional technical process so that it will not be forgotten or lost.

The poem also exemplifies the idea that process explanations are a critical part of our everyday lives and reminds us that processes evolve.

© Brandon Cole/Visuals Unlimited

Sockeye salmon are *anadromous*, which means they migrate from the ocean to spawn in fresh water. During migration, sockeye typically have bluish back and silver sides. Then during spawning, the adults typically turn bright red, with a green head. The name "sockeye" is most likely a corruption of the Indian word "sukkai."[15]

Nora Marks Dauenhauer
How to Make Good Baked Salmon from the River[16]
for Simon Ortiz, and for all our friends and relatives who love it

It's best made in dryfish camp
on a beach by a fish stream
on sticks over an open fire,
or during fishing
or during cannery season.

In this case, we'll make it in the city,
baked in an electric oven on a black
    fry pan.

INGREDIENTS
Bar-b-q sticks of alder wood.
In this case the oven will do.
Salmon: River salmon,
current supermarket cost
$4.99 a pound.
In this case, salmon poached from river.
Seal oil or hooligan oil.
In this case, butter or Wesson oil,
if available.

WEBLINK

For a close-up visual story of the largest sockeye salmon run in the world, in the Adam's River Run, in British Columbia, go to www.english.wadsworth.com/burnett6e for a link to this remarkable natural process.
CLICK ON WEBLINK
CLICK on Chapter 16/salmon run

598   Part IV Understanding the Communicator's Strategies

DIRECTIONS

To butcher, split head up the jaw.
    Cut through.
Remove gills. Split from throat down
    the belly.
Gut, but make sure you toss all to
    the seagulls
and the ravens, because they're your kin,
and make sure you speak to them
while you're feeding them.
Then split down along the backbone
and through the skin.
Enjoy how nice it looks when it's split.

Push stake through flesh and skin
like pushing a needle through cloth,
so that it hangs on stakes
while cooking over fire made from
alder wood.

Then sit around
and watch the slime on the salmon
begin to dry out. Notice how red the
    flesh is,
and how silvery the skin looks.
Watch and listen
how the grease crackles, and smell
    its delicious
aroma drifting around on a breeze.

Mash some fresh berries to go along
    for dessert.
Pour seal oil in with a little water.
    Set aside.

In this case, put the poached salmon
    in a fry pan.
Smell how good it smells while it's
    cooking,
because it's sooooooooooooo important.

Cut up an onion. Put in a small dish.
    Notice
how nice this smells too,
and how good it will taste.
Cook a pot of rice to go along with
    salmon.
Find some soy sauce to put on rice,
or maybe borrow some.

In this case, think about how nice the
    berries
would have been after the salmon,
but open a can
of fruit cocktail instead.

Then go out by the cool stream
and get some skunk cabbage,
because it's biodegradable,
to serve the salmon from.
Before you take back the skunk cabbage,
you can make a cup out of one
to drink from the cool stream.

In this case, plastic forks,
paper plates and cups will do,
and drink cool water from the faucet.

TO SERVE

After smelling smoke and fish and
    watching
the cooking, smelling the skunk cabbage
and the berries mixed with seal oil,
when the salmon is done,
put salmon on stakes on the skunk
    cabbage
and pour some seal oil over it
and watch the oil run
into the nice cooked flaky flesh
which has now turned pink.

Shoo mosquitoes off the salmon,
and shoo the ravens away,
but don't insult them, because
    mosquitoes
are known to be the ashes of the
    cannibal giant,
and Raven is known to take off
with just about anything.

In this case, dish out on paper plates
from fry pan. Serve to all relatives
    and friends
you have invited to the bar-b-q
and those who love it.

And think how good it is
that we have good spirits
that still bring salmon and oil.

TO EAT

Everyone knows that you can eat
just about every part of the salmon,
so I don't have to tell you
that you start from the head,
because it's everyone's favorite.
You take it apart,
bone by bone,
but be sure you don't miss
the eyes,
the cheeks,
the nose,
and the very best part—
the jawbone.

You start on the mandible
with a glottalized alveolar fricative
    action
as expressed in the Tlingit verb *als'óos.*'

Chew on the tasty, crispy skins
before you start on the bones.
Eiiiiiiii!!!!!!
How delicious.

Then you start on the body
by sucking on the fins
with the same action.
Include the crispy skins, and then
the meat with grease oozing all over it.

Have some cool water from the stream
with the salmon.

In this case,
water from the faucet will do.
Enjoy how the water tastes sweeter
    with salmon.

When done, toss the bones to
    the ravens
and seagulls, and mosquitoes,
but don't throw them in the salmon
    stream
because the salmon have spirits
and don't like to see the remains
of their kin thrown in by us
among them in the stream.

In this case, put bones in plastic bag
to put in dumpster.

Now settle back to a story-telling
    session
while someone feeds the fire.

In this case,
small talk and jokes with friends will do
while you drink beer.
If you shouldn't drink beer,
tea or coffee will do nicely.

Gunalchéesh for coming to my bar-b-q.

Who are the audiences for this poem? How does their prior knowledge affect their understanding? Their response?

The poem explains a traditional process for preparing salmon. How could this process — part of an oral tradition — be preserved in a recipe? How would a recipe change the process and the product?

What tribal knowledge is embedded in the poem? In what ways is culture always part of a process explanation?

How does tribal knowledge accommodate itself to change? How does the poem show such changes?

Individual and Collaborative Assignments

个人作业和小组作业

1. **Evaluate a process explanation.**
   (a) Read the following explanation about the operating process of a hydrogen/oxygen torch ignitor.
   (b) Identify the probable audience(s).
   (c) Evaluate all aspects of the process explanation, including the effectiveness of the organization, the visual, and the language choices.
   (d) Create a rubric for assessing this process explanation.

HYDROGEN/OXYGEN TORCH IGNITOR[17]
This reliable device can be used to ignite a variety of fuels.
Lewis Research Center, Cleveland, Ohio

The figure illustrates a hydrogen/oxygen torch ignitor that is reliable and simple to operate. This device is the latest in a series of such devices that have been used for more than 20 years to ignite a variety of fuel/oxidizer mixtures in research rocket engines. The device can also be used as a general-purpose ignitor in other applications, or as a hydrogen/oxygen torch.

The operation of this device is straightforward. Hydrogen and oxygen flow through separate ports into a combustion chamber in the device, where they are ignited by use of a surface-gap spark plug. The hot gases flow from this combustion chamber, through an injector tube, into the larger combustion chamber that contains the fuel-oxidizer mixture to be ignited.

The pressures and flows of hydrogen and oxygen are adjusted to obtain a pressure of about 135 psig (gauge pressure of 0.93 MPa) in the combustion chamber during operation. The pressures and flows are also adjusted for an oxidizer/fuel ratio of 40 to obtain a combustion temperature of 2,050 K, which is low enough that there is no need to cool the combustion chamber if the operating time is short enough.

Some of the flow of hydrogen is diverted to the annular space surrounding the injector tube to cool the injector tube. The rate of this cooling flow is chosen so that when it mixes with the hot gases at the outlet of the injector tube, the resulting oxidizer/fuel ratio is 5. The resulting flame at the outlet is about 12 in. (about 30 cm) long and its temperature is about 3,100 K.

The Hydrogen/Oxygen Torch Ignitor can be used as a general-purpose ignitor or as a hydrogen/oxygen torch.

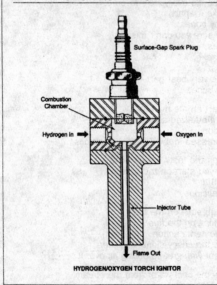
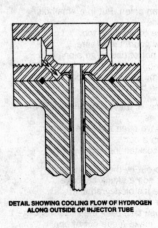

2. **Write a process description.** Select one of the topics below or choose one in your field or discipline. Identify the intended audience and specify the purpose of the process explanation. Analyze the audience to determine ways to increase (a) accessibility (for example, headings and subheadings, labeled steps), (b) comprehensibility (for example, content complexity; active or passive voice; first, second, or third person), (c) usability (for example, clear definitions, relevant visuals).

birth of a calf or foal	installation of a wood-burning stove
breeding of genetically pure lab animals	inventory control
creation of a silicon crystal	maintenance of a spinning reel
depreciation	manufacture of carbon fibers
design of a dietary program	operation of a laser
development of genetically modified organisms	operation of a rotary engine
	operation of a septic tank or leach field
development of hybrid varieties of corn	operation of a transit
development of a hydrogen engine	packing a parachute
energy audit of a house	refinishing a piece of furniture
extrusion of polymer parts	regeneration of tails in lizards
fabrication of metal optics	self-regulated pain control (e.g., biofeedback)
formation of a weather front	
formation of kidney stones	test/inspection procedure
formation of plaque on teeth	thermal aging process
grafting of plants	welding or brazing

3. **Design a visual to depict a process.**
    (a) Consider one of the topics in the preceding list. Identify the intended audience and specify the purpose of the process that you can present in a visual (the way Figure 16.5 explains acid rain). Design the visual so that it is both accurate and appealing.
    (b) Write a direct, brief caption that explains and supports the visual.

4. **Evaluate a Web-based process explanation.**
    (a) Visit the following Web site: **www.howstuffworks.com.** Choose a procedure to evaluate.
    (b) Identify the definitions and descriptions that are embedded as part of the process explanation.
    (c) Evaluate the process explanation by considering whether the information is effectively explained and organized (including whether the site is navigable), how visuals are used, and what language choices are effective (or ineffective).

(d) Create a rubric to identify the criteria you'll use for evaluating the process explanations.

5. **Analyze a brief process explanation.** What features of the following sentence qualify it as a process explanation?

   Routine maintenance involves changing the filter when it's dirty and making sure the heat exchanger and smoke pipe are clear of accumulated creosote.

6. **Design a brochure to explain a process.** The Equal Economic Opportunity Commission's (EEOC) enforcement guidance on harassment by supervisors recommends questions to be asked during the process of investigating a harassment complaint.[18] However, this list of questions doesn't by itself explain the process of an investigation or encourage any complainant to come forward. Search the Web to check the EEOC enforcement guidelines on harassment. Create a brochure that provides a process explanation for employees about harassment by supervisors, including the following questions. The brochure should be accessible, comprehensible, and usable.

   For the complainant — who, what, when, where, and how:
   - Who committed the alleged harassment?
   - What actually occurred or what was said? When did it occur? Is it ongoing?
   - Where did it occur? How often did it occur? How did it affect you?

   Determining employee reaction:
   - What response did you make when the incident(s) occurred or afterward?
   - Effect of harassment: Has your job been affected in any way by the harasser's actions?

   Collecting relevant information from other sources:
   - Was anyone present when the harassment occurred? Did you tell anyone about it?
   - Did anyone see you immediately after episodes of harassment?

   Determining a pattern of harassment:
   - Do you know whether anyone complained about harassment by that person?
   - Are there any notes, physical evidence, or other documentation regarding the incident(s)?
   - How would you like to see the situation resolved?
   - Do you have any other relevant information?

   Getting input from the alleged harasser:
   - What is your response to the allegations?
   - If the harasser claims that the allegations are false, ask why the complainant might lie.

- Are there any persons who have relevant information?
- Are there any notes, physical evidence, or other documentation regarding the incident(s)?
- Do you have any other relevant information?

For third parties:
- What did you see or hear? When did this occur? Describe the alleged harasser's behavior toward the complainant and toward others in the workplace.
- What did the complainant tell you?
- When did she or he tell you this?
- Do you have any other relevant information?
- Are there other persons who have relevant information?

The EEOC lists some factors to consider when determining credibility:
- Is the testimony believable on its face? Does it make sense?
- Did the person seem to be telling the truth or lying?
- Did the person have a reason to lie?
- Is there witness testimony (eyewitnesses, people who saw the person soon after the alleged incidents, or people who discussed the incidents with the complainant around the time the incidents occurred) or physical evidence (written documentation) that corroborates the complainant's testimony?
- Does the alleged harasser have a history of harassing behavior?

Chapter 16 Endnotes

[1] U.S. Department of Energy, Wind Energy Program. (n.d.). *Find out about how the turbine works.* Retrieved November 16, 2003 from http://www.eere.energy.gov/wind/feature.html

[2] Rude, C. (1994). Meaning publications according to legal and ethical standards. In O. J. Allen & L. H. Deming (Eds.), *Publications management: Essays for professional communicators* (pp. 171–187). Amityville, NY. Baywood.

[3] Crowell, T. After Toramura: Ratting on Japan's Nuclear Sloppiness. *Asia Now.* 13 October 1999. Retrieved 2001, from http://cnn.com/ASIANOW/asiaweek/intelligence/9910/13

[4] Modified from Noce, T. E., & Holzer, T. L. *U.S. Geological survey* (S. L. Scott, Graphics) (Fact Sheet 028-03). Retrieved October 25, 2003, from http://geopubs.wr.usgs.gov/fact-sheet/fs028-03/

[5] Phillips, W. (1998, February 3). Flow charting and technical writers. Message posted to TECHWR-L electronic mailing list, archived at http://www.raycomm.com/techwhirl/archives/9802/techwhirl-9802-00133.html

[6] ISO 9000 Maps. (n.d.). *Packaging map: ISO 9002*. Retrieved November 25, 2003, from http://Elsmar.com/9000maps/packagng.htm

[7] Oltsch, F. M. (n.d.). *Bog development*. Becket, MA.

[8] Shields, J. P. (1992, August). Thermal inkjet preview, or how do dots get from the pen to the page? *Hewlett-Packard Journal, 67.* © 1992 Hewlett-Packard Company. Reproduced with permission.

[9] How acid rain is formed. *Lowell Sun.*

[10] Slafer, L. I., & Seidenstucker, V. L. (1991). INTELSAT VT: Communications subsystem design. *COMSAT Technical Review, 21* (Spring), 61.

[11] Zecarias, N. C., Iowa State University.

[12] Office of Protected Resources, NOAA Fisheries, National Marine Fisheries Services. (2003). *Sockeye salmon*. Retrieved on November 18, 2003 from http://www.nmfs.noaa.gov/prot_res/species/fish/sockeye_salmon.html

[13] Alaska Seafood Marketing Institute. (2002). *Alaska Federation of Natives: Subsistence facts*. Retrieved on November 18, 2003 from http://www.alaskaseafood.org/aboutus/salmonwk2003.htm

[14] Alaska Fishing on the Web. (n.d.) *Fishing and the Tlingit Indian*. Retrieved on November 18, 2003 from http://www.alaskafishingontheweb.com/tlingit_fishing/

[15] Office of Protected Resources, NOAA Fisheries, National Marine Fisheries Services. (2003). *Sockeye salmon*. Retrieved on November 18, 2003 from http://www.nmfs.noaa.gov/prot_res/species/fish/sockeye_salmon.html

[16] Dauenhauer, N. M. (1998). How to make good baked salmon from the river. *First Fish–First People: Salmon Tales of the North Pacific Rim*. Seattle, WA: One Reel/University of Washington Press.

[17] *NASA Tech Briefs*. (1995, December). 58.

[18] Long, S. E., & Leonard, C. G. (1999). The changing face of sexual harassment. *HR Focus,* (Oct), p. S1.